22/12/93

To:-

With the Authors

Complements and

Best Wishes.

John M Gardner

This journal has been compiled over a period of some 6 or 7 years and remains as originally written. Events do move on regardless and so do personalities and organisations mentioned within these pages; who I trust will accept the diary of events to be a true record at the time they were first written.

Portions of the text in this volume and some photographs have been previously published by the Milngavie Herald and other sources, and I wish to thank the considerable number of people and organisations who have provided useful assistance during the books preparation.

The impressions, opinions and viewpoints expressed are highly individualistic and I accept full responsiblity for any omission, inaccuracies or opinions mentioned.

ISBN 0 9518134 0 4

Typeset by Mouse House, Cambuslang.
Production and printing by BDC Printing Services Ltd., East Kilbride.
Bound by James Gowans Ltd., Glasgow.

THE EXPERIENCE OF A LIFETIME

JOHN M. GARDNER

Ex~Senior Bailie ; J.P. of Milngavie

CONTENTS

STOP
LOOK
BEFORE
NEIL
PBELL
J.M.GARDN
PLUMBER
ELECTRICAL & HEATING EN
CHEMIST
ILFORD

FOREWORD

"Milngavie" was one of the first unusual words I learned to read. My father always made a point of explaining the pronunciation to me when a tramcar passed us in Maryhill Road bearing the Milngavie destination plate.

I recall the bluebell woods of Sunday School trips from Lansdowne Church and the many nostalgic stories told by my parents of camping weekends in their youth, which started and finished at Milngavie. A truly magical place for those surrounded by city grime - not perhaps at the end of the rainbow, but certainly just beyond the tram terminus.

This was "my Milngavie" when I was appointed in January 1985 as head teacher of Milngavie Primary School. Clearly not enough for my own needs and most definitely not sufficient to structure our environmental programme which over the seven primary school years would provide the pupils with an intimate knowledge of their village - past and present. Books there were, but the need to talk to Milngavie people with a love and knowledge of the village and its growth - particularly since the Second World War - was needed. Requests in the local paper for such persons had produced no response.

As happens, whilst making a purchase in Gardners the Plumbers in Station Road, I met Mr. John Gardner who was "visiting". Neither of us is short on conversation and we quickly established each other's identity. Yes, Mr. Gardner had read the request for help but wondered if he knew enough about Milngavie to meet our needs. He would be delighted to help where he could.

Well, there was an understatement if ever I had heard one: Mr. Gardner went out of his way to help, imparting his vast knowledge to staff and pupils alike. What a find! What a treasure! The pupils loved hearing him talk and enjoyed firing very testing questions at him. He was never caught out.

Some months later I was delighted to learn that Mr. Gardner had decided to write a book about his Milngavie. This book you now hold in your hand. Enjoy it and learn as we did about this fascinating village.

Christine Reid

Mrs. Christine Reid
Head Teacher
Milngavie Primary School

"THE EXPERIENCE OF A LIFETIME"

by Ex-Senior Bailie JOHN MITCHELL GARDNER J.P.
of Milngavie, Glasgow

EARLY DAYS

My parents were married on 19th June 1884 in Glasgow and came to live at No 36 Main Street, Milngavie in 1885, just 100 yards from the grain mill of Davie Guy "Millbrae Farm" Main Street. The family consisted of four sons and three daughters, the youngest member of the family being John Mitchell Gardner, born six years after his sister Emma on the 2nd of October 1907 at Main Street. The house consisted of two rooms, one kitchen, inside toilet, a sink in the kitchen with running water tap for cold water and a small tank at the side of the kitchen fireplace to be hand-filled for hot water, quite modern really. Bath time was usually Thursday and Friday evening with a fairly large basin made of galvanized metal with two handles, laid out in the centre of the kitchen. Sometimes I had to share the water with my older sister, so much for sanitation. As you can imagine it was quite a busy house going in and out the various apartments so there had to be special arrangements for privacy.

My father was born in the Cranstonhill District of Glasgow and as a boy was employed by a grocer in that area, later he delivered groceries etc. to Milngavie, was a guest in the Black Bull Hotel for the night and returned to Glasgow next morning. This was found rather inconvenient. Since he knew quite a number of people in the village, my parents decided to live in Milngavie and started a small grocers shop in Main Street.

My mother was born in the Isle of Skye at a place called Dunvegan, but had to come south to Glasgow at an early age because of difficulty in obtaining employment. She met my father and they were married in 1884 when she was nineteen years of age. My mother looked after the shop and the family with assistance of a woman who helped in the house. My father had employment at Tambowie Distillery, Craigton. He was termed in those days as a handyman and did various jobs thereafter to augment the finance of the family. My parents were both hardworking, it was their intention to better the circumstances in which they found themselves and they succeeded in due course. For some reason, they were members of New Kilpatrick Parish and are buried in the Cemetery at the side of a small brook at the corner of Drymen Road.

One of my early escapades happened, I am told, when I was three months old. My second oldest brother Archie, on arriving home from school one afternoon, was delegated to take baby John in the pram to the public park, to be left at the side of the field as they played football. In the excitement of playing the game, darkness descended, the players went home and I was forgotten about. However, about two hours later a courting couple coming through the park noticed the pram with a baby in it. I was thereafter transferred to the local police station, consisting of one small office and one cell, and deposited in the cell. In the meantime consternation at home, the baby is missing; a next door neighbour Mrs Provan called at the police station to report the matter, to find a baby in a pram in the cell sucking milk from a stone ginger bottle with a rubber teet. Great relief to all concerned, life can be rather peculiar; many years after that I was appointed a senior magistrate dealing with the same police station.

Shortly after that episode, I understand we removed to a larger house consisting of four rooms and one kitchen also a bathroom, immediately above what was then known as " Innes Pub", later the Talbot Arms in Main Street where we lived until at the age of five I reported at Milngavie Public School. This was much to the relief of older brothers and sisters as I always appeared to be obstructing their progress one way or another during washing floors or other domestic problems.

On my first day at school it was the opening of a new world to me. I was taken there by my older sister Emma, six years older than I was and already a pupil in what was known as the big school. I was enrolled in the original or Lower School in what was known as the baby class. There I met a number of other small boys and girls, approximately thirty. The seat given to me was between two other boys. One of the boys, Andrew Hannah, was the son of the Art Teacher in the school, the other was Robert McLellan who in after life became a well known writer of Scots plays and poems in Scotland; he used to recite a poem in the school "Play up, Play up and Play the Game", very talented, I remained very friendly with the two boys most of our lives.

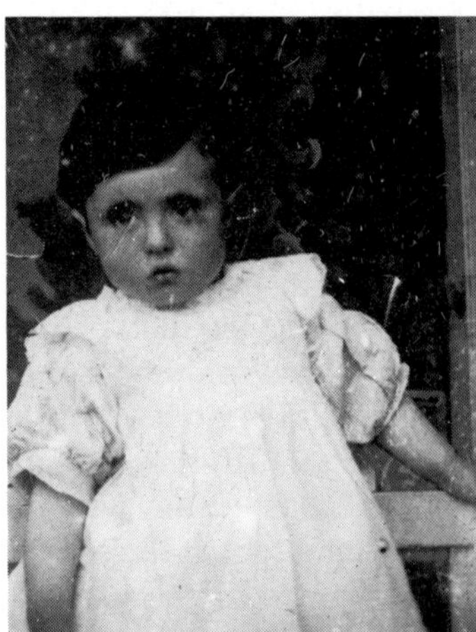

Author, age 2

The Head Mistress of the Lower School was a Miss Williamson and my teacher was a Miss Young, who was my teacher right up to the Qualifying Class. At the beginning life was a game, but as life went on it became a much more serious affair.

I liked my teacher very much and do not recall getting into any trouble. Life went by like a song, sometimes I used to get into trouble playing football in the playground and wearing out my boots more than I should by my mother, they were called tackity boots and were very strong. I loved gymnastics and sport.

At the age of ten I received rather a set back with illness. Diptheria and Scarlet fever kept me in hospital for two months at Duntocher Hospital with the result that on sitting my qualifying examination I obtained a poor result and had to re-sit the exam; but on the second attempt obtained very satisfactory results after some hard work, which stood me in good stead at a later period in my education in supplementary classes.

My duties were to deliver pies on a Saturday to the local mansion houses in a huge basket, later to be followed with a type of bicycle with a basket holder. It was quite a good job but I did not like the large dogs in some of the houses. The people were nice. I can remember some of the family houses yet, the Carricks family, Risk family, Dykes family, Hunter family, Burnside family, etc. My working hours on Saturday were 8 a.m. to 4 p.m. My wages were a half crown plus two pence for my rail fare to Mulguy and a refreshment of one pie with a cup of tea. The lady in charge of the shop was a Miss Lang. Her father looked after the Schaw Hospital. These were happy days.

During the next four years until I left school life became rather hectic, it was at the time I became interested in the working of the Grain Mill and Farm Dairy at Millbrae. This was now the property of James Watt, grain miller and farmer and one of the original members of the formation of the Burgh of Milngavie in 1875. The population at that time was 2184. I was fascinated by the working of the machinery driven by a large water wheel and the manufacture of the oatmeal into large canvas bags. I was allowed to take the trace horse down Milngavie Road to meet the horse and lorry bringing in the grain from Glasgow. My first part time job, the milking and feeding of cows was another attraction. My first real job was to take the milk to Millbrae Dairy in Main Street about 100 yards from the farm. Thereafter I had what was called a milk run with cans of milk on a barrow, my district being Tannoch Drive and Strathblane Road, for which I received two shillings for a seven day morning run. Sometimes I delivered hand made scones made in the dairy by Miss Watt, the only bother was I had to get up early each morning to be back for school. An extra was a new made scone for a play piece at 11 o' clock.

At the age of eleven I joined the lst Milngavie Boys Brigade under the command of Captain Arnold Wilson. He was one of the original founders of the Boys Brigade Movement. My religious life was quite busy, on a Sunday at 9.00 a.m. I attended the B.B. Sunday Class for Bible Study, thereafter three other Sunday Schools, Church of Scotland, Allander Hall mission and St Andrews Church. I think the idea was to keep me out of mischief.

The B.B. Hall was in Douglas Street. It consisted of a drill hall with the addition of two large rooms. It was here most of my evenings were spent in Drill with wooden rifles, before being withdrawn as too warlike. During my time in the company, until I was seventeen years old, I was fortunate to gain a few honours. Our holiday summer camp was held at Lamlash in the Isle of Arran, happy days. The only setback was when another boy and myself arranged with two Girl Guides to go with them to a dance in the village at night after hours, we were caught by an Officer, given a reprimand, but allowed to proceed. So much for that.

Life had become much more serious for me at the age of 15 years, and I had to leave school in 1922. There was what was called a trade recession, jobs were very difficult to find and unemployment bad. This was in the dark days after the 1914 - 1918 First World War with a great loss of life. It affected my own family. My oldest sister Helen lost her husband James Clark in a battle in France after only six months of marriage, thereafter she took care of my father and mother assisting in house duties. Shortly after my oldest brother got married and started a carpenter and joiners business in Mugdock Road Milngavie, followed by my second oldest sister who married a local Police Officer, Robert Hutchison. My second oldest brother married a local lady, his employment being at the Singers Sewing Machine Factory at Clydebank and later on Inspector of Works at Barr & Stroud, Scientific Instrument Makers at Anniesland.

This left only a brother Norman who was employed in the North British Railway Company. He also married and lived in Milngavie leaving my sister Emma who got a job in Barr & Stroud. She married an Engineer, Mr Campbell, living at Scotstounhill Glasgow, leaving myself with no employment for a period of nine months. I continued my education by attending evening classes in Engineering at Milngavie Public School. During the day I was responsible for shopping for my parents and had a pal by the name of Jim Forrester, who like myself was unemployed. We used to go walks, did swimming in the local stream called the Allander near a pool adjacent to Milngavie Golf Course, and sometimes we were allowed to caddy for some of the golfers for a fee of one shilling. At that period little did I know how much sport would come into my life later. It was at this time while swimming in a pool called the Lynn near the golf course about four p.m. one summer afternoon, we had a call from Mr Goodley the Clubmaster asking us if we would caddy for two golfers, one being the Captain of the Club, Mr Eadie Taylor. Jim Forrester had caddied for him before, the other gentleman was a visitor who was playing over the course for the first time. We were delighted to earn a shilling for pocket money, Mr Taylor was club champion at the time and to our great surprise the visitor offered to give Mr Taylor three bisques or better known as three strokes. This to Jim and myself was fantastic and never heard of before, however on going round after a few holes I became quite friendly with him, the explanation I received was that after the first world war in 1918 he had just finished his education at Edinburgh University, this being 1922. It turned out he was one of the finest Amateur Golfers in Britain, and had recently won the French "Open" Championship. He asked me if I would ever play golf and I had to reply that my parents were quite poor and could not afford to let me play and of course I was unemployed. He was very sorry and said he would like to help me, but he was going off to America shortly to have an operation to one of his eyes that had been damaged in the 1914 - 1918 War, when he was an officer in the Royal Scots attached to the "Royal Tank Corps" in a mustard gas attack, and this would probably be his last game of golf in Britain. He gave me a little advice when he said "John, if you ever play golf and you can go round any golf course in level fours you will be a match for anybody." How right he was and I remembered that all my life, what a wonderful golfer and a privilege to go round with him. He became one of the world's most famous golfers as "golfer and teacher". His name was Tommy Armour. Here is an extract from a book he wrote by one of the Golfing Masters who had lessons from Tommy Armour.

Written on the back page and here I quote.

A note about Tommy Armour

After winning many Amateur golfing events in Europe as well as the French "Open", Armour went to the United States shortly after the first war and became a "professional golfer" in 1925. In 1927 he won the U.S. Open Championship and the Canadian Open. Subsequently, he went on to win every major Championship of the day, including the British Open, the P.G.A., the Western and the Metropolitan. He was acclaimed the greatest "Iron Club" player in the history of golf.

In 1929, he became professional at the Boca Raton Club in Florida, he took much pleasure in helping beginners to "break 100" as he does in brushing up the games of the top tournament professionals when they cannot iron out their own difficulties. Armour claims that the teaching part of his career has been the best - the part he has enjoyed the most.

It is a fact of life, evolution takes place, and now in 1987 so many changes have taken place with modern equipment and the playing of golf by golfing giants of today, who go round in figures well under fours and many scores in the sixties are common place to win major tournaments, so much for the moment in the game of golf.

Growing up to adult life

Before leaving my day school days I should make reference to the effect on my life with the rather good result in my qualifying examination and a heart to heart talk with Mr Lindsay my Headmaster, who advised me that education should be my main concern from now on and how right he was. In the next three years I had various teachers who gave me very great assistance, Mr Cruickshank the assistant headmaster took Mathematics and Algebra etc., he also took charge of the new formed football team. Mr Hutchison took Science, Mr Scott English and Languages, Mr Brown took woodwork, Mr Hannah Art and Mr Diack took Music. Needless to say I could master all the subjects with the exception of Music which I was hopeless at, although I improved a little in later life. All this plus Boys' Brigade made me rather busy until I left school at 15 with no job. However after a period of nine months I received a job with the local plumber, gasfitter, hydraulic and sanitary engineer, Mr R. Currie, 31 Station Road in Milngavie, to serve six years as an apprentice. It was always a job. The firms hours were from 7 am in the morning till 5 pm with a break of 1/2 an hour for breakfast and 1/2 an hour for dinner. In the evening I had to attend classes on the above subjects at the Stow College in Glasgow.

In the meantime my family had several change of houses from Main Street to Stewart Street, from Stewart Street to 36 Douglas Street, from Douglas Street to Barloch Terrace in Moor Road, from where I started my apprenticeship, after two years to a bungalow at Keystone Quadrant where I resided until I was married. All members of the family by this time had been married with only my parents and my sister Helen, who was widowed and, left to look after the house; changed days indeed. One other change I have omitted was for a period at No 12 Claremont Gardens, we seem to have been living all over Milngavie. The bungalow at Keystone was called "Dunvegan" as that was where my mother was born. My father now retired after a variety of jobs; from Tambowie Distillery to Woodburn, a local builder, to a new dam at water works, to the railway station at Milngavie, to Ellangowan Paper Coy to Blackie Book Binders in Glasgow on to Barr and Stroud Instrument Makers at Anniesland from where he retired. He seemed capable of turning his hand to most things. There were not so many unions in those days.

Ellangowan Paper Mill

Sergeant M. McDougall and author,
1st Milngavie Boys Brigade, about 1923

Mother's home at Dunvegan, Isle of Skye

Father

First church in Milngavie, on Kirk Row

MILNGAVIE FROM ROMAN TIMES

In order to continue with my own experiences in adult life I should like to give a rough idea as to the growth of the village to a town, the Estates and Industrial Life.

The district in old pre-Roman times was on the border land which separated the wild Caledonians of the North from the ancient Britons of the South, and the particular tribe who inhabited it were called by the Romans the Damnii, perhaps the most powerful and prosperous of the tribes of North Britons. Little is known with certainty of either their mode of life or religion and so we pass to Roman times. During occupation of this country by the Romans about the Year of our Lord 139 we saw the completion by the Romans of the Great Wall of Antoninus Pius. This was the vast rampart between the Firths of Forth and Clyde to guard the more settled southern districts from the fierce incursions of the men of the north for a period of years when the Romans left the country.

The spot where Milngavie now stands was on the verge of a great loch, or rather series of lochs, partly natural and partly artificial, which lay to the north of the wall and covered all the low ground from Kilpatrick village to Kilsyth.

The wall itself was in full view, and traces of it are still to be seen distinctly, particularly opposite Hillfoot House and the "Stickit Kirk" on the road from Canniesburn to Milngavie.

This great wall was a high bank of turf and earth, probably faced with stone, and with a deep ditch in front. Every mile or two there were small forts erected on it, and on the south side a military road extended from end to end.

At New Kilpatrick there was a large and important fortified camp, of which the traces were, till comparitively recently, very distinct. It lay a little to the east of the village, and the site of the tent of a wartime Roman centurion is in many instances now occupied by the comfortable villa of a peaceful Glasgow trader. At the very spot where the station at Bearsden now stands, was an old Roman burial place belonging to this fortress.

To the north of the wall on the high ground, about Craigmaddie, Mugdoch, and at other points on the Kilpatrick hills, were detached forts, the remains of which can in some places still be traced. These are supposed by antiquarians to have been forts of observation built by the natives, and by others more probably, to have been outposts of the Romans.

Be this as it may, there is no doubt this district was aplace of some importance to the Romans, guarding as it did one of the great passes from the north; and the Damnii of Milngavie could not fail during the long period of the Roman occupation of Britain to profit by their vicinity to them, and to learn in some degree the comforts of civilisation, and to cultivate under the shadow of their protection the arts of peace.

In fact, it must have been rather a gay and fashionable neighbourhood here in those remote days, and the large barracks at Bearsden, well filled as they were with handsome young Romans, must have made it "fair times" for the lovely fair-haired Damnian maidens of Milngavie up to the fifith century, when the Romans finally left the country.

The departure of the Romans was doubtless a sore blow to our district, for immediately on its taking place a rush of the savages from the north followed, and all traces of order were quickly obliterated.

Milngavie was a small centre of civilization and a bright spot of light on the edge of the dark and endless forests which lay beyond and covered the whole north and west of Scotland. After this period there follows a long and gloomy period in the history of our country with terrible conflicts between rival races and tribes who strove for mastery, the scene of bloody encounters between the Picts of the north and the Strathclyde Britons of the south.

Mugdock appears to have been the centre of much activity with a large battle at Ardunan near Strathblane where a curious group of stones on Craigmaddie Muir, called the Auld Wive's Lift, are situated as being erected in memory of some such event; with an unusual number of ancient graves in the vicinity in the Parish of Baldernock. After another long period of unrest Christianity was introduced to the Kingdom of Strathclyde by St Ninian and later by St Mungo.

We now come to a period when Saxon Princess Margaret of England became the Queen of Malcolm Canmore towards the end of the 11th Century. The influx of Saxons and Normans from England was the means of bringing English customs to Scotland. These settlers quickly set to work to arrange the manors, baronies or larger districts of country which were assigned to them, on the model of those they left in the south. One of the first improvements was to settle the church on a firm basis. Each baron made a grant to the church and a parish was formed, such as the Parish of Kilpatrick which was formed out of the great district that comprised the Earldom of the Levenax or Lennox. The whole Shire of Dumbarton with the addition of the Parishes of Fintry, Kilsyth, Campsie, Strathblane, Baldernock, Balfron, Drymen and Inchcalleoch, now

Buchanan, was the probable extent of the vast Earldom at this early date.

The Earl's principal castle at first was Dunbarton, but this was early resigned to the Crown, the five fortified castles of the Earldom were Balloch, Inchmurrin, Cotter, Ballagan and Mugdock.

The Earls of Lennox were the first known proprietors of our district here, and before going further, I may briefly dispose of them by reminding you that Duncan the 8th and the last of the old Earls of Lennox, was, along with Murdoch, Duke of Albany (his son-in-law) and his two sons, executed at Stirling in 1425 soon after the return of James I from his long captivity in England, on a charge of treason and misgovernment of the country in the King's absence.

After the Battle of Flodden in 1513 many changes took place. The Earl of Montrose allocated most of the ground associated with the Earl of Lennox, the Earl of Montrose living principally at his houses Mugdock, Garscube and Kincardine, parts of the Earldom being in Dumbartonshire and Stirlingshire. A descendant of the family, a cousin, Sir John Graham, became the new owner of Mugdock Castle, a huge part of the district of Dumbartonshire and a smaller part of Stirlingshire. He seems to have been much occupied latterly with domestic matters and spent a good deal of his time in golfing and archery, he was much addicted to tobacco, the golf being played over the now Milngavie Golf Course.

Factor of Mugdok," and also the accounts of the Factors on the other estates. I give here a few extracts—

ITEM given the 12d of Marche, 1625, to Patrik Lytstone for ane dusone goiff balls to my Lord,..iij lib.

Item for two dusone tobacco pypes the said day,..............viij. s.

Paid to Patrick Lystsone.

After the restoration the Castle of Mugdock was the only residence of the family till they removed to Buchanan Castle about the beginning of the 18th Century. All that now remains around the old Castle of Mugdock is High Park Farm and Laigh Park Farm.

Having now sketched slightly the state of this district while a part of the ancient Earldom of Lennox and also an account of the Duke of Montrose and Lord Graham, I shall now tell you a little of the different estates in the neighbourhood which were formed out of these great baronies.

Estates of the neighbourhood
Dougalston Mansion and Estate

This place originally formed part of the Barony of Mugdock and before it was granted to the Grahams, was in Dumbartonshire. Its name appears to have been taken from Dugald son of Alwin, second son of the Earl of Lennox. For many generations Dougalston was in possession of a family of Grahams, cadets of the Mugdock Grahams being leading merchants in Glasgow and one was Dean of Guild in 1650 and all of whom gave or left money to charitable institutions of Glasgow. In 1707 John Graham, then laird of Dougalston, built a new house in the same place as the existing one, the foundation stone was inscribed that he and Margaret Nisbet had done so. This stone was found later when preparing the site of another house on the same place. A further inscription incised upon it was "Robert Ker and Elizabeth Johnstone 1876". In between times, one in the name of John Glassford had purchased Dougalston. He came from Paisley, the son of a wealthy man. James Glassford came to Glasgow just as the Virginia trade in tobacco was opening up and did a wonderful trade. He was known as one of the "Tobacco Lords". He planted trees, formed lakes and gardens, a banqueting house and greatly added to the old house making it a magnificent mansion. He died in 1783, 68 years of age and Dougalston having been disentailed, was sold by his sons to Mr Robert Ker, himself a great glasgow tea merchant. It is now many years since the mansion house of the Grahams and Glassfords was burnt down, and for long Dougalston and its policies stood neglected and forlorn, but things have changed and under the new laird this fine old place is rising from its ashes renewed and beautiful, thanks to Mr Ker who had the tragedy of losing a fortune at Monte Carlo only to regain it the following year. Later he left Dougalston for another mansion at Bardowie, called "Bogha", and from there he lived at Eastertoun House, Mugdock. A very respected family. The house at Dougalston was bought by Mr. Connell a shipbuilder on the Clyde, who lived in it for many years till he died after World War 2. His widow lived there until she died, it was purchased and later demolished to make way for a golf course and housing estate by Reo Stakis, hotel owner.

Kilmardinny Mansion House Estate

The above property was part of the Barony of Mugdock and was taken out of Dumbartonshire and put into Stirlingshire to suit the Grahams. It was alienated by them, but in 1465 Sir John Colquhoun of that ilk had one part of it and the remainder belonged to the Lennoxes of Bolcorrach, an old family descended from the Earls of Lennox. The next family in possession were the Grahams, a branch of the Grahams of Dougalston. The next owner being the Rev Andrew Gray, minister of New Kilpatrick and afterwards of St Andrews

Parish in Glasgow. A very excellent man, Mr Gray had been presented to the parish in 1730, but for some reason certain members were not pleased and a serious riot took place at the church one Sunday morning. The Lairds of Mains, Garscube, Kilmardinny and Kilmanon with their sons and servants, and with other parishioners, took possession of the Church, pelted the pulpit with stones and barricaded the door. The objectors for the time were triumphant, they were obliged, however, soon afterwards to humble themselves before the majesty of the law, Mr Gray was settled and did very well. On Mr Grays death his nephew John Gray, minister of Strathblane, succeeded to Kilmardinny. He did not keep it long, but sold it off in four lots, the principal part with the mansion house being bought by Mrs Helen Colquhoun, widow of Wm Colquhoun of Garscadden. Later a Mr Brown improved and added to the old house and it is now a very handsome and commodious mansion. Today it is the property of Bearsden and Milngavie District Council for art and theatre etc. for local functions.

Mains Estate, Mansion House

The Douglasses of Mains have lived in this parish for fully 500 years, and with exception of the Grahams of Mugdock, now the Dukes of Montrose; They are the oldest family in the neighbourhood. Except for very short intervals they have always lived on their property and taken their proper share in county and parish work. The Douglasses came to Mains by the marriage of Nicholas Douglas in 1373 to Janet, one of the heiresses of the Galbraiths. Nicholas was the youngest of six sons! The eldest was Sir James Douglas, Lord of Dalkeith and the third was Sir Henry, the ancestor of the present Earl of Morton. Their sister was Margaret who married William Elphinstone of Blythswood, who was the father of the well known Bishop Elphinstone of Ross and Aberdeen. Without attempting a complete history of the Mains family, herewith are some of the more prominent members.

In 1549 Mathew Douglas succeeded as 5th Laird of Mains. In 1571 under the leadership of his neighbour Captain Thomas Crawford of Jordanhill, and along with friend and connection John Cunningham of Drumquhassel, who was then the proprietor and apparently occupier of Killermont, and others, he took an active part in a daring exploit, the surprise and capture of Dumbarton Castle.

At this time this strong fortress was held for Queen Mary, but the Regent Lennox was very anxious to obtain it, and Crawford Douglas and their companions volunteered to attempt its capture. They did so by means of a surprise and carried out their project in a most daring manner, scaling the rock at the most difficult and therefore least defended part, using ladders where possible, and climbing rock to rock with difficulty where they could not be used, till they reached the summit. The son of this brave old soldier was Malcolm Douglas, who married a daughter of Cunningham of Drumquhassel and Killermont, his father's companion.

Malcolm Douglas was much engaged in the public affairs of the day, but along with his father in law, who was a most active and daring spirit, he was apprehended by the then all powerful James Stewart, Earl of Arran, on the suspicion of being engaged in the raid of Ruthven and other treasonable conspiracies. This Earl of Arran's proceedings were very high handed and violent, and Mains and Drumquhassel had little or no trial. They were condemned and beheaded at the Cross of Edinburgh in 1585.

Another member of the family who rose to eminence was Robert Douglas, second son of this unfortunate Malcolm. Very early in life, he was in the household of Prince Henry, eldest son of James Vl. On the death of this Prince he continued in the services of his father, the King, and on Charles 1 succeeding he was promoted to a higher rank at Court and made a Privy Councillor and created Viscount of Belhaven, dying without issue on l4th January 1639. From this time onward the Douglasses have lived upon their property and taken their due share of the business of life. The Campbells of Blythswood are connected by marriage with the family under review and in terms of the Blythswood and Mains entails, the Douglasses have several times supplied heirs to this fine property of Blythswood, so that the Campbells of Blythswood may almost be said to be cadets of Mains. The Douglasses like many other families in the neighbourhood of Glasgow had town houses in the fashionable Briggate of Glasgow. Mains Mansion is not the original mansion of the state. It stood about a mile in the south and is still a picturesque and interesting old place, the present house was purchased along with some land from Mr McNair by Mr John Campbell Douglas, the present Mr Douglas' father, who built a very fine addition and changed the whole from Balvie to Mains. Balvie was a very old place owned by Earl Maldoven of Lennox granted to the Galbraiths. A daughter married Mr Logan and got with her the lands of Balvie, then a large estate. The Logans were cadets of the Restalrig family near Edinburgh and were an active, enterprising and somewhat lawless race, and in troublesome times when they lived at Balvie were much engaged in public affairs before being sold to Mr John Campbell. In modern times the present Douglas family moved to Aberfoyle and the house was demolished to enable a great number of smaller modern houses to be built all over the estate by private builders, changed days. Some of the street names are called after the Campbells and Douglasses of Mains.

Clober Estate and Mansion House

This has long been a separate estate and was part of the Barony of Mugdock. It was one of the estates taken from Dumbartonshire and put into Stirlingshire to please the Grahams about the beginning of the century. It belonged to the Grahams of Dougalston who were a great family and in 1773 the laird of Dougalston sold it to James McGregor, merchant in Glasgow and he built the original part of Clober House.

Mr Robert Dunlop succeeded his uncle and made large additions to the house. His son, Alexander Dunlop, advocate to Edinburgh was the new proprietor.

There is a peculiar interest attached to Clober, from its being the scene of some of the works of the celebrated natural philosopher and engineer James Watt, the inventor of the steam locomotive. The bleachfield here which has long been famous was planned by him for his father-in-law, Mr McGregor, and during its construction he superintended the making of the water courses and the erection of the machinery, and worked successfully for many years by Messrs Pender and later by Major Drew, his brother and sister, until they died. It was idle for a considerable time and the old water wheel and machinery was admired for many years until the local Town Council filled in the Clober Dam to make a public coup of it, thereby destroying what would have been one of the most important historical features of our town, what a disgraceful thing to do. Where the works were is now the site of the Bowater Factory, cardboard box manufacturers and other small factories. So far as Clober Mansion is concerned it was lived in by the Blackwood family who owned the Craigton Bleachworks for many years until the family died. Like Douglas of Mains the house was demolished to make way for new houses covering the estate, with some roads in it named after the Blackwood family.

Part of the estate and Clober Farm was taken over by Walter Barr Lyle and made into an eighteen hole golf course, at first as a public course, but now a private club.

Craigallian House and Estate

Craigallian has long been a separate estate and being an old part of Mugdock it consists of a farm. It could be termed a mixed farm of the dairy type with cattle and also sheep grazing on a substantial area with a forest of beautiful trees and a mansion house. About two centuries ago it belonged to a family of Brysons. There used to be remains, and very picturesque they were, of the original mansion house. A few years ago they were removed and the present mansion house was built by a new owner Mr Alan Barns-Graham, who had coal mines in Lanarkshire and treated the place as a country mansion. Later, the house and estate was acquired by Messrs Connell, shipbuilders on the Clyde. There were two brothers who employed quite a staff, having Rolls Royce cars that could be seen daily going to, and coming from the shipbuilders yard on the Clyde. The estate was inherited by a nephew, Sir Charles Connell and family. Sir Charles' son now occupies the mansion house, part of which are now offices, the firm having been removed from the Clyde some time ago. He also runs the farm, his sport appears to be pheasant shooting and horse riding. It is surrounded by beautiful scenery and can be termed the gateway to the north, as the West Highland Way from Milngavie to Fort William goes through the ground.

Craigend Estate and Castle

It was formerly called the Gallowknowe, from the Gallows of the Barony just above the Castle at approximately 300 feet. It was rather unique when you ascended the hill as you were faced with a small loch as if a volcano at sometime had left the inside of the hill hollow and the depth of water was quite considerable, in fact it was used as the water supply to the castle. It must have been like an artesian well. It was laid around with a beautiful garden with all kinds of plants, most of which appeared to be foreign.

In early times, after trial, the executions were carried out at Gallows erected at Gallowknowe Hill. It was for male persons only, female persons were drowned at the Gallows foot. Around 1500 it was tenanted by a family named Smith and members of it, as traditions in the family tell "were out" with the Great Marquis in his wars, though of course in a subordinate position.

After the death of the Great Marquis, James the Second known as the "Good Marquis" found that in consequence of the loyal exertions of his great father, his estates were greatly burdened with debt.

To clear this off he was obliged to sell a further part of the Barony and about 1660 Robert Smith bought Craigend a small house which then stood on the site of the present mansion.

Towards the end of the century the Craigend family acquired property in the West Indies, some of them went there and others went into business in Glasgow. They were upon the whole prosperous, and John Smith, the then laird, made a considerable addition to the old house and added to the property by several purchases. On his death his son, who had succeeded to several uncles' money, built the present house about 1815. The last Smith laird of Craigend was John who sold it in 1891 to Sir Andrew Buchanan C.C.B., who became Ambassador to the Court of Vienna.

Craigend has vastly improved since the growth of the timber. It was formerly a very bare muirland place. Later Sir Andrew Buchanan rented the castle to Sir Harold Yarrow the Clyde shipbuilder for quite a number of years, before leaving for Kilmacolm. It lay idle for some time until the house and estate opened as a zoo with all kinds of animals. It had to close as it did not pay and has now been unoccupied for a number of years and is derelict. It has now been taken over and is in the process of becoming a Country Park.

Craigmaddie Estate and Mansion House & Castle

This Estate is a small part of the old Barony of Cartenvenoch or Bardowie; the old Castle of Craigmaddie is about 300 yards from the original small house built at the end of the last century by James Black, Lord Provost of Glasgow, who also laid out the grounds with much taste. It was the ancient seat of the Galbraiths, James Black afterwards built what may be called the beginning of the present Mansion House.

The succeeding proprietors were General Peters of Glasgow; Rev Dr Mc Turk, Professor of Church History in the University of Glasgow; Henry Gordon, afterwards Henry Gordon Glassford of Dougalston:- James Spens Black of the Printfield in Milngavie:- and Major Graham Stirling of Craigbarnet - all of whom made additions and improvements. It was bought from the Major by Mr Ker of Dougalston and is now the residence of Mr Charles T. Higginbotham and his wife who is a daughter of Mr Ker. They, like all their predecessors, had their hands in the mortar tub.

More recently it was taken over by Captain Arnold Wilson, who was one of the original members along with Mr Smith who started the Boys Brigade movement. He was also the man who started the lst Millguy Boys Brigade and was Captain for a nunber of years. The writer has many happy memories of our reception and sports on visits to the mansion house, enjoying hospitality at New Year and summer sports at this house, where the place and grounds are beautiful and the actual house so commodious, after our walk from Milngavie to Craigmaddie and back to Milngavie, rather tired after playing the bagpipes and bugle band home. Today, it is owned by a Mr Struthers.

Bardowie Estate and Castle

This is rather a beautiful old place on the margin of the loch of the same name with the castle outstanding as viewed from the Balmore and Torrance main road. It is in the parish church of Baldernock, the scene of that famous play "Bunty Pulls the Strings", the bell on the roof being pulled from outside the church.

The castle was a principal residence of the great family of Galbraith, and on the breaking up of their Barony it passed, by the marriage of Janet Keith one of the co-heiresses of the Galbraiths, to John Hamilton, of the family of Cadzow, of which the Duke of Hamilton is now head. The east part of the castle is very ancient and is a fine specimen of the massive and faithfully built mansions of that early date. The writer has had some experience of this old castle and above the front door there is a stone sticking out from the wall about 3 feet, where I am told executions were carried out.

From the fourteenth century when we first hear of them until 1526, we know very little of the Hamiltons except that they duly married, and as duly had heirs who carried on the line. In that year the monotony of the family history was broken by a quarrel with their relatives the Logans of Balvie. The Logans and their friends finally murdered John Hamilton of Bardowie and his son John, for which they were punished by a very moderate fine of £100 Scots Pounds.

Allan Hamilton of Bardowie who succeeded, also met a violent death, he too quarrelled with his neighbour Colin Campbell of Auchenhowie and Dowan, he too had the worst of it and got killed.

In 1550 the Hamiltons who had been living up to this time at Craigmaddie removed to Bardowie. Craigmaddie Castle was allowed to fall into ruins, with Bardowie being added to and preserved.

Unfortunately, the families of Bardowie and Dougalston fell out and had a violent quarrel. It was patched up and John Hamilton signed a bond at Bardowie, wherein he engaged that "James, Mr Allan, and Umphra Hamilton his sons shall not molest Walter Graham of Dougalston or his tenants from that date." To the present time the history of the family has been uneventful, until Dr Francis Buchanan Hamilton established his claim to be chief of the clan Buchanan. The present laird, his son, is thus John Buchanan Hamilton, head of the ancient family of Hamilton of Bardowie.

MILLGUY OR MILNGAVIE IN MODERN TIMES

Millguy is the child of the Allander.

From the time this stream leaves its heathery bed there are two main tributaries, one from the Auchineden area and another from the Carbeth area via Craigallian Loch. There are also numerous springs until the waters reach Millguy and onwards, until it sinks into the River Kelvin. It is a thing of beauty now, rushing through the rocks and brackens, now meandering in the meadows, now gliding through the copse wood. Milngavie has good reason to admire the old stream which has made her what she is today "Thing of Beauty" as she is. For a time our great neighbour of Glasgow obtained water by a channel from a reservoir in the Dunbarton Muir before embarking on her own world famous water supply from Loch Katrine to the newly constructed reservoirs at Milngavie, before being despatched by huge water mains from the original No 1 Reservoir at Barrachan near Mugdock.

The water from the Allander was very important for the life line of Milngavie in early times, the water could be taken by gravity or pumped for the use of industrial purposes. The law was that use could be made of the water, provided it was allowed back into the Allander at a lower point, hence the use of water wheels and pumps etc.

Agriculture and Industrial Growth

For hundreds of years a corn mill stood on the stream. Here and to it, many of the lands in this part of the barony were thirled, although the Montrose family parted with most of their lands here, they still held on to the old mill, and it is only in comparatively modern times that it passed out of their hands. There is no doubt this mill was the beginning of Milngavie.

Round it a few houses gradually rose, but so slow was the growth of the place that in 1793 there were only 200 inhabitants After this, however, the rate of increase became quicker. Small farms were also coming on stream with the disposal of lands by the Montrose family. The growth of agriculture was quite considerable.

The bleachfield at Clober and other work being established, that by 1831 - 1162 inhabitants, in 1895 there were 1871 inhabitants, and shortly after over 2000.

At the beginning of this century and for a considerable time afterwards there were small bleachfields on the Allander. Here matters were conducted in a very primitive fashion. A level piece of ground being intersected by trenches filled with water from the stream, which men with long ladles poured from time to time upon the articles to be bleached; Clober, formed about the end of the last century, was the first of the large works.

It was partly laid out by the great James Watt. The large cotton spinning works - now the paper mill - soon followed. They were erected by James Donaldson & Co, on a feu on the farm of Cloberhaugh granted by Henry Glassford of Dougalston and by the side of the Allander. These works afterwards belonged to Kibble and Mc Kerrals. In 1825 it passed into the hands of Messrs Robert Mc Gregor & Co, a firm, in its different forms, well and favourably known for long here. Later it was called Ellangowan Paper Company managed by Colonel Birrell. After his death it was taken over by Clyde Paper Co, but eventually closed to be a scrap yard until taken over by the local Town Council, who built a number of houses on the site.

Block Printing Works were first introduced to Milngavie by Mr Weir, whose daughter is still resident here. It was afterwards carried on with other printing on a large scale by James Black & Co. In the large works on the Allander known now as Clober Crescent. Many employees were employed in these works, and from them sprang the men who formed the genesis of the Mechanics Institute (now defunct) the oldest social and literary agency in the neighbourhood. The site was used for quite a few purposes, a hall for Boys Brigade, Ellangowan Masonic hall, Billiards Rooms and production of a local paper called the Milngavie Herald.

It is in the Mechanics Institution this association was formed, in the autumn of 1836 and had for its objective "The dissemination of useful knowledge, by the delivery of public lectures at such times and on such terms as would enable all who felt inclined to participate in the advantages which must be derived from the spread of general knowledge."

The first president was Mr Alexander Dunlop of Clober, a fine old gentleman. He opened the Institution with an inaugural address with great success, it was published and had a large circulation.

The institution had an honorary president and an honorary committee of 12 with an ordinary president and committee of 16. The first president was Mr Henry Ross.

In 1837 a library was formed in connection with the Institution and contained 1000 volumes of books. The fortunes of the Institution were varied, the membership at times falling to 17 in number and at other times as many as 70 and 80, there having been some excellent courses of lectures. The library sometimes was very well used. Then a large new hall was formed for their lectures and other purposes, a living and lively affair, and a centre of good to the inhabitants of Milngavie. You must make things attractive and amusing as well as solid and sensible or you will not succeed. After many years the Printing Works closed and with it went the Mechanics Institution and the library, a great loss to the community at that time.

The dye works at Burnbrae, though not exactly in the town, were now a very important addition to its industries.

There was also formerly an annual fair or market here for the sale of cattle, horses, sheep, pigs, hens, and also for the sale or rather niffering or exchange of wives - a peculiar institution and a practice which, in some instances, might perhaps have its advantages, but, upon the whole, would likely complicate the state of matrimony. The stance of this market was at the Cross Trees near to where the City of Glasgow Bank was situated. The last fair was held here the summer before cholera appeared in this country - about 1830.

Station Road

With the advent of steam, the Railway Company opened a line between Glasgow and Milngavie. It extended past the Ellangowan Paper Co. The idea to continue the line to Strathblane and the north never materialized, but with the coming of the Railway the town began to prosper and grow in intensity.

The start of the Glasgow Corporation water supply from Loch Katrine brought over many Irish families. Also, during the clearances of the Highlands many good families from the north west found work with the industries in the town. This in turn called for houses and shops of all kinds.

Coal was found in abundance at Baljaffray Pit. There was a Gas Works in the centre of the town, and building materials came from local stone quarries. The West of Scotland Laundry one of the best equipped in Scotland. Also Strathdee's Ginger Beer Works at the side of the Allander; McAulay haulage contractors and Milngavie Co-op Society. With the production of whisky at Dumgoyne Distillery and Tambowie Distillery at Craigton, plus the whisky made in houses by our friends from the Highlands. With the march of time we had the oldtown of Main St, Douglas Street, Cheapside Street. Mugdock Road was the centre of the town, whilst the new town comprised mainly of Glasgow Road, Strathblane Road, Baldernock Road, Tannoch Drive, Heathfield Drive and Montrose Gardens, where there were numerous villas, the residences of the Glasgow business men, who enjoyed leisure far from the city's "fume and fret". Later we had the lands of Crossveggate and Keystone being developed on the south side with Dougalston and Barloch on the east side, on the west side the lands of Craigdhu and Mains Estate including Clober Estate. It is at this stage one soon discovers what town-planning means in the modern erection of houses, commercial, and industrial premises with roads and bridges etc.

Having given a rough sketch of Milngavie from early times before going again on to my own experiences, I should like to quote a passage from a lecture given by the late J. Guthrie Smith Esq. of Mugdock Castle, to the Milngavie Mechanics Institution on 15th January 1878.

"There have always been a number of very good people in Milngavie, and there have always been a number of very different ones. With all its fine water it has never been very clean, though I am bound to say that hitherto in spite of this it has been usually very healthy, but this should not be presumed upon too long. There has always been a great deal too much whisky drunk here, and I think that in this Milngavie is as bad as ever, or perhaps worse, but I am not disposed to be a croaker, I see no reason at all why Milngavie should not mend its ways - why with its churches and its Sunday schools, and week day schools, with its municipal institutions it should not be made one of the pleasantest places for business or residence in the West of Scotland. It is beautifully situated with a fine southern exposure, and it has plenty of good water, churches, schools, shops and other conveniences of life - all that is wanted is to improve off the face of the earth the indifferent people, to go thoroughly into a good system of sanitary reform, and stick to it, to drink less whisky, and to encourage in every possible way rational and innocent amusements among the rising generation reverently, as our fathers did before us, on the ordinances of religion, and to be regular at service in our churches, be what they may, and to show an example in our private households from the good old men who dwelt of yore in the Highland Row of Milngavie!"

Herewith is a list of Public Houses and Hotels with a Licence known to the writer during his lifetime:-

Black Bull Hotel, Main Street. Original Hotel in Millguy.
Innes Public Bar, Main Street. Later known as Talbot Arms.
Auld Hoose Pub, corner of Main Street and Douglas Street (Demolished).
Cross Keys Pub, corner Station Road and Mugdock Road.
Woodlands Bar, Mugdock Road (Demolished).
The Railway Inn, Station Road (Now a chemist shop).
The Newtown Vaults, Glasgow Road and Baldernock Road.
Browns Public Bar, Strathblane Road (Demolished).
B J Young Grocer, Douglas Street Licence.
Approximate population 10,000 in 1936.

Churches Various

Herewith is a list of Churches known to the writer during his lifetime. Religious services on second Sunday, July 1788 in the open air, later known as the Preaching Braes on Barloch Moor. Near this site was built the first church on Mugdock Road. The minister was Rev Mr Mc Naughton, later a most beautiful Church was built in a corner site between Buchanan Street and Cairns Drive, known as Cairns Church of Scotland.

In the first instance *The Relief Church* 1788-1847.
United Presbyterian 1847-1900.
United Free 1900-1929.
Church of Scotland 1929 onward.
New Kilpatrick Church, Bearsden Parish Church 1830.
New Branch Church, Milngavie Parish Church 1840-1906, corner of Station Road and Hillhead Street.
The new Church of Scotland, Saint Pauls Church of Scotland 1906.
Free Church of Scotland, St Luke's, at corner of Station Road and Buchanan Street 1896. Branch of Baldernock Free Church.
Christian Brethren Church, Allander Hall, Douglas Street 1890.
St Lukes Church, opened at new church built in the Mains Estate at Clober.
A Continuing Free Church was built and opened in Craigdhu Road.
The first Roman Catholic Church in Milngavie dedicated to St Joseph, was opened in Woodlands Street 1872.
St Andrew Episcopal Church, opened in Park Road 1896.
St Lukes Church, Buchanan Street and Station Road, now a Catholic Church.

ADMINISTRATION OF THE TOWN

The Burgh of Milngavie and formation of the Town Council. I now turn to the administration and formation of the Town Council that played a large part in my own life at a later period.

Milngavie was declared to be a populace place within the meaning of the Act on 10th May 1875, the meeting of householders to consider the advisability of adopting the Act was held on the 31st July of that year in the old Parish Church where Sheriff - Substitute Sconce presided.

The first meeting of the Commission Board was held within the Bridge Street School on the 27th September. The members present on that occasion were Mr Robert Crawford of the Railway Inn, Mr James Watt of the Grain Mill, Mr James McAulay, Contractor, Mr D McGregor, Grocer and Mr William Hunter, Education Representative, Mr John Woodburn, Builder and Mr John Strathdee, Post Office.

At this meeting Mr Robert Crawford was elected chief magistrate later to be first Provost of Milngavie 1875- 76, while Mr James Watt and Mr James McAulay were appointed junior magistrates. The first clerk to the Commissioners was Mr Robert Mackenzie, who held the office for a brief period and then resigned, being succeeded by Mr John Cranmer. Mr Charles Bissland of the Douglas Arms Hotel was the first honorary treasurer of the burgh, while the post of active treasurer was held by Mr Hugh Carmichael from 1875-1888. He was Inspector of Poor for the Parish of New Kilpatrick in 1888. The dual offices were undertaken by Mr John Cranmer and carried on by him until the time of his death.

The population at the formation of the Burgh in 1875 was 2184, and the assessable rental £4072.

Owing to the development of the Burgh the surrounding districts were extended in 1901 and again in 1912. At the census of 1921 the population was returned at 4434 and the assessable at £42,288. The Town Council consisted of a Provost, two Magistrates and six Councillors. At a later date Lieut Colonel Robert Kyle C.M.G., D.S.O., was for many years Town Clerk of Milngavie.

The Council Chambers were on the first floor of the Burgh Hall in Station Road, with the Police Station next door. Unfortunately during the Second World War the Burgh Hall was turned into a cleansing station and A R P centre. A fire took place and destroyed the hall, and a new town hall, and art gallery was built called the Lillie art gallery, for their generosity towards the building of it. The Lillie family were very well known artistes; The offices were originally in the Burgh Hall, where the first Burgh Surveyor was Mr Frank Preston, but were transferred to premises in Grange Road. Jimmy Shannon was the local bell ringer for information going round the streets. He had a great voice "Here ye, Here ye".

The Burgh Coat of Arms

According to the late Marquis of Bute K.T., the arms of the Police Burgh of Milngavie, which are said to have been designed by the late Mr Guthrie Smith of Mugdock Castle as drawn upon the official seal are very difficult to describe heraldically. It is however apparent they have been compiled so as to combine historical allusions.

Within the circle bearing the legend is a large heraldic rose, which is said to be taken from the arms of Lennox "because Milngavie and district belonged to the Grahams, and the district is still The Lennox".

The arms of the Earl of Lennox of Auld, as given by Sir David Lindsay, are argent, a saltire between four roses, gulls. He represents the roses a four-leaved, without barbs, but seeded argent. In the case of the seal also the rose is the ordinary five-leaved heraldic rose, and it is barbed presumably proper; but adds the Marquess, being the Lennox rose, it must be gulls, and, indeed, appears to be so scored upon the seal; and if it be treated as an heraldic charge, the field must be argent. Within this is another circle which is fimbriated, within this again, and touching it, is a peculiar figure, something between a quatrefoil and a cross aiquisee: and this again has a peculiar border somewhat like a fimbriation; in the four spaces left by this figure are as many scallops, the rounded or lower side of each of them being turned towards the centre.

These scallops are taken from the arms of Graham, and are introduced in this device to show that the Grahams were the founders of this mill. The arms of Graham are or, on a chief sable three escallops of the first.

They must be therefore, says the Marquess of Bute, and be upon colour which may be most naturally supposed to be sable. Upon the device as a quartrefoil is a cross molene gulls square-pierced.

This device has been assumed because this so-called cross represents a millrend or "Water Wheel", being after the form of an iron instrument fixed in the nether stone of a mill. This device is therefore a play upon the name of the Burgh, which is commonly interpreted to mean Mill of Guy, it is all very complicated.

The Glasgow Corporation Water Works

Herewith I give you some details of the Glasgow Water Works as my life from now on is much concerned with water and water supply and with civil engineering etc.

Perhaps the outstanding feature of interest in Milngavie is the Glasgow Corporation Water Works situated at Mugdock and Craigmaddie. The original reservoir was called the Mugdock reservoir as the water entered at that area through a tunnel and pipes conveyed from Loch Katrine. The Reservoir has a water surface of 60 acres, and at an available depth of 40 feet, has a capacity of 489 million gallons.

The Act of Parliament authorizing the Craigmaddie Reservoir was obtained in 1882 and the operations were in progress for twelve years. The Reservoir has a water surface of 86.25 acres and an available depth for the supply of the City of Glasgow of 40 feet, and at this depth contains 700 million gallons.

Craigmaddie Reservoir contains 14 days supply, at the rate of 50 million gallons per day, and Mugdock Reservoir nearly 10 days supply, twenty four days supply in all.

The embankment of the Craigmaddie Reservoir is nearly one mile long and is 93 feet above the bed of a small stream, which at one time flowed through the site.

This reservoir formed part of a scheme for duplicating the water works, in order to provide a supply of 100 million gallons per day to the city, and was constructed with a view to fulfilling the same purpose as the Mugdock Reservoir - that of maintaining a regular supply of water to Glasgow while the customary and necessary repairs were being made upon the aqueduct from Loch Katrine.

The turning of the first sod in connection with the construction of the Craigmaddie Reservoir was performed by Provost McOnie, on the 20th November 1883.

The operations in connection with the Reservoir were started in July 1886, having been entrusted to Messrs Robert Carlyle & Co, at a sum of £104,552.

This firm, however, only executed £22,000 worth of work when after eighteen months, they surrendered their contract. The work was re-let to Messrs Morrison and Mason in May 1888, and this firm carried it to completion. The cost of the reservoir, including land, but exclusive of interest, was about £300,000. The construction gave jobs to many Highland and Irish families, who remained in Milngavie after, and became very good citizens. A monument erected to Mr Gale, chief engineer can be seen at the junction of the two reservoirs, a fitting memorial.

The original Mugdock Reservoir was opened in 1859 by Queen Victoria.

Author at "Craigenure", Innellan, Cowal

Reproduced from above booklet produced in 1930

St. Luke's Church and Milngavie Burgh Hall

Station Road Bearsden

Robert Crawford,

First Provost of Milngavie 1875 - 1876

Mrs T. R. Ker M.B.E.

Craigend Castle

The old mill

Hilton Park Golf Course

Back of McAuley's

Milngavie Cross (Author lived above shops as a boy)

NOW WE MOVE TO ADULT LIFE

At the age of sixteen I was engaged to commence an apprenticeship of six years with the local firm of R Currie, Plumbing, Gasfitter, Hydraulic and Sanitary Engineer at 31 Station Road, Milngavie, doing business with most of the building, domestic, commercial and industries in quite a substantial area of the County of Dumbartonshire and Stirlingshire. This was the biggest challenge to my life so far. I can recall my first day at work. The tradesman I had to assist was Mr Robert Leitch, a first class tradesman. We started off with a messenger push bicycle with a huge roll of lead pipe walking to a mansion house called Westerton House at Mugdock, the property of Professor Barr partner in the firm of Barr & Stroud, Scientific Instrument Makers, Anniesland. We took turn about to push the bike and I was glad to reach our destination to have a cup of tea. Our job was to install a hot water installation and a new bathroom at an alteration in one of the lodges. At that time sanitation was taking an upturn to the benefit of the occupants in many houses in the district, thereafter no matter what I did it was clear to me that if I had to make progress in life, education was a must. With this in view I worked very diligently at evening classes after my days work at the Stow College of Building in Glasgow, usually three evenings per week, one evening for practical work, one evening for theory, one evening for drawing. My wage for the first year was Nine Shillings per week and if successful in gaining the certificates of merit you got a rise in your weekly wage each year in addition to your standard rise. I was fortunate as my employer paid for my travelling expenses usually to travel to Glasgow, it was an incentive to do well.

After carrying out a few smaller contracts with my tradesman Mr Leitch we secured a large contract to install a mains cast iron water supply from the Torrance Water Company. This was for the excavation of ground, fitting in pipes on the main road from Allander Toll where the water works pipes were to Bardowie, Balmore, Torrance of Campsie and to terminals near Kirkintilloch, with a branch line to Baldernock, a branch line at Balmore through the village, also branch lines at Torrance. This was a great boost to each of the villages and houses as they had no piped water and, the only water was from springs or wells in the vicinity, this in turn allowed the existing houses to do alterations with the supply of bathrooms, hot and cold water, and sanitary appliances etc., creating a great deal of employment and changing conditions. All the excavation work was carried out by a Mr Branigan who employed a squad of experienced men in that type of work. When this was complete, we carried out works at Craigton Bleaching Company, Clober Bleaching Company, Ellangowan Paper Company, West of Scotland Laundry, Burnbrae Dye Works, most of the estate mansion houses, Garvie Lemonade Works, schools, commercial premises, and shopping premises, housing both private and municipal, churches. In 1925 we had an unusual assignment, my oldest brother during and after the First World War was manager of a firm at Old Kilpatrick on the Clyde, called the British Motor Marine and Launch Company, they made seaplanes and motor launches for large liners being built on the Clyde. They drifted on to making large motor cruisers with all domestic appliances and berths etc. The first one my firm did, was all the ships plumbing for a millionaire director in a firm, Coats of Paisley, and two others before returning to our usual works of plumbing and electrical work. We certainly did a good variety of work. Not long after that we were doing a job of renewing leadwork on the roof of St Pauls Church in Milngavie and when my boss was inspecting the roof he fell through a rotten part of the woodwork and I just managed to catch him by the shoulders to save a drop of some 40 feet. I think I got a bigger shock than he did with no bones broken or damaged, it was a lesson to me thereafter on the care to be taken on high roofs with proper scaffolding. My boss must have been about 50 years of age at that time.

It was about this period great changes were taking place in the design and materials coming forward. Lead piping was on the way out with light gauge copper pipes taking over with asbestos pipes, plastic pipes, and aluminium materials all coming into vogue. The use of zinc sheeting was departing from the scene. It meant new jointing materials and fittings, stainless steel was becoming popular over electro plating, the advancement of radio and later the introduction of the motor car and mass production, the start of television, and we were in a new world. The reconstruction of roads was to follow, it appeared to be never ending.

Modernisation with telephone communication, the great liners of the sea, electrification of railway communication, development of air transport, the world appeared to becoming smaller, everything seemed to be speed and science, and high technology was the order of the day.

Period of Change

The Glasgow Corporation had run tramcars from the city to Killermont Bridge as early as 1906, then again in 1923 the tram track was pushed out to Hillfoot with the avowed object to further the extension to Milngavie, but a prolonged dispute over the erection of a new bridge over the railway delayed this final stage until 1934.

The motor car has always played a prominent part in the life we live today, after a number of years the extended tramcar track to the Milngavie terminus was dispensed with as uneconomical. It was closed with the removal of the track from Milngavie into Maryhill terminus, and at a later stage, right into Glasgow with a new mode of transport taking over.

We were entering a period of change. The original industries like bleaching of cotton at Craigton and Clober were transferred to England, the Ellangowan Paper Coy. was taken over by the Clyde Paper Coy. but closed down later with the business transferred to England. Printing Works had long since closed down and Tambowie Distillery closed after fire had destroyed most of it.

So much for the advancement of science and technology. We were left with little industry, although Bowater Cardboard Box Manufacturers opened a large factory at Clober. Some small firms started up such as John Jamieson (Glasgow) Ltd., Scientific Instrument Makers, West of Scotland Laundry expanded, Ardrolic Engineering Company at Clober, Douglas Ltd, Bedding Manufacturers, James Garvie & Sons Mineral Waters, Weir Maker of Spectacle Frames, Milne Paint Coy., Alexanders Transport Garage as a bus depot, Messers Halleys Car and Caravan site, Messers Duncan Greenhouse and Garden Centre, Liddell Garage expansion of showroom for cars and the expansion of the Shopping Centre. With such a change in industry one could say we were about to suffer a trade recession, but on the other hand there was a great influx of people to Milngavie from the decentralisation of Glasgow, who with the arrival of the motor car preferred to live outside the City of Glasgow and travel in daily to business by car or train and of course by passenger bus. This caused great expansion of new housing estates, with all the modern planning required for road and sewers, the enlargement of services including new Sewage Purification Works, changes in the environment, cleansing, and public health, building control, open spaces, parks and halls, streets and lighting, with recreation grounds and sports facilities. By this time the Town Council had twelve members, including the Provost, four Magistrates, Honorary Treasurer, Dean of Guild and five Councillors, The Council Chambers and Municipal Offices were at 3 Buchanan Street.

Few places were better adapted for a garden city than Milngavie and as already stated in these days when the average businessman prefers to toil in the city and reside in the country. It is not anticipating too much to state that one day this quiet neighbourhood may become a great residential place, where commercial princes will spend their leisure in what has been fitly termed "The Gateway to the Highlands", especially to those who are interested in nature, or, in walking, or who wish to get away from the turmoil of the city for a peaceful interlude in the country setting without having to go too far afield. Unfortunately due to a change in politics both local and national with the result that work usually done by private firms changed, when the local authority started employing labour direct, this also applied to County Councils cutting out work to the private contractor for education, municipal housing and health, and by 1929 a depression in trades was the order of the day. It so happened the completion of my apprenticeship ended in 1929 and being the youngest member of the staff my boss found it necessary to letter me on 30th July 1929 as follows :-

> *The Bearer, John Gardner has been employed by me from 19th March 1923 to March 1929 as apprentice Plumber and Sanitary Engineer and since then as journeyman. During that time I have found him, capable, diligent and trustworthy. I regret having to part with him owing to depression in trade and can with confidence recommend him to anyone requiring his services.*
>
> *Signed*
> *R Currie*

I was most fortunate, it was not unusual in those days when an apprentice had served his time with one firm to go to another firm. Within one week, with my experience and qualification from the Stow College of Building, I obtained a job with a Glasgow firm doing a contract with Glasgow Corporation Housing for approximately 300 council houses at Scotstounhill, Glasgow. After a period of a few months I was given the job of testing the houses before being handed over to the Corporation. The firm doing the work was called Messrs Millar & McCrae. It so happened Mr Millar, one of the directors had a father in law the name of Devine, who had a plumbing business in Cambridge Street, Glasgow. He had a substantial contract to do at the Agricultural College in Bath Street, Glasgow and required a foreman, I was asked to take on the job, and gladly accepted it. This went on for a few months and when completed Mr Devine asked me to do a job for the Lord Provost of Glasgow, Sir Thomas Kelly, in a mansion house in Great Western Road, Glasgow. This was a first class job with all the latest appliances, an excellent job to do. After completion a surprise was in store for me, my original employer asked me if I would come back and work for him. After due consideration I agreed, and explained my situation to Mr Devine who thanked me for the help given him and wished me good luck. This was now 1930, little did I know then I had made a very good decision.

In the meantime I had continued my education at the Stow College and gained all the necessary qualifications with honours. It was at this point in time Mr Cunningham, the head teacher at the College had a long conversation with me and advised me to go on with my education at The Royal Technical College in Glasgow, with a view to take a position of a Sanitary Inspector or Surveyor in Local Government. This I agreed to do and for the next few years

I studied various subjects, which I will explain later with my other qualifications.

In the meantime with my original firm, I started another branch. In addition to plumbing & sanitary engineering, I became interested in electrical installation and central heating, both coming very much to the forefront.

During the last few years for recreation my sport at week-ends was playing amateur football in the Scottish Junior Football League. I was given the opportunity to play for St Johnstone in Perth, or a trial with Celtic Football Club, but my parents were against the idea, especially my mother, who said it would be a short life and I would probably suffer from injury. How right she was, so I took up ballroom dancing and bought a motor cycle for £5 from a local garage; In addition to this I happened to go one Saturday evening with my brother to Clober Golf Course to carry his clubs, instead my brother Norman allowed me to play the last few holes with his clubs. Now another change was about to take place in my life. At the last green, the local Secretary of the Artisan Club at that time was standing nearby, his name was Jim McKechnie, he said to me, "I did not know you played golf, I understand you to be a footballer", my brother said to him "you are quite correct, but he is not allowed to play football anymore", so the Secretary said, "John, give me 5 shillings and I will make you a member", but my reply was I could not do that as I only got one shilling pocket money a week, so my brother paid the five shillings and I was a member.

When my mother heard of this she gave my brother the five shillings. She was so pleased about it I was given a pound note to go into Glasgow and buy clubs, here I was in trouble again - where could you get clubs for a pound?

On the Monday after coming home from work my tea was on the table ready for me, I was then despatched into Glasgow by tramcar costing one halfpenny, I came off in Maryhill and made straight for "John' s Pawn Shop" to get second hand clubs. It must have been one of the greatest deals of all time with one pound in my pocket to buy a set of golf clubs.

The gentleman in the shop was just about to close the shop when I arrived, and after some persuasion I managed to get him up into the top attic of the premises and there before my eyes were the most awful dilapidated golf clubs covered in rust with wood hickery shafts. The first question I was asked was what type of clubs did I require, my reply was I was not sure as I was just starting the game, the owner of the shop then told me what I required to start.

He laid out a wooden club called a driver, then another called a baffy, three iron headed clubs called, a mid iron, a mashie and a putter. When I asked him if he had a piece of string to tie them up, he replied "goodness gracious, have you no bag either?" By this time I was nearly crying, he then gave me an old canvas ladies bag with a big hole in the side of it. When I produced my pound note he smiled and said, "by jove, you do want a bargain". However when he saw the state I was in, he accepted the pound, gave me the clubs, the bag and 2 gutty golf balls along with two silver king rubber type balls to start me off. He asked me where I came from when and I left the shop to catch a tramcar back home, he shook hands with me and wished me the best of luck, what an experience.

Next evening when I went along to my new golf club as a member with my set of clubs, the clubhouse was a fair sized wooden hut with lockers all round, with quite a few members in it. I was stopped at the door. I could not enter as I had no proof of membership, and after a short time the Secretary arrived and I was allowed in, apparently my name had not come before the committee. The next hurdle I had to overcome was that although I knew one or two of the members, none of the menbers would play with me because they said I had only a bag of scrap iron and not proper clubs. So the position was quite clear, my mother would not let me play football, she had spent money on me to acquire the clubs, plus the fact that she was so pleased I had joined the Clober Golf Club. I had no alternative but to make the best of it. My brother could only play on a Saturday, so for the first year I had to play during the week on my own until two friends allowed me to play with them. Later I started to play in club competitions and a new sport had opened up for me. Thereafter I became quite proficient at the game, helped by the advice given to me as a boy by the great professional Tommy Armour.

During this time my parents bought a property at Innellan on the Clyde Coast between Dunoon and Toward Point. It consisted of six houses and two attics of the tenement type. One house was kept for family holidays and it was called Craigenure. After a few years they bought a double villa, stone built, very substantial. One of the houses was called "Roselea" and the other "Rosslyn". The family had Roselea for a holiday house and Rosslyn was occupied by a Mr McCormack, the local master plumber in the village. It was quite convenient for a sail down the Clyde in one of the paddle boats for the weekend.

I had another idea, having bought a second hand "Imperial Motor Bike". It was rather old fashioned, so I tried to make it modern by cutting the handle bars, did various alterations, fitted a pillion seat, painted and polished it, and it looked quite nice. After some experience in driving the bike on the open roads I was ready. Quite proficient in driving, my first long trip was from

Milngavie to Innellan for the weekend. It turned out to be quite an experience.

The route from Milngavie was by Dumbarton, Craigendoran, Helensburgh by St Catherines to Dunoon and on to Innellan.

After making up a sandwich on Saturday morning I set off at 8 am in the morning. My first stop was just past Helensburgh at a small village called Rhu on the Gareloch. It so happened my second oldest sister with her husband, who was the local policeman, lived in a cottage on the main road so I called in to see them. After having a cup of tea with them I was about to restart when my brother in law on inspecting my motor, pointed out two deficiencies, a crack in the framework, and a leak in the petrol tank, and recommended I should not continue my journey. However I got them both patched up and continued on my way with a warning that if I was stopped by the police on the road I could be charged with an offence. Everything continued alright until I arrived at a place called the "Rest and be Thankful". The bike appeared to be travelling rather slow, but on looking back I discovered I had been travelling up a vast incline. Having got to the top of the hill, I inadvertently turned into the wrong road. I was on my way to Lochgoilhead instead of St Catherine. On going on into the glen my footbrake jammed and after another running repair I managed up out the glen on to the main road for Dunoon, chasing some sheep on the way. After a long and tiresome journey I arrived at Dunoon at approximately 6 pm in the evening, stopping at the first garage to enquire if they could assist in repairs. The manager looked at the motor bike and then myself, to address me as follows, "Well son, there is only one person can help you at this time of night, put up a prayer to God". Thereafter there was nothing for it, but to travel on to Innellan in a slow steady pace to arrive there at 7 pm rather tired and hungry.

After a good meal in the house, my father had a look at it and he proposed that the both of us just lift it down to the beach and throw the motor bike into the sea, but I took great exception to this idea, made some more repairs, ready to start on my journey back next morning. On Sunday morning I set off from Innellan at 8. 30 am and had a steady, but rather eventful trip back to Millguy. My nerves were shattered and after putting the bike into an outside coal cellar I retired to bed, did not wake until 10 am the next morning, late for work. That was the last I saw the motor cycle for a period of two months when I restarted the repairs for another reason I will explain later. As this was the start of a very exciting period in my life I will describe in chronological order from my diary of events. My education, sports and pastimes, business affairs, war service, associations, politics local council, county council and national, holidays and tours at home and abroad, hospital and retirement, letters of thanks, from 1922 to 1979.

Extract from Milngavie and Bearsden Herald 1958

Honour for Mr John M Gardner

Congratulations to Mr John M Gardner who has been appointed President of the Glasgow and West of Scotland Master Plumbers' and Domestic Engineers Association.
The last time this honour came to the district was in 1902 when a Bearsden Plumber Mr Thomas Day was appointed President.
Mr Gardner has been a Director of Association for the past eight years and has filled the posts of Honorary Treasurer and Vice President. He is also a member of the Institute of British Engineers.
Mr Gardner is a well known local figure having been born and bred in Mingavie. He was educated locally, at Stow College and the Royal Technical College, Glasgow. He took over his present business from Mr R Currie about fourteen years ago.
A keen sportsman, he is a past Captain of Milngavie and Clober Golf Clubs and in earlier years was a member of Milngavie Junior Football Team. Registered with the Worshipful Company of Plumbers London as R.P., also a Member of the Institute of Plumbing London M.I.P..

From My Diary, with summary of Events in Chronological Order to 1979

<u>Education:- School education and certificates etc</u>

Milngavie Secondary School: Intermediate Certificate

Milngavie Evening Classes: Engineering Certificate

Plumbing etc :

Stow College:	Glasgow Courses 1,2,3,4 Classes 1st Class Certificate Practical
Stow College:	1,2,3,4 Classes 1st Class Certificate Theory
Stow College:	1,2,3,4 Classes 1st Class Certificate Drawing
Stow College:	1&2 Classes 1st Class Certificate Electrical Engineering

1930 Registered R.P. with Worshipful Company of Plumbers London R.P.

Royal Technical College Glasgow:-

1st Class Certificate	Sanitary Engineering
1st Class Certificate	Sanitary Inspection and Legislation
1st Class Certificate	Municipal Engineering
1st Class Certificate	Town Planning
1st Class Certificate	Building Superintendence and Professional Practice

Profession:-

Apprenticeship R Currie, 19th March 1923 to March 1929 as Plumbing, Sanitary, Heating and Electrical Engineer - 6 years.

1943	Started business taking over from above firm
1949	Subsequently the business of McAdam, Blanefield
1945	Member of Employers Plumbing etc., Association West of Scotland, also Member of Benevolent Fund
1958/59	President of Glasgow and West of Scotland Master Plumbers and Domestic Engineers Member of the Scottish Federation of Master Plumbers Member of Electrical Contractors Association Member of Electrical Contractors Inspection Council Member of Institute of Plumbing, London M.I.P. Member of Institute of British Engineering M.I.B.E.
1974	Partnership with my son Iain McDonald Gardner, the firm known as John M Gardner & Son
1979	Retired from business after 42 years in the trade

Sports and Pastimes:-

Football, Golf, Yachting, Bowls, Curling, Swimming, Athletics.

1st Milngavie Boys Brigade Football Team
Milngavie School Former Pupils Football Team Glasgow, played Amateur Football Woodside and Kilmun Thistle
Milngavie, played for British Legion and Milngavie Athletic Clubs
Milngavie Scottish Junior Football Team in Scottish League

Maryhill Junior Team (Lochburn)
Offer to play for St Johnstone (Perth) by Tommy Muirhead, Manager
Offer to play for a place in Celtic Football Club by James McGrory
Parents refused both offers, not allowed by parents

Golf:-

1927 Started playing golf at Clober Golf Course being a member of the Artesan Club, played for a period of five years and became a low handicap player, handicap two. After 3 years became temporary secretary of the club for one year, the fee being one guinea. Resigned after one year. Elected Captain of the club 1932.
Ran a Stop-Watch Competition and presented the club with a Silver Trophy of that name. Resigned from the club, given a presentation of a Westminster Chiming Clock.
Joined Milngavie Golf Club 1933/34 season with a handicap of one, and reduced to scratch the following year. This was the start of a more distinguished career as follows:-

Events:-

Milngavie won 4 monthly medals in succession, a record for the Club (1935).

1935 Winner of Dumbartonshire Union Championship
at Helensburgh, presented with Silver Rose Bowl
Winner Carrick Cross, Milngavie
Winner Quaich Cup, Milngavie
Winner Young Trophy, Milngavie
Winner Rotary Cup, Milngavie

Represented Milngavie Golf Club for 19 years in team matches.

1976 Made Honorary Member of Milngavie Golf Club

1977 Presented Milngavie Golf Club with a Silver Challenge Trophy to be played over 36 holes scratch as John M Gardner Stroke Play Championship

1979 Winner of Open Greensome Tournament at Milngavie in partnership with Mr A Seymour, Manager Royal Bank of Scotland and Captain of Bearsden Golf Club with a scratch score of 72 less 12 of a Handicap Nett 60 and a record for the course and with a prize value of £160

1982 Elected Honorary President of Milngavie Golf Club at the Annual General Meeting of the Club

1983 Chief Guest at Annual Dinner Dance

1986 Chief Guest at Burns Supper

1977 Made an Honorary Member of Dougalston Golf Club by Mr Reo Stakis, owner of the golf course for services rendered and advice on golf and construction of the golf course on the sudden death of the American Architect with three holes to be finished

1959 Winner of Scottish Building Contractor's Cup at Gleneagles. Bearsden and Milngavie District Council Golf Section won Competition at Ardeer with a record 66 strokes when 66 years of age

Notable Tournaments played in with some success:-

Tennant Cup, Glasgow Golf Club - 3 Times Qualifier
Eden Tournament, St Andrews - 3 Times Qualifier
Elgin Tournament, St Andrews - 3 Times Qualifier
Moray Open Tournament - 3 Times Qualifier

Various Champion Golfers I have played with as partner:-

Hector Thomson, British Amateur Champion 1936,
Glasgow Golf club in Tennant Cup
Eddie Hamilton, 3 Times Scottish Champion at
Milngavie Golf Club, 1937
Major David Blair at Nairn, Scottish Champion and
Walker Cup Player

Putting at Milngavie Golf Club

Sir Robin Cater in Tennant Cup Glasgow Golf Club, 1935
Walter Lyle, Clober Scottish Professional Champion
James Forrester, Balmore Scottish Professional Champion

Minor Trophies:- West of Scotland Plumbers, various in golf section

Scoring:- At the age of 72 in 1980, June Medal scored 71 scratch, Milngavie Golf Club, one stroke less than age. At the age of 75 in 1983, scored 73 scratch less 2.

Other Activities:-

Bowls Outdoor: Joined Milngavie Bowling Club in 1969, but did not participate very much until I retired from Milngavie Town Council in 1979. Made quite good progress and won the Triples Cup in 1981. My partners were R Maitland and Jack Hayes.

Played a number of team matches and in 1986 reached the final of the Club Pairs, my partner being William Bradburn. Prize valued at six pounds.

Bowls Indoor: Joined Indoor Bowling Club in 1978 at the Allander Sports Centre, playing ordinary members League and Senior League, also Triples League with reasonable success.

Badminton:- Badminton Parish Church Team at 16 years of age
Tennis:- Former Pupils Milngavie School at 17 years of age
Swimming:- From the age of 10 years, no fixed address
Curling:- West of Scotland Plumbers (Curling Section).
Played in various outings - Glasgow, Dundee, Falkirk, Aberdeen and Perth.
Yachting and Cruising:- Loch Lomond from McFarlane Yard at Balmaha. In 1964 purchased 30 ft Seamaster fibreglass yacht. Sold same after a number of years and purchased a 15 ft fibreglass day boat cruiser with Yamaha Engine in 1978 and a rowing boat.

lst Milngavie Boys Brigade: Douglas Street, Milngavie
Joined at 11 years of age and gained the following:-

3 years Service Anchor Badge
Sergeant Star Badge
Bugle Badge
Gymnastic Badge
Ambulance Badge
Best Drilled Sergeant
Kings Badge "Senior Honour"
Colour Sergeant

War Service 1941 - 1945:-

Royal Engineers Technician to Deputy Commander, Cameron Barracks, North Highland Area, Inverness, Civilian Mechanist, Electrical and Mechanical Engineer, Invernesshire - Responsible for water supplies, electrical installations, heating installations and mechanical works.
Promoted to Fort William as Acting E&M Garrison Engineer, before returning to Inverness. Responsible for West Coast Inverness, Sutherland, Rosshire, Caithness, Morayshire, part Aberdeen, North of Perth for North Highland Area as Technical Advisor Deputy Commander Engineers, later transferred to Glasgow before release.

Associations:-

Ellangowan Masonic Lodge No 716, Life Member
Founder Member Milngavie Toastmasters Club, later known as Speakers Club
Founder Member Milngavie Rotary Club

Religion:-

Member St Pauls Church, Strathblane Road, Milngavie

Dwelling House:-

Purchase of Dwelling House, known as "Clavie", No 2 North Campbell Avenue, Milngavie. House built 1930. Purchased on 15th July 1955, purchase price £2850 from Osmund Anthony Goulden, fue from Campbell Douglas of Mains Estate.

Municipal Election 1964

5th May 1964. Copy of first election address to the electors. At this stage in my life I now enter the world of local government. I do so after consultation with my own family and their backing, as an Independent Candidate in Milngavie Town Council, with knowledge that the existing Independents are agreeable, and that two of number namely Robert H M Kennedy and Dr John S Park will be my partners in this election.

Herewith is the first circular sent out to the electors in 1964 as under.

Election
1971 Senior Bailie
Convenor of Planning Milngavie
Member Swimming Pool Joint Committee with Bearsden
Election
1972 Senior Bailie
Member of Dumbarton County Council, Roads and Planning
Convenor of Planning Milngavie
Member Swimming Pool Joint Committee
Member Scottish National Housing and Planning
Election
1973 Senior Bailie
Member Dumbarton County Council, Roads, Planning, Police
Convenor of Planning Milngavie
Member Swimming Pool Joint Committee
Convenor Licensing Court
Senior Magistrate Police Court
Election
1974 Justice of the Peace J.P. and Senior Magistrate
Member County Council, Roads, Planning and Police
Convenor of Planning Milngavie
Swimming Pool Joint Committee
Election
1975 Senior Bailie, Justice of the Peace, Dumbartonshire
Member County Council, Police, Planning, Roads, General Purpose
Member Scottish National Housing and Town Planning
Chairman Final Meeting Police Court

Pedestrianisation of Central Area Development

In 1970 Central Development proposals approved by Secretary of State for by-pass road.

In 1973, owing to hold-up of by-pass road, a request for a meeting with Mr Gordon Younger, Secretary of State was granted.

Bailie John M Gardner headed a delegation to St. Andrews House, Edinburgh, the outcome of which was that £75,000 was granted for the by-pass road, to be commenced within six months, this was duly carried out.

Bailie Gardner retired from Milngavie Town Council on demise, in 1975, due to Regionalisation and the formation of Bearsden and Milngavie District Council, being undefeated in all elections. Asked to stand as an Independent for Bearsden and Milngavie District Council.

Bearsden and Milngavie District Council

Elected member of District Council representing Ward No One, Barloch, and became founder member.

1975: Positions held:- Magistrate and Justice of Peace
Convenor of Planning and Building Control
Member of Policy and Resources (Finance)
Member of Housing Committee
Executive of Scottish National Housing and Town Planning

1976: As above with responsibility for Milngavie Central Area Construction of new Golf Course (Dougalston), "Fine Fare" Hillfoot Shopping Centre, Ledcameroch Development Bearsden, etc.

1977: Executive of Scottish National Housing and Town Planning
Convenor of Planning and Building Control
Member of Housing, Policy and Resources
Magistrate on Bench, Licensing Court and Court of Appeal
Refused Chairmanship as President of Scottish National Housing and Planning.

May, 1977 : Retired from Bearsden and District Council being undefeated in all Elections since 1964.

Invitations and Honours

<u>While serving on Milnoavie Town Council, Dunbarton County Council and Bearsden and Milngavie District Council</u>

The Provost, Magistrate and Councillors of the Burgh of Milngavie request the pleasure of the company of Dean Of Guild, John M Gardner and Lady at the Town Hall, Milngavie on Tuesday, 29th June 1965 at 10.00 am
on the occasion of the visit of

Her Majesty the Queen and His Royal Highness the Duke of Edinburgh.

Invitation accepted with pleasure.

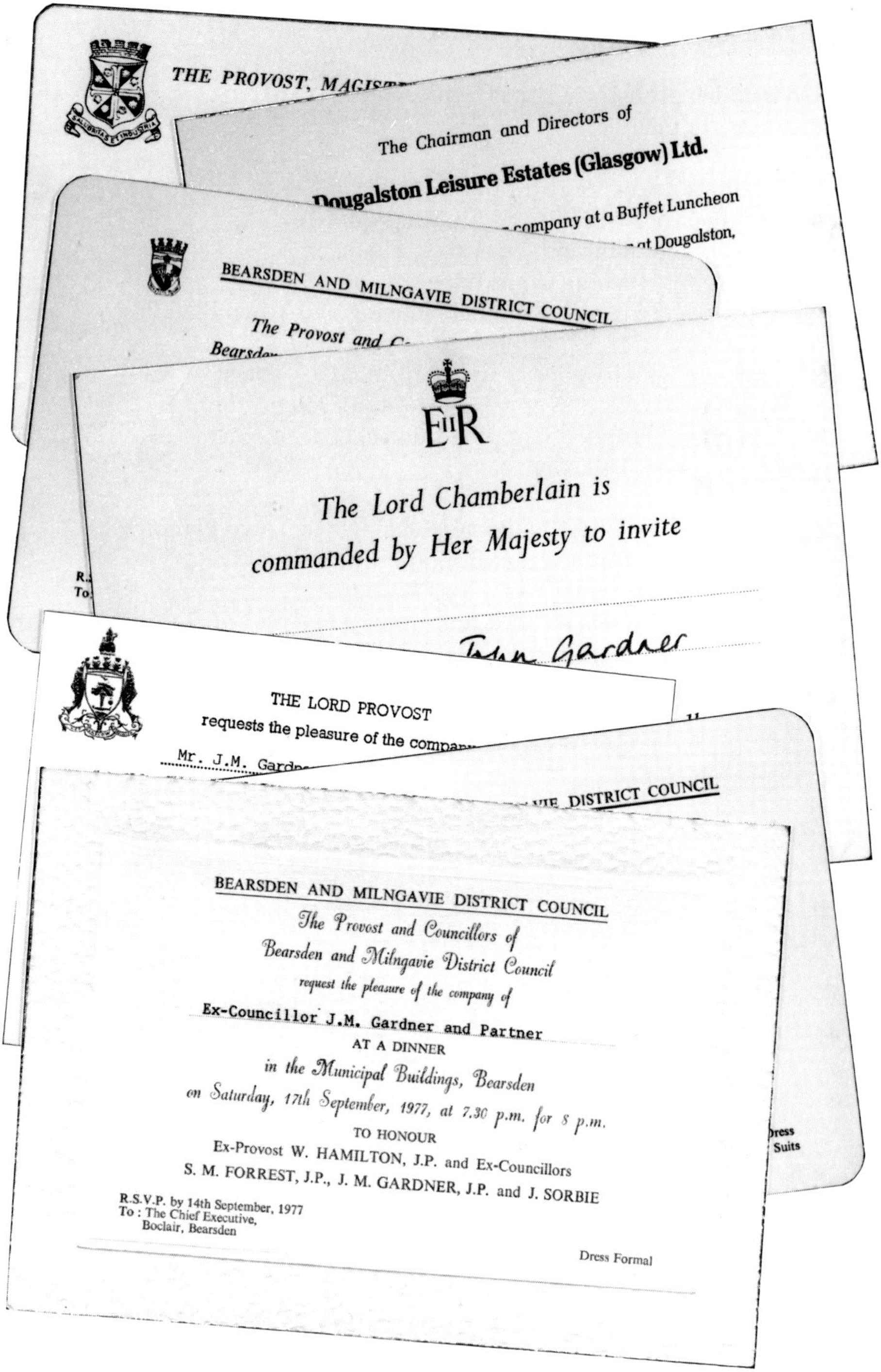
THE PROVOST, MAGIS
The Chairman and Directors of
Dougalston Leisure Estates (Glasgow) Ltd.
company at a Buffet Luncheon
at Dougalston,
BEARSDEN AND MILNGAVIE DISTRICT COUNCIL
The Provost and C
EIIR
The Lord Chamberlain is
commanded by Her Majesty to invite
John Gardner
THE LORD PROVOST
requests the pleasure of the compan
Mr. J.M. Gardn
DISTRICT COUNCIL
BEARSDEN AND MILNGAVIE DISTRICT COUNCIL
The Provost and Councillors of
Bearsden and Milngavie District Council
request the pleasure of the company of
Ex-Councillor J.M. Gardner and Partner
AT A DINNER
in the Municipal Buildings, Bearsden
on Saturday, 17th September, 1977, at 7.30 p.m. for 8 p.m.
TO HONOUR
Ex-Provost W. HAMILTON, J.P. and Ex-Councillors
S. M. FORREST, J.P., J. M. GARDNER, J.P. and J. SORBIE
R.S.V.P. by 14th September, 1977
To : The Chief Executive,
Boclair, Bearsden
Dress Formal

The Chairman and Directors of Dougalston Leisure Estates (Glasgow) Ltd. Mr Reo Stakis, Chairman, 21 Woodside Terrace, Glasgow
request the Pleasure of your company at a Buffet Luncheon to mark the opening of Dougalston Lounge Bar and Golf Course at Dougalston, Milngavie
on Friday 29th October 1976 at 1 PM.
Guests are invited to play golf thereafter before Monday 1st November.

Invitation Accepted with pleasure

The Lord Chamberlain is commanded by Her Majesty to invite
Councillor John M Gardner J.P.
to an Afternoon Party in the Garden of the Palace of Holyrood House
on Thursday, the 26th May 1977, from 4 to 6pm

Invitation Accepted with pleasure

The Provost and Councillors of Bearsden and Milngavie District Council request the pleasure of the company of
Ex-Councillor J M Gardner and Mrs Freda Millar
At the opening of the Allander Sports Centre by Her Royal Highness the Princess Anne, Mrs Mark Philips
on Friday 28th of April 1978 at 11.30am

Invitation Accepted with pleasure

The Provost and Councillors of Bearsden and Milngavie District Council request the Pleasure of the company of Ex Councillor J M Gardner and Partner
At a Dinner in the Municipal Buildings, Bearsden
on Saturday 17th September 1977 at 7.30pm for 8.00pm
To Honour
Ex Provost Wm Hamilton J.P. and Ex Councillors
S M Forrest, J.P., J M Gardner J.P. and J Sorbie

An Introduction by Bearsden and Milngavie District
Council to the Electors of the District
First Ward Barloch
Councillor J M Gardner J.P. No 2 North Campbell Avenue,
Milngavie
Member of Milngavie Town Council 1964-1975
Served as Convenor of Planning, also Public Health
Was Dean of Guild and served two terms as Senior Bailie
Member of Dunbarton County Council
Convenor of Planning and Building Control Committee of
the Bearsden and District Council
Spare time is spent playing golf to a very reasonable
handicap

J M GARDNER M.I.P., M.I.B.E., J.P., R.P.

The final circular to the Electors Ward One 1974

"Clavie"
2 North Campbell Avenue
Milngavie

To the Electors

Sir or Madam,

For the past ten years I have had the honour and privilege to serve continuously as your representative in Ward One as an Independent member of Milngavie Town Council and more recently in Dumbarton County Council, now that a change to District representation under Local Government re-organisation is taking place I offer myself for re-election in Ward One where my business premises are situated. I have served on every Committee and have gained considerable knowledge of the affairs of our District.

I have held successively the Offices of Dean of Guild, Senior Bailie for two terms, and in addition those of Convenor of Public Health and Cleansing, Convenor of Parks and Halls, represented the Burgh as a member of the Electricity Consultative Council. At the present time I am Convenor of Planning and Future Development. At Dumbarton County level I am on the Police, Planning, Roads and General Purposes Committees.

During my term of office as Convenor of Public Health and Cleansing, the new Sewage Purification Scheme was completed and an arrangement between the Burghs of Bishopbriggs, Bearsden, and Milngavie for Refuse Disposal. While Convenor of Parks, Landscaping, Drainage and a Paddling Pool were completed and now as Convenor of Planning and Future Development, Central Re-Development of Milngavie is in progress. This requires very careful consideration to preserve the village atmosphere and yet cope with modern development of traffic. It should be done with as little cost to the ratepayer as possible.

I believe that with my business experience and knowledge of the building and civil engineering industry, together with my associations in the District over many years could be of value, especially now, when there would appear to be important projects under contemplation.

It has always been one of my aims to try and bring together the people of the community new and old, it was with pleasure the Town Council adopted my idea of a "Milngavie Week" in so doing, engendering a greater communal spirit within the Burgh.

I have endeavoured at all times to further the interest of all sections of the community and have refrained from bringing politics into the scheme of things.

If you agree with my policy I ask your support on Polling Day, Tuesday May 7th, and I assure you I will do my utmost to warrant your trust, please vote.

Yours faithfully,

John M Gardner.

Duly elected

R. CURRIE,

Registered Plumber,
Gasfitter, Zinc Worker, and
Lead Merchant

MILNGAVIE, 30th July 1929

The Bearer John Gardiner has been employed by me from March 19th 1923 to March 1929 as Apprentice plumber, & since then as Journeyman. during that time I have found him capable diligent & trustworthy. I regret having to part with him owing to depression in trade & can with confidence recommend him to anyone requiring his services

R Currie

ROMANCE 1931

After my return to my original employer with my additional experience, I seemed to have more confidence and matured both in my occupation and private life. This must have been around 1931. At this time a new private nursing home was opened up by two local doctors, they were the brothers Dr John and Dr Ronald Reid, and a Glasgow surgeon, Mr Moore; It was Cloberfield Nursing Home. Very convenient since patients did not require to travel into Glasgow. At one time it was a private house and was easily converted to enable operations and convalescence to take place; it was very popular for a number of years.

By chance I was delegated to inspect a cold water storage tank at the nursing home where dampness was discovered in the ceiling of one of the main rooms. It was found that the tank was of wood with a lead lining. The lead was defective and it was found necessary to cut out the old lead and re-line with fresh sheet lead. To do this is rather expensive, unfortunately it was the main source of supply for the nursing home and I was given the assistance of two apprentices to keep the cost down. I was busy explaining this to the matron when a nurse came into the room, took a good look at me, smiled and left the room.

Next day the same nurse met me on the main stairway. We both smiled at each other, said hello at the same time and continued on our way. On the following day, when I was walking on my way towards the nursing home, I again met this nurse coming towards me. This time we stopped. had a short chat, and exchanged names. Her name was Miss Munro, assistant to the Matron and had trained in the Royal Samaritan Hospital in Glasgow. She came from Burghead, Morayshire, where her father was the local hairdresser. In return, I informed her we were only 200 yards from where I lived at 12 Claremont Gardens. To my surprise she said that she knew, having been told by the local postman who delivered the mail to our house and the nursing home as well.

The following evening on my way to Clober Golf Course, I met Miss Munro coming in my direction with a letter to post. We had a longer chat and I asked her if she would care to go for a run on my motorcycle, it was under repair and should be ready in few days. Her reply was, provided it was safe, she had no objection. If I would phone when the bike was repaired she would let me know her first evening off duty.

It is wonderful how your life style can change, here I was in my early twenties living, as I thought, a full life. My pal at the time was a chap called

Cowden Kyle. We both played football together. Our social life consisted of going to dances and concerts. We were both qualified tradesmen now. He was an engineer in the Albion Motor Car Company in Glasgow and I was in the plumbing, electrical and heating business. We were in quite a steady job and getting not bad a salary so we could afford a little enjoyment, in fact Cowden Kyle was being trained as a singer and used to make a few bob at concerts.

After playing football on a Saturday afternoon we used to go ballroom dancing at Greens Playhouse in Glasgow. I suppose we flirted about with one or two of our girl friends, but had always to catch the last bus home from Renfrew Street. It was at this period I had to give up football and concentrated on golf, hiking was another of our pastimes.

Back to the motor cycle caper, now becoming quite famous, it was all stripped down for overhaul and repair, which must have been completed in the record time of four days with new pilion seat with footrests etc., a phone call was put through to the nursing home and a I got date for Friday evening, 6 pm, with Nurse Munro.

Friday evening arrived. I called at the nursing home as arranged and we started off along Clober Road, Craigton Road on to Drymen Road. It was a lovely summer evening, eventually arriving at Balmaha, had a cup of tea at the wee shop there, and went on to Rowardennan Pier, watching the pleasure boats and having a long chat. We returned home after a most enjoyable evening. We seemed to have much in common, even the motor cycle behaved well, yes it was the start of something good.

We became very good friends and made good use of the motor bike on Nurse Munro' s day off. At weekends with a picnic basket we spent happy days around the West of Scotland. I reduced some of my activities and continued my education at the Royal Technical College in Glasgow. Golf now appeared to be my main sport and pastime as it was convenient. I was now a regular visitor to the nursing home and if the weather was inclement we spent our time in the recreation room in the home. When it came round to my birthday on the 2nd October 1931, I received from my girlfriend the present of a beautiful book. It was "The Good Companions" by J B Priestley, the cover covered with velvet and with my initials in gold print, J.M.G. On the inside, "Wishing you many happy returns of the day October 2nd 1931" and a short poem as follows:-

In the distant unknown future
as the lamps of life burn low
these pages will remind you
of the days of long ago
and as through these pages you ponder
thinking of the days that were,
of the days that are now vanished
will you sometimes think of me.

Jessie Sophia Munro.
2nd October 1931.

We became engaged to be married in 1934.

We were married on 3lst day of October 1935 at the Station Hotel, Elgin, Morayshire.
Taking up residence at No 7 Strathblane Road (Tannoch Place) Milngavie.

My wife was born on January 4th 1909 at 51 Granary Street, Burghead in the County of Moray. Brought up in Burghead, educated at Burghead Public School, thereafter served as a probationer nurse in Forres Hospital for 12 months before going to train as a nurse in the Royal Samaritan Hospital of Glasgow. Completing her training she took up an appointment as assistant to the Matron at Cloberfield Nursing Home in Milngavie, going back to Bishopmill Nursing Hospital in Elgin to be nearer home until her marriage at Station Hotel, Elgin, in 1935.

My wife's father and mother Mr and Mrs Robert Munro came from Forres, where her father was a foreman on a large farm. Unfortunately, when a young man he saved the life of a railway employee outside Forres working on the railway, with the result he lost part of his leg. For his bravery he was given a gold medal and £100 reward presented to him the day Marshall College was opened in Aberdeen by King Edward IV. He married the nurse who looked after him in hospital, a Miss Georgina McRae. After the marriage they took up residence at 51 Granary Street, Burghead, and started business as a hairdresser next door, and carried on the business for forty five years.

I spent two very enjoyable holidays in Burghead before my marriage to

Sophia, his eldest daughter, there being a younger brother Tom and a sister Rhoda. I made quite a number of friends in the Broch as it was called for short. Mr Robert Munro was a very popular and brave man.

The day of our marriage was memorable for more than one way. It was a lovely ceremony by Rev Theodore Lamb of Burghead. On leaving the hotel for our honeymoon, coming down the main stairway I got separated from my wife and some of the male guests got hold of me to carry me to the train about 100 yards away. In so doing, the case I was carrying came up and struck me quite severely on the nose so that the loss of blood for a few minutes was considerable, however some of them must have been menbers of the Red Cross Association, they quite quickly doctored me up, an apology for the accident was forthcoming and I finished up a hero.

On arrival at the Bon-Accord Hotel in Aberdeen, other than a swollen nose I was alright. What a start to a honeymoon! The following morning at breakfast the table maid asked my wife if I was Benny Lynch the famous boxer, right enough my face was a little black and blue.

We left our luggage at Aberdeen Station and did a bit of shopping, one of the purchases being a parcel of fish, it was haddock. When we arrived home the next morning my wife suggested fish for breakfast. Before I left for work the fish was put on a gas grill while we went through to the living room to set the table. After a few minutes some smoke was coming into the room, on rushing back to the kitchen the room was full of smoke, the haddock was now a burnt offering. My poor wife was never used to gas and had the gas tap full opened. The upshot was, with a cup of tea and a jeely piece, I was off to work. It was not funny at the time, but we did have a good laugh about it later. She actually turned out to be an excellent cook. What is the saying "a bad start to a good ending". And so it turned out to be.

In 1932 my parents removed from 12 Claremont Gardens to the first bungalow being built by Gordon the builder at Keystone on the main street. It was called "Dunvegan Cottage" after my mother who came from Skye. It was the showhouse, four apartments with kitchenette and bathroom. By this time all members of the family were married except myself, my parents being looked after by my widowed sister Mrs Clark. It was from this house I got married.

It was about this time I resigned from Clober Golf Club and joined Milngavie Golf Club in the season 1933/34, having been Honorary Secretary in 1931 and Captain of the Club in 1932. I must state I had made many friends at Clober, being friendly with the Lyle family who owned the Golf Course, especially with Mr and Mrs Lyle senior and the three boys, Walter, Alex and

George Lyle. Mr Lyle and myself had a number of long talks about the course and its future. I remember one summer evening sitting on the outside steps of the clubhouse from 10 pm in the evening to 3 am in the morning discussing the new clubhouse to be built and drawing the rough proposed plan on sand laid out on the ground. Although I resigned from the club in 1933 he kept in touch with me and the clubhouse was ultimately built on the lines we discussed that night.

The Lyle boys were a little younger than I was, but I played with them quite a lot, especially Walter the oldest boy. He later turned professional with the Littlehill Golf Club in Glasgow. Alex also turned professional and went down to England; George the youngest of them turned professional and he was local professional with the Clober Club. It gave me very great pleasure when I learned Alex Lyle who went to England, that his son Sandy Lyle had won the British Open Championship. I met him in the Tennant Cup at Glasgow Golf Club. He was not successful, but put up a good show. It so happened I was at the presentation that year with the Provost of Milngavie and Bearsden District Council in an official capacity.

My wife and myself fitted in very well at No 7 Strathblane Road. Our house was now quite well furnished. We had 2 rooms, 1 large scullery, with hot and cold water, and a bathroom. The kitchen had a fitted-in bed and kitchen range with gas grill. One room was a bedroom and the other was a drawing room. We were now about a year in the house. One evening we had a visit from the local police inspector, George Stevens, with a request to know if we could allow two new recruits to live with us until they went to the police school, It so happened to be that the Inspector's wife came from Burghead where my wife came from, ultimately the arrangement was they could come temporary under the circumstances. One of the recruits came from Banff, the other from Peterhead.

They occupied the smaller bedroom. Sometimes they would be on shifts so that only one used the double bed most of the time. They were no bother and I became quite friendly with them, after all they were away from home for the first time; in fact I used to do physical exercises with them in one of the rooms to keep fit. Mind you they were two of a kind. One of them, Willie Clubb was always reading detective novels. I used to say to him 'Willie, I think you could become Chief Constable' to which his reply was 'or Assistant Chief Constable'. He ultimately married a Milngavie girl and his first appointment was at Loch Sloy, where a large Hydro Electric Scheme was being carried on. Later in life he retired as Inspector of Police at Dumbarton where he now lives. Iain Thomson from Banff was the other constable, but entirely different he was, more of a sportsman, and a member of Duffhouse Royal Golf Club at

Banff.

When he was informed that I was a member of Milngavie Golf Club he put out a challenge game with myself. Nothing much was discussed until we arrived to play the game, after playing the first hole in which I took one over par, I was offered a few strokes, which I declined, as my handicap was very low. The outcome was Iain was defeated quite heavily, after that he was more subdued, and I was treated with much more respect. He was appointed to the Helensburgh district, and later in life married a Miss Lyle of Clober. He also retired as an Inspector of police at headquarters and took an appointment at Edzell Golf Club as Clubmaster with his wife, an aunt of Sandy Lyle the famous golfer.

At this time I was doing some research work on the art of soldering aluminium metal, which was very difficult and was quite successful. I was endeavouring to sell the idea to Bulpett Aluminium Manufacturers, but could not come to an agreement on price. Shortly after war broke out and my life suddenly changed. I suppose it was a chance missed as I was unable to continue at a later date.

It was about this time my wife was pregnant, the recruits had to find alternative accommodation, they were being posted to their first appointment in the county as police constables. My oldest daughter was born on the 28th day of December 1936, so we now required all the accommodation we had. It was another experience for me as I was the youngest of my family, however I soon learned the art of being a father, my wife previously being a nurse was most valuable.

My now famous motor bike had to be dispensed with and in its place I bought a second hand push cycle at a place called the Barrows in Barrowland, Glasgow. It had drooped handlebars like a racing model. I used it mostly for going from the house to Milngavie Golf Course. I found it most convenient and it lasted me for about 10 years, when I bought a motor car, life was being lived to the full.

By this time I had gained all the honours I set out to achieve at the Royal Technical College in Glasgow, so my education had now more or less terminated. The College eventually changed its name to Strathclyde University. For the next two years I tried to obtain a job with the qualifications I had as a Sanitary Inspector or Burgh Surveyor. I was finding this quite difficult. The reason being unless you started your apprenticeship in a Local Government Office you were not quoted, unless your father or a close relation was in the business before you. In any case the war clouds were gathering and my wage at the time was quite adequate for our purpose. After two years we had on 5th December 1938 an addition to the family called Freda, a sister for older daughter Evelyn, with a further girl born on 26th March 1940. We were now quite a family.

Our annual holiday was always spent at Burghead, where my wife and the girls used to spend a months holiday with her parents and managed to get a rest. It was always in July. I usually managed the second fortnight. It was ideal for a young family, with a lovely sandy beach round to Findhorn on the Cromarty Firth although Burghead is situated on a peninsula. The other side was rather rocky, round to Duffus and Gordonstoun, the ground being fairly flat. Inland was convenient for walking, the town itself was really a fishing village with a very good harbour and the outlying district forestry. It had its usual compliment of visitors and was ideal for yachts. I always had my golf clubs with me and used to play in the fine golf courses of Lossiemouth, Elgin, and Forres, entering for and playing in the local tournaments with some considerable success, making friends with many of the local people. We were most fortunate with my father in law being the local hairdresser, we were never without company, especially when the fishing boats arrived back in the harbour.

Father in Law, Robert Munro of Forres

WORLD WAR TWO

In 1939 at the beginning of the year, what a transformation was about to take place in all our lives with outbreak of World War Two in September of that year, Germany's attack on Poland, followed by the entry of France and Britain in fulfilment of their guarantees to Poland.

Great activity took place over the country with the north east of Scotland aerodromes at Lossiemouth, Kinloss and Dyce, around Burghead a new wireless station with all it complies with training centres and housing, storage of ammunition etc. The towns of Inverness and Aberdeen became garrison towns. My own family were never evacuated to another part of the country. I was employed in the erection of our air raid shelter and alterations to building, cleansing and the protection for gas attacks. I was also the member of a fire and rescue team. My first taste of War was when Clydebank on the Clyde was blitzed in 1940 with all the horrified aspects of war brought home with bombardment, by day and night bombing, and the long hours in the air raid shelters with my family sleeping and living under rather nasty conditions.

In 1941-1945 I was called up for service in the Royal Engineers and with my special qualifications put on a list of specialist occupations. I was despatched to the Cameron Barracks North Highland Area, Inverness, to the Deputy Commander of the Royal Engineers as a Technician Civilian Mechanist Electrical and Mechanical Engineer Inspector of works. I was responsible for Water Supplies, Electrical Installations, Mechanical Works and Heating Installations for the garrison town of Inverness. It was six months before I again saw my wife and family.

On my arrival at the Cameron Barracks, Inverness, I had an interview with Colonel Dunn, Deputy Commander of the Royal Engineers. He was a Glasgow man and was a director of Quantity Surveyors known as Gray, Dunn and Baxter. He knew of the firm I worked for in Milngavie, which was quite a good start. After a long conversation with him in the main office I was introduced to the staff in the office quarters where I would operate from. There was a Garrison Engineer and about twelve Clerk of Works with whom I would be giving advice when the occasion arose.

The next step was to be taken around the various headquarters and installations within the town of Inverness. For transport purposes I was given a staff car with a sergeant in the A.T.S. as my driver. On completion of this and other private documents my permits made out and I was ready for business.

My first assignment was rather unusual, I was to investigate the cause of death of a civilian at an anti- tank firing range of the automatic type at Fort George, with a report for Scottish Command and to appear at the Sheriff Court in Inverness as a witness. It took me about one week to collect all the information and forward the necessary report. Later I did appear in court to give an explanation of the working of the apparatus and was duly thanked by the Sheriff for my explanation.

The next operation to be carried out was the plans for the installation of transformers and bell circuits for the new headquarters at the Palace Hotel in Inverness, and thereafter extensions for the various camps, including central heating at a local mansion house. It really was surprising the amount of work I was doing, everything was urgent or very urgent. It was done mostly by contractors or direct labour with the sappers themselves.

After six months I was informed that due to expansion taking place my district would be the County of Inverness and I would be given the necessary staff to cope with the additional work. I was given two experienced Staff-Sergeants for the office and outside staff. By this time I was getting quite used to the methods and the carrying out of works by the Royal Engineers. It was most interesting and testing my ability to the full. The larger the area the more staff was required and assistance was coming along nicely. It seemed all services were expanding at a terrific rate.

My next experience was quite considerable with the coming of Commando training at Achnacarry by the army and later commando training at Lochailort by the Marines. I was selected to take over the needs of the services now being formed right up the west coast with the inclusion of Morayshire, Rosshire, Sutherland, Caithness and the outer Isles. With this in view I was being transferred to new headquarters in Fort William, given the post of acting Garrison Engineer E.M. and to co-operate with the American forces in training west coast. This was by now the most urgent training and important large area anywhere in Scotland, and probably anywhere in Britain, however it is wonderful what can be done when necessity calls for additional effort. I had now travelled a long way in a short space of time, thanks to the education at the Royal Technical College and Stows College in Glasgow.

Despite all the changes, and hard work, at times bad, at other times good even amusing, it kept us going. The Commander at the new headquarters in Fort William was a Colonel F R Wray, a London architect pre-war, with considerable experience. Being the chief technical adviser I became very friendly with him. I was to discover later he was a friend of Winston Churchill through the Constitutional Club in London. He appeared to be very influential, well known in the upper class, well off financially, and about the same age as the

Prime Minister.

I was now given considerable scope as I still had Invernesshire on my plate, but relieved of the town owing to the distances I had to travel. The A.T.S. girl was sent back to Inverness and I was given a Staff-Sergeant with a difference, in that Scottish Command allowed me to drive as and when necessary. I was still not allowed uniform as sometimes it was necessary for me to deal with Officers above my rank, it worked out very well.

With the increase of troops in the area we were given extra staff and after clearing a backlog of work done by private contractors and not having payment for over a year, I had to concentrate on measurement of work done at gun sites with underground and overhead cabling etc. After that I was dealing with larger operations, although I had a special dispensation to travel anywhere in the restricted area. I had about six or seven special permits I had to carry due the changing of troops these were so necessary; Telecommunication helped considerably and wireless.

It was usual for me to contact the Officer in Command before operations were commenced, normally he would have been advised before our arrival. I seemed to be dealing with all kinds of problems, troops coming and going, what they called marching in and marching out, causing what was known as barrack damages. Arbitration was necessary sometimes and I wondered if I should have been a legal representative.

Fort Augustus Abbey, The Benedictine Fathers of the English Congregation

For example this incident happened at a small place called Fort Augustus on the Caledonian Canal. At that point there is a large Abbey called Fort Augustus Abbey with a large residential school. They were more or less self-contained with large gardens, and farm animals, They also had a small hydro-electric scheme and provided electricity for the Abbey. In addition, the village and hotels were supplied with electricity.

We had troops in most of the hotels, and were dependant on them for a supply of electricity. Tragedy struck the scheme when the tail race collapsed. This was made of wood, no wood for the repair was available and we were called in to help them. Under the circumstances I managed to get the wood and the renewal was carried out to the satisfaction of the Abbey. In the meantime I became friendly with Brother James the electrical engineer and used to have lunch with him at any time I was in the area.

Storm over Lower Banavie, entrance to Caledonian Canal

Loch Lochy, close to the site of Achnacarry House

At a later date we were asked by Scottish Command to lay on water tanks at the side of Loch Ness. The Army under General Ritchie were having an exercise from the North of Scotland south to Falkirk. It included the Highland Light Infantry. The idea of the tanks were so that the troops would not bother anyone trying to get a bed or food when resting at night. Passing through the villages there could be anything up to two or three thousands troops with all the necessary gear, including rations. The morning after they had passed through Fort Augustus I had an urgent telephone call from Colonel Wray to make my way as quickly as possible to the abbey, as there appeared to have been some trouble during the night, and contact Brother James. Within a period of 2 hours I arrived at the abbey and had contacted Brother James at his lodge house. His complaint was, three of the soldiers from the H.L.I. had broken the rules, pleaded with him for shelter, being unaware of the circumstances he offered them a bed for the night, only to discover next morning his Rolls razor had disappeared, but much worse, his pig had been stolen.

This was important to him as it could not be replaced because of restrictions imposed on pigs during the war. I offered to get the money for his pig. But money was no use to him, it was the scarcity of a female pig he depended on for food and a litter was now not available. So I had to retrace my way back to the C.R.E. Office with haste and advise Colonel Wray. After telling the unfortunate story, it turned out Wray himself was a former pupil in the Abbey College and the top monk was a friend of his, so he had to take action. While he was in touch with the powers that be, the troops had passed through Fort William that morning and were nearing Kinlochleven; so I was dispatched in a fast car to overtake the troops, and advise General Ritchie of the circumstances, he would probably be in his caravan.

Having duly arrived at Kinlochleven, the main body of troops were passing through Glencoe. On arrival I had an immediate talk with the General explaining the circumstances, he was very understanding and offered me twice the value of the pig in what was termed in the army as barrack damages. When I advised him it was not money Brother James required but a pig. His reply was 'Well Gardner, the pig is no more. It would have been taken, turned into ham and eaten, possibly by the soldiers he had been far too kind to by taking them into his house. We shook hands and I made my way back to Fort William.

On arrival I told my story. In the meantime Wray had been in touch with Scottish Command in Edinburgh. A search was made by the agricultural people and no pig was available in Scotland, however, in the afternoon a pig had been found in the north of England and it was being brought to Scotland by despatch riders in a motor cycle and side car.

The despatch riders arrived early in the morning at the C.R.E. Offices, only the pig could not walk because of cramp. After a little exercise it was fed and watered and it was left to me to lead the despatch riders to Fort Augustus. On arrival Brother James could not believe his eyes when the pig was released and on its way to the pig-sty. The riders made their way back after we had breakfast in the abbey. I compensated Brother James for the Rolls razor which was 110 volts and no use to the soldiers who stole it anyway, and the transaction was completed.

I retraced my way back to Fort William to get on with the job I was supposed to be doing, after all you had to turn your hand to many things, there was a war on. It was one of many experiences.

It was always very difficult on changing headquarters to obtain living quarters. Here I was rather fortunate to obtain a billet next to the Royal Hotel. It was a house called "Glenan", a type of boarding house run by a Mrs. Morrison, and her daughters, with real highland hospitality. There were three of us, the local schoolmaster, Mr McGregor, a Captain in the R.E's. and myself. Little did I know another experience was about to take place. Mr Mac, as I called him, came from Kingussie, his father being an ex-provost. He lived in Fort William and went home during the holiday period.

He was a very keen mountaineer, we were good pals and when I was off duty on a Sunday he would arrange an expedition to climb some mountain, I even had special boots etc., for the job, he was an expert.

On the Saturday night he would have the maps out and plot the route ready for Sunday. We always finished at the Tartan Hotel, Kinlochleven and had a good - what he called a tightener - of bacon and eggs. He would never let me pay as that was my prize for being his companion.

Ben Nevis, the Mamores and Glencoe were some of his favourites. He was a bachelor at the time and used to tease me about being an old married man. However, I turned the table on him at a later date when he got married to one of the lady teachers. He was not a bad chap, a good companion and we were both very fit. I have many happy memories of our expeditions, sometimes I was not always available.

My next experience was not such a happy event. I had been at a place called Roshven on the west coast making arrangement for a water supply and electrical installation of works, where Lord Lyle V.C. and some specially selected small number of men were doing special training for a particular job of the utmost secrecy, arriving back home very late. At 4 am in the morning

I was called on to go with the C.R.E. to a fire that had started at No 1 Commando Training Centre Headquarters at Achnacarry Castle near Spean Bridge. It was the home of Sir Donald Cameron of Lochiel, a most important place of training.

My job was to inspect the site, make out a report of the damage. This was not anything unusual to me, but I could see from my first glance of the damage that it would be a most expensive business. The whole roof had gone, considerable amount of flooring, electricity and water supply were obsolete, the main walls and partitions intact and in sound condition. I made contact with Lord Lovat and Colonel Vaughan, who were C.O.'s of the headquarters and training. After a short talk they appeared to think the fire started in the power house, where the electrical plant and generation equipment were. It was made clear to me the importance of the situation as training had to go on as usual and I would be given every assistance with labour. I did not commit myself to a timetable and did not intend to until I had made my inspection and report for a court of inquiry, which I knew would be set up, and I would be a witness.

In fact after an intensive inspection, it turned out not to be an electrical fault, but from a flue pipe in the boiler room of the central heating boiler, where officers put their wet clothing after training. The boiler thermostat was set so high that the clothes caught fire setting light to the wood lathe under the plaster. The quickest way to get started was to erect a temporary corrugated roof so that the inside work could be done and the rooms that were used as offices to be occupied as soon as possible. It was a twenty four hours a day job and I must admit it was done in record time. After three months I did attend a local inquiry, but the final settlement could not take place until after hostilities had ceased.

There is a war memorial at Spean Bridge in honour of the soldiers who sacrificed their lives.

My next call was not so urgent, but important just the same. It was with the American troops. They occupied a site at a place called Glencripsdale near Salen and had only 5 weeks to complete their training. The complaint I got was the electricity supply had gone so low they could not read any of the manuscripts. This time I got a speed boat with crew from the navy at Fort William as the quickest way was by sea to the site. As usual I contacted the C.O. and was given a description of their troubles. It was a small hydro electric plant and on testing the generator with a techometer I found the revolutions were far below the standard and the inflow of water not at its usual force.

In company with one of my assistants and an American officer we began climbing the hill to the reservoir. On the way up I noticed what appeared to be a galaxy of water spraying into the air. On getting nearer the water pipe track it was water spraying alright, with half inch holes in the pipes. We discovered the troops had been firing at targets laid against the pipes, being above ground on concrete blocks. It was like Blackpool on a Saturday night, there must have been dozens of holes. To add insult to injury they were special turned and bored faucet pipes that could not be replaced and even if we did have pipes there were no ships in the Clyde available to get them there. Here again money was no object, it was immaterial. After a great deal of discussion and phone calls it was left to me to decide, there was a time factor here.

It was clear to me that improvisation was necessary and from my past experience in plumbing I suggested lead rivets to be turned out at the Navy Base in Fort William. They had a lathe to turn them out and they were agreeable. We obtained lead from the local plumber Mr Campbell and had a batch of 100 lead rivets made very quickly. After making arrangements with the C.R.E. on the tradesmen required, six men were despatched to Glen-rippsdale with the rivets and had them caulked into the holes. A second batch was necessary and the job was complete in about four days, to the satisfaction of all concerned.

The upshot of this lot was after the war about 20 years later, I was taking my family through Fort William on holiday to my father in law in Burghead, I stopped at Mr Campbells plumbing shop in the main street to ask him if he had ever been back at Glenrippsdale. He said yes and that the lead rivets we had put in were still there and satisfactory, all I could say was it was a miracle.

My next experience made me rather angry. After travelling about 100 miles to investigate an electrical fire and assessment of damage, it was found on arrival there was no electric supply within 20 miles. The nearest approach to lighting was an old acetylene plant with a few old batteries lying around, the value being nil. It was at a place called Tomdown away in the highlands, it could have been a fake phone call or a complete misunderstanding of the message and yet it could have been something important. To me it was a complete waste of time.

However my next visit was to a place near Kincraig called Glenfeshie, There had been a great deal of tree felling in the area, there was also a snow and mountain warfare training centre, along with a camp called Torwood with a number of Italian Prisoners of War. The water supply had failed, I arrived there one Saturday morning as we had some engineers there as well. After investigation the water supply pipes were disconnected and the pipes cleared of obstruction with material that had been washed down from the hills. As I was having lunch in the canteen and being Saturday afternoon, it was suggested I should wait a short time and play for the army football team as someone had heard I was a player at one time. After a bit of teasing I agreed to play. It was hard to believe, but the prisoners had made a football field between two mountains in the glen. The game ended in a draw. Although I was fit for mountain climbing this was a different kettle of fish. However after a wash down and an invitation for tea which I accepted, it was off for me down a six mile trek on a very scraggy road, not really suited for a car, to the main road with a rather late return to Fort William.

For the next fortnight I was confined to office work as a number of new schemes were imminent and a rather large recreation centre comprising two giant nissan huts had to be erected just outside the Alexandra Hotel where our offices were. I had to draw up plans for a heating system and electrical installations with costs for grant purposes. If only approximate, and included; concert hall with stage effects, dance floor, reading rooms, writing rooms, badminton, billiards and a library with the usual Naffie requirements. It was quite an undertaking as it had to suit all the troops in the area. It took about six months from start to finish and was opened by Lord Alexander and many of the stage stars of that era. I can remember Dame Sybil Thorndyke, Claud Dampier and many others. It was a huge success and to crown it all I acted as compere one evening. I had no idea what I would be asked to do next.

It was about that time I asked for a fortnight leave which was granted. Colonel Wray gave me a railway ticket home and suggested I should bring my wife and family for a holiday when I was returning, this I did. We got fixed up with Mrs. Morrison at "Glenan" as Mr. Mac was on holiday at the time. I did mostly local business for a time with my assistants doing the long distance runs, after all, I had been over most of the counties by now and knew the various Chiefs of Staff.

The next long distant trip was rather amusing, I was asked by Scottish Command to arbitrate in a difference of opinion between the navy and the army at a commando training centre at Lochailort, where two Russell Newbury 60 kw Engines were being installed in the power house. Colonel Wray was with me to see fair play. We left Fort William at 4pm and arrived at Lochailort around 6pm. I was introduced to Commander McEwan the O.C. and proceeded to the power house. To my astonishment the place was full of top brass, so I requested Colonel Wray if the place be cleared and one representative of either service be left with himself and Commander McEwan. I explained the situation giving each representative their say. It finished up briefly, the navy wanted a chain drive and the army a belt drive. I produced various designs of plants in the area and after further discussion my decision from a safety point of view was that it should be a belt drive. The reasoning behind it was if a fire started in the Power House with the chain drive there was every likelihood of an explosion, whereas the belt drive would slip off and cause no damage. This was readily agreed on and we proceeded to the Officers Mess for refreshment and dinner. I made it clear I only took a soft drink and did not smoke, thereafter we sat down for dinner. By now it was nearing 9 pm and Commander Mc Ewan asked for silence as they always listen in to Lord "Haw Haw" with an announcement as follows, 'This is Germany calling. We regret to announce that this afternoon H.M.S. Lochailort of 25,000 tons has been sunk with great loss of life', nobody said a word and then Commander McEwan turned round to me sitting close to him and said 'Goodness gracious Gardner, your sunk, as H.M. Lochailort was a Castle.' You can understand the uproar of merriment for the rest of the evening. Wray and myself waited overnight and returned to Fort William in the morning.

Later I had occasion to visit Lochailort again in a few months time, to find a huge camp around the castle and everything working to the satisfaction of all. This time I was going on to Roshven and had to be transported by Mc Donalds ferry boat. There was a lady passenger on the boat and when introduced to her it was none other than Wendy Wood the Scottish Nationalist, who stole the flag by climbing the pole at Stirling Castle. I asked her if that was true and she admitted all she did during a dark night was to unhook the rope and the flag came down of its own accord, she of course took possession of it before returning it at a later date, she was a character.

After another six months most of the major works were on hand. My assistants were all over the place, leaving me to deal with any sudden requirements such as smoke screens over Loch Treig, important to the aluminium works at Kinlochleven. The works at Fort William had a stack of 3 Bombs dropped near the tail race of the water supply, two never went off, the third went right under the pipes and never went off either.

At Foyers Aluminium works in Loch Ness they were not so lucky. Three bombs were dropped, one going through the side of the power house, the other two never went off, they landed in Loch Ness. However, the damage was quickly repaired and production started in a short time.

We also had the arrival of prisoners of war, mostly Italians and later German prisoners arrived. They were accommodated mostly at prison camps in the far north with the usual protection by electricity etc., and put to work.

In 1944 when most of the troops had done their training and were abroad in Africa or transferred to other camps, we were about reaching the crest of the wave, the situation was at a climax. I was posted back to Inverness Headquarters in preparation for the run down of the services, transfer of equipment south. It was now a question of marching out instead of marching in, with all the work entailed in inventory procedure. The war was coming to a climax, Italy had unconditionally surrendered in September 1943 and at the end of 1944, Germany was being overwhelmed at the same time. I was to experience another change in my life.

Scottish ex-Presidents and guests at "top table" of Glasgow and West of Scotland Plumbers and Domestic Engineers' (Employers) Association Dinner, January 1959

Mr & Mrs John M Gardner at Trades Dinner, Kirkcaldy

STARTING BUSINESS

At the end of December in 1944, I received a letter from Mr Leitch the foreman with my old firm in civilian life, stating that my old boss had died and the business would be up for sale. If I was prepared to purchase the business Mr Leitch would carry on the business until I was able to get out of the Army. Having slept on it for a night I decided to have a go.

I asked Colonel Wray for a weekend pass to go home. By now it was only a matter of form. I was also allowed a few days extra. I did not at the time tell him my intentions. I reached Milngavie on the Friday afternoon, made contact quickly with Mr Leitch and he was delighted about the outcome. I then contacted the lawyer, who was the same name as myself, I was John M Gardner and he was W Reid Gardner, no family connection in any way, although he was also glad to know I would put in an offer. I then proceeded to see Mrs Currie's married daughter and she was pleased to see me as well, so much so, that she would advise her mother and if I could come near the offer asked for, I would be given preference.

I arranged a meeting with Mr R Gardner, the Solicitor, on the Monday. In the meantime I had a good idea what I could afford, after some discussion I was £100 short of the amount I required but I thought if he gave me a couple of hours grace I could get the money. After one hour and a quiet word with Mr Leitch, the foreman, I had the money from him on loan. So back I went to Mr Gardner, the solicitor, and who was in the office but the late Mr Currie's married daughter. I produced the £100, handed it over, Mr Gardner shook me by the hand and confirmed the business would be mine. Mr Currie's daughter shook me by the hand, gave me a kiss and started to cry she was so happy, saying her mother would be delighted as she had known me as a boy. The documents were then duly signed and the deal completed.

It was only natural my wife was over the moon, that was on the 10th of January 1945. There we were, standing in the living room of our house, we had ten shillings between us, how could we manage, I did not get my wages cheque until the end of the week. With 3 girls and my wife to feed for the rest of the week, my wife suggested I take the ten shilling note with me as I might need it going back to Inverness and that she would get groceries from the shop across the road until the weekend. What a predicament! However it turned out all right. Going back in the train to Inverness I wondered if it was all a dream and what would be my next experience, it was not long before it happened.

On arrival at Inverness, the ten shilling note still in my pocket, what would I say to Colonel Wray. I had one night to think it out.

Having given it some thought there was only one way, to make a clean breast of it. This I did and to my surprise he was quite sympathetic to my aspirations, the difficulty would be to get out of the forces as I was a specialist in a very important area. The only thing he could not understand was my intention to go back to such a small town with a population of 12,000 persons. I had to explain about the industrial area and the Milngavie and Bearsden business type of people there.

He suggested I should go back with him to London and start up there as he did, working for hospitals etc., or I could go over to Germany and remain in the forces in connection with the rebuilding of Europe. My answer to that was my wife would not be prepared to go abroad with a small family. By this time I had convinced him of my intentions and his reply was 'I will not stand in your way if I can possibly help a very good friend and adviser'. The air was now cleared for another few months at least.

The news from home was quite good, the business was thriving due to a heavy frost in January and February. The trouble was lack of labour as most tradesmen were in the forces or munition work. It was quite obvious, assistance was required, so I had to make a move, the only way out was, now that the main job was mostly a clean up operation and getting much quieter, I put in for a transfer nearer home, it would be either Stirling or Glasgow. After using the influence of the C.R.E. Colonel Wray I was given a transfer to Glasgow in a months time. This suited me very well. Due to my past record I was to be allowed to work in the forenoon for the C.R.E. Kirklee, Glasgow, and the afternoon at my own business. At last things were now working out a bit better. It was sad for me to leave all my friends in the north who were so loyal to me, but I suppose that is life, yet coming home to a new future was very important to my wife and family.

The first six months at my business was very hard work, but the situation became much better when some of our tradesmen were released from the forces. After a time I was given a complete discharge from the army and with additional staff I managed to build up about fifteen tradesmen, mostly electrical and plumbing with central heating experience. The great difficulty now was transport, I had to give tuition for driving to a few of the men and with the purchase of a few vans we were now getting settled. Most of the men were local so it helped considerably. Some of them like myself were born and brought up in Milngavie, so we knew the people and the district. There was no shortage of work and the business was expanding quite rapidly, especially with jobbing work neglected during the war years, new housing, both local authority and private housing due to expansion in Milngavie and Bearsden.

In July 1949 I purchased the business of Alex McAdam in Station Road, Blanefield, under the name of Alex McAdam, Plumber, Sanitary Engineer and Grate Builder with possession of premises, publication of sale, a complete list of all clients past and present, with a list of any contracts, outstanding work to be carried out and the introduction to clients where possible. This now covered the area of Killearn, Drymen, Balmaha, Balfron and Blanefield. This turned out to be a very worthwhile transaction. In 1946 I became a member of the Glasgow and West Scotland Employers, Plumbers and Domestic Engineers Association. After that as a firm we became quite well known in Glasgow with the trade and Merchant Warehousemen.

I also became a:-

Member of the Scottish Federation of Master Plumbers
Member of Electrical Contractors Association
Member of Electrical Inspection Council for Contractors
Member of Institute of Plumbing, London
Member of Institute of British Engineers

In 1958/59 I was elected as President of the Glasgow and West of Scotland Master Plumbers and Domestic Engineers Association.

By this time the staff in my office was very satisfactory and I had a very good foreman in Mr Leitch to look after our affairs when I was doing my rounds. This left me with more time to attend conferences and dinners connected with the building trades. I suppose that in reaching the top of your profession you were expected to make speeches at dinners and meetings. At the annual routine of Glasgow, Edinburgh, Perth, Dundee, Aberdeen, Inverness and Ayr it was quite a task, due to this I met many top people in industry and politics. At this time my wife was most helpful by attending functions with me.

In July 1955 we purchased a dwelling house known as "Clavie", 2 North Campbell Avenue, Milngavie. It was quite a large self contained Bungalow for the sum of £2850. It was built in 1930. Our family had increased to four girls and one boy who was the youngest; We required the six rooms, and with the assistance of a part time housekeeper, my wife was able to travel with me on my various escapades.

It was on January 1959 at the Annual Dinner of the Glasgow and West of Scotland Master Plumbers Association held in the Grosvenor Restaurant that was to test my ability to speak as Chairman. There were eighteen presidents from all over Scotland attending, not including the chief guests from various walks of life, with approximately two hundred ordinary dinner guests. It was indeed the most important night in my life so far.

Toast List

The Queen:- The Chairman
The City of Glasgow:- Mr James McAulay, Chief Constable Paisley
Reply:- Mr Andrew Lawson J.P., Deacon Convenor of The Trades of Glasgow
Glasgow and West of Scotland Employers Association
Major Sir Guy Lloyd D.S.O., D.L., M.P.
Reply: -The Chairman
The Kindred Associations and Guests:- Lieut Col. David Yuile, Kilmarnock
Reply:- Messrs H Hewerine and Mr Harold McKinlay, Scottish Federation
The Chairman and Croupiers: Mr William Anderson Jr
Reply: - The Chairman

Message of Thanks to Mr Grant, Secretary and Treasurer of
West of Scotland Employers Association

From Major Sir Guy Lloyd D.S.0., D.L., M.P. House of Commons, London

21st January 1959

Dear Mr Grant,

I just want to send you a line to express my very grateful thanks to you and the President for the splendid hospitality you provided last week.

I so much enjoyed the evening and would like to take this opportunity to congratulate you on an obviously very contented united Association.

yours Sincerely,
Guy Lloyd.

Message of Thanks:- Mr Ian Grant, Solicitor, Secretary and Treasurer, Glasgow & West of Scotland Plumbing Employers Association.

From: - Alexander Lawson J.P., Deacon Convenor of Trades, Glasgow.

Mr Dear Ian,

I feel inpelled this morning to ask you to please convey my warmest thanks to the President for his bountiful hospitality last night.
It was quite a privilege to be present to contribute to the Toast List and, no doubt you will agree, that thanks to the genial chairmanship of the President, the whole evening proved to be a complete success.

With warmest regards,
Yours sincerely,
Andrew Lawson J.P., Deacon Convenor
of the Trades of Glasgow.

Extract from The Glasgow Herald, 17th January 1959

Plumbing in van of progress
Modern Developments

There was a great future for the plumbing industry as technical progress was made with space heating and other modern developments, Mr John Gardner, President of the Glasgow and West of Scotland Plumbers and Domestic Engineers (Employers) Association, said last night.

Major Sir Guy Lloyd M.P. for East Renfrewshire, said that the plumbing industry had made an immense and far reaching contribution to the health, comfort and amenity of the community over the past 100 years, they had been in the van of progress.

Other speakers were:- Mr James McAulay, Chief Constable of Paisley, Mr Andrew Lawson, Deacon Convenor Trades of Glasgow, Lieutenant-Colonel David Yuille, Vice-President of the Association and Mr Harold McKinlay, President Scottish Federation.

I had arrived. From then on, after becoming a director of the Scottish Federation I had many requests and invitations to conferences and dinners all over Scotland. I tried my best to fulfil as many as I could but it was most time consuming although very rewarding. I made many good friends throughout Scotland.

On the brighter side of the business I was asked and played in many sports outings such as golf, bowling and curling between the various associations in team matches, it was most enjoyable.

A lot of my work, estimating and such, was being done at home in the evenings. Later I had to curtail some of my aspirations as my family required more of my time especially at weekends. My wife did her best to cope, so my family now had to come first and with a home help we were doing not so bad.

Tragedy

However in 1960 my wife took ill with serious trouble within the Intestine and after a major operation, carried out at Canniesburn, never appeared to be the same. This went on until the beginning of January 1961 when she took a sudden stroke, an operation being carried out in Killearn Hospital. The left side of her body was now paralysed and suddenly on the morning of the 12th January 1961 at 1.30 am she died.

It all happened so quickly and was a terrible shock to myself and the family. Death had been caused by an aneurysm of the left caroted artery, Cardia Respiratory failure. She was cremated at the Maryhill Crematorium.

I cannot describe my feelings for some time. My oldest daughter had just commenced her training as a nurse at Ruchill Hospital and my son was eleven years of age, the other three girls were still at school. Mr Peat, the minister of St. Pauls Church was a great help to me at this time, but life had to go on. It was difficult to understand why this should happen to us. I had to take a grip of myself. My life had changed so suddenly. I had my family to work for and I had never shirked anything in my life.

After a time it became clear what I had to do. Whether it was independence or determination, I do not know which, but I had to get organised and this I did by resigning from all associations and clubs to concentrate only on my family and business. There is no doubt this paid off. The only club I continued to pay my dues for was Milngavie Golf Club where I was a past captain.

I allowed my oldest daughter, Evelyn, to continue her training as a nurse. My second oldest girl went to a typing school and then obtained a job in Barr & Stroud. My third oldest girl, Rhoda, had a job at Bowater but became unwell through loss of confidence and had to go for treatment to a hospital. Cynthia, my youngest girl trained as a hairdresser and got a job in a hairdresser in Byres Road, Glasgow. That now left my son, who eventually started his apprenticeship in our own business. So things were beginning to take shape again. I still had a lady as a home help. I learned to do cooking and before long we had a system going satisfactory to all. I had more time to deal with my clients again on a personal note. Business was continuing to be quite good and I had started playing golf again.

Freda, my second oldest girl, left Barr & Stroud to come into our own business, with her experience in typing and book-keeping she was a tremendous help.

My oldest daughter, Evelyn, who had been Captain of the 1st Milngavie Girl Guides, had to relinquish her post due to her training as a nurse. Not long after my second oldest daughter, Freda, took over as Captain of the 1st Milngavie Company of the Girl Guides and Cynthia later became a Lieutenant in the same company. My family were now becoming more mature and independent.

Authors 30 foot fibreglass yacht on Loch Lomond

Another experience was about to start with the purchase of a "Seamaster" fibre glass yacht, coloured blue with white sails, with an engine capable of about 15 mph. The yacht was 28ft long with a small boat and a Seagull outdoor motor for trailing purposes. We had an anchorage at McFarlanes Boat Yard, Balmaha, Loch Lomond. It was convenient for weekends and summer evenings for the next few years. With my family now growing up Loch Lomond was ideal for experimenting, sailing the yacht, exploring the various islands and picnics with friends, generally a very enjoyable experience. Later my son Ian purchased a speed boat and became interested in jet skiing. The family now had their own interests, I was most fortunate in that I was never in any trouble so far as my family was concerned.

I had to interest myself with a garden around my house and, although it was altered so that a good percentage of it was put in grass with a lawn at the front and back of the house, there was always plenty of work to do on it, so all the spare time I had, and that was not much, was spent as best I could in the garden. Although my name was Gardner I was never really an expert Gardener.

I suppose at this stage of my life something was to happen and change my life into the most exciting time so far in my lifetime. I was approached by at least three different town councillors to enquire if I would take up politics by standing for the Milngavie Town Council. At first my family were rather amused at the idea, but later became quite serious about it as it would fill up a void in my life. After much discussion with my family and a visit to the house of the Provost Dr John L. Park, it was decided practically for me. My election address went out and I was duly elected an Independent Councillor on 5th May 1964.

I should have mentioned that in 1956 I purchased a caravan and during the summer months we had a pitch at Kinkell Braes, St Andrews, from May until October when the caravan site closed for the season. Sometimes I would trail the caravan up north during July for a fortnight to Burghead, we called that our annual holiday. It was then returned to St Andrews. My wife used to live for a period in the caravan during the school holidays and I travelled through at weekends. It was excellent for the family growing up right at the seaside. St Andrews was one of our favourite places, in fact I became a member of St Andrews Golf Club taking out what was known as country membership, these were happy days for my wife and the family.

In 1959 it was suggested by the family that I should buy a dog. It would be convenient as a watch dog and they would look after it, After searching around I got in touch with a breeder Mrs J. Gillespie, and with my oldest daughter, paid her a visit. The upshot was, she offered us a golden cocker spaniel puppy born on the l8th September 1959, this was now the middle of October. It was a pedigree dog male, his parents being Sunkist Sir Harold, the sire, and Golden Chorus Girl, the dame. The registered number of the sire was 61052/57 and the number of the dame was 90713/59. Little did we realize until some time after they were both champions. Our puppy was called Caesar after a dog my father-in-law had in Burghead. At first my wife was not very keen having it inside the house until it was trained. A fairly large garden shed was equipped for the purpose. After a week the dog was sick with something he had eaten and he was allowed, with his basket, into the house temporarily, but he never returned to the shed. After another few weeks he could be found lying in front of the living room fire, but always fed in the kitchenette. It was many months after that I discovered he was sleeping overnight in the living room on the best chair. I was always first down in the morning and when he heard my footstep he was off the chair like a shot before I entered the room. It was a long time before I discovered this and by accident I noticed the seat of the chair warm, I thought it was very clever of him so I told nobody about this and he had his lovely bed for a few years, in fact for as long as I can remember. He was very clever, when my wife was sitting on the armchair he would jump on her lap and put his paws on her shoulders, after that she spoiled him, at a later date he used to like coming with me in the car.

We had a system I used to take him for exercise to Drumclog Moor and he had a fine old gallop, thereafter he would wait with me in the car front seat until we came home for lunch. He remained at home in the afternoon under the watchful eye of the family.

It became rather amusing, he occupied the front seat of the car alongside of myself and he would not permit anyone to use his seat. He had the nicest way of shoving them off, until all the tradesmen knew it was the backseat for them. He used to look out the window of the car as only a cocker spaniel could. He was attractive no doubt.

Author with "Caeser"

During my visits to the various estates and mansion houses, some ladies are attracted to canine pets and two ladies had a special interest in Caesar.

Dowager Lady Edmonstone of Lettre House, Killearn, was one of our clients and when I called at the house she would open the door of the car and ask me for Caesar's lead. I was advised to go into the house and have a coffee with the butler while she had a stroll with Caesar, meantime I would be taking instructions from the butler.

Another lady, Lady Wilson of Killearn House did exactly the same. I remember having a telephone call one Friday evening from Lady Wilson wondering if she could have Caesar on loan for a day as her son would be coming up from London for a shooting expedition on the estate, unfortunately I had to advise her that Caesar was not trained for that purpose and if a gun shot went off he would run for his life, as it was not unusual to find him lying in front of the living room fire, anyway Caesar and her ladyship were always good pals.

The other great attraction for Caesar was to go with me to Loch Lomond. He would sit at the bow of the boat as if it belonged to him, and when on the Islands he would romp about until he was tired. I used to feed him on dog food called Chum, thereafter a sleep on the seat at the stern was called for until he was ready for home. Sometimes, although not often, we had a tent and stayed overnight on one of the islands. We also had a very detailed map of Loch Lomond giving depths in fathoms at the various places, we found that very necessary, even as a guide to the islands, glens and mountains.

Ceasar was all that could be expected from a dog, He was a beautiful dog and an excellent companion, always in good health for thirteen years, when he took a heart attack and died. He is buried in the front lawn of our house where, as a pup, he used to sit and wait for me coming home at night. I could never have another dog I thought so much of my Ceasar.

My daughters were now being married between 1962 until in 1974, only my son, Iain, and myself were living in our house. We were not using the Seamaster boat so much now, and with my other political affairs, I did not have the same time to spend on boating. Iain had bought a speed boat for himself and was more interested in parascending and giving tuition in other forms of water sports, so I sold the large boat, but kept the small rowing boat with the Seagull engine.

POLITICS

Now come my experiences in the world of politics in Local Government. At the Town Council meeting I was given the post of Convenor of Public Health and Cleansing, a member of the Dean of Guild Court, Parks and Halls and became Milngavie's representative on the Electricity Consultative Council, Clyde Area.

During the first year the replacement sewer in Balfleurs Street was completed, alterations necessary to prevent flooding by duplication of sewer from Crossveggate to main outfall were in progress. After very protracted negotiations a start was made on the new Sewage Purification Works. That completed my first year as a Councillor.

In 1965 Milngavie as a Burgh had been split into Wards and voting took place on Tuesday 4th May. Being duly elected again the first meeting of the Council took place on 7th May 1965. On this occasion my responsibility changed slightly, I was now Convenor of Dean of Guild Court, Convenor of Cleansing and Public Health, Member for Streets and Lighting and Member Electrical Consultative Council Clyde Area.

Burgh of Milngavie
New Sewage Purification Works

As this is possibly one of the most important works ever carried out in Milngavie and as Convenor of Cleansing and Public Health, herewith is a description of the various works carried out.

The new works replace works originally constructed in 1906. The latter consisted of septic tanks and contact beds and by 1962 their condition had deteriorated to the extent that they were being by-passed and the sewage was flowing to the Allander Water untreated.

The Town Council, well aware of their statutory obligations were faced with two possibilities, they could either construct modern treatment works or they could arrange for the sewage to be conveyed to the sewerage system of the Corporation of Glasgow.

After investigation it was found that the connecting sewer from Milngavie to the Glasgow system would be so long as to be uneconomic. Moreover, the scheme depended upon the Glasgow Sewerage System extending to a certain point and there was no immediate prospect of this for various political reasons.

The Town Council therefore decided to proceed with the construction of new works.

The population of Milngavie in 1962 was approaching 9,000 and the planned population for the Burgh was 15,000. Growth is so rapid in the area that it was decided to design for the latter figure. Space is available within the works area for duplication of the plant.

The flow was measured at about 500,000 gallons per day and a design flow of 750,000 g.p.d. was adopted. There was no major industry in Milngavie and this was borne out by chemical analyses.

The fall between the inlet sewer and outfall was restricted and would not permit the use of percolating filters of reasonable depth without pumping, it was therefore decided to adopt mechanical aeration.

The sewage in Milngavie is mainly domestic and is collected in the main outfall sewer which follows the Allander Water to the site of the sewage purification works at the south east corner of the Burgh.

By arrangement with the Clyde River Purification Board all flows up to twelve times dry weather flow (12 x d.w.f.) are taken to the Purification Works, while flows in excess of this are passed to the Allander Water.

<u>The Sewage Purification Works comprise the following main units:-</u>

1. Detritus Channels, Screening and Flow Measurement Equipment.
2. Primary Settlement and Storm Tanks.
3. Aeration Tanks.
4. Final Settling Tanks and Activated Sludge Return Pumphouse.
5. Primary Sludge Pumphouse.
6. Sludge Storage Tank and Road Tanker.
7. Administration Block.

1. Detritus Channels, Screening and Flow Measurement Equipment

The purpose of the detritus channels is to extract organic-free grit from the sewage. The channels are designed to maintain a constant velocity of about 1 foot per second at all levels of flow. At this velocity, grit, sand and similar heavy particles are settled, but organic matter is carried through to be dealt with in later units. The channels are cleared by mechanical dredging equipment.

The screens intercept papers, rags and "stringy" matter present in the sewage. This material is then disintegrated before being returned to the flow. In this form it will be less liable to choke pipes and pumps in later processes.

The flow is measured in a flume and a chart records the variations throughout the day.

2. Primary Settlement and Storm Tanks

Three similar tanks are provided, each 60ft in diameter and each holding 125,000 gallons. The primary tank and the first storm tank are interconnected and both are equipped with sludge scraping equipment. The piping and channels allow the first storm tank to take over the duty of the primary tank should the latter be emptied for maintenance or repair. The second storm tank is also equipped with a scraper. Sludge settling on the floors is swept to conical hoppers at the centre of the tanks from which it is led by gravity to the sludge pump house.

3. Aeration Tanks

It is in these tanks that the biological process of purification takes place, oxygen being supplied to the purifying organisms by mechanical means.

The two tanks are each 30 feet square and 14 feet deep and have a total capacity of 150,000 gallons.

4. Final Settling Tanks and Activated Sludge Return Pumphouse

The effluent is finally purified in these units and is then in an acceptable condition for discharge to the Allander Water.

Part of the function of the tanks is to arrest purifying organisms escaping from the aeration tanks and to pass them back to those tanks via the activated sludge return pumphouse.

In the event of a surplus of sludge accumulating, this can be diverted back to the primary tank to be mixed and settled with primary sludge. The final tanks are 45 feet in diameter and each has a capacity of 85,000 gallons. Facilities are available for emptying the final tanks and aeration tanks.

5. Sludge Pumphouse

Sludge settled in the primary and storm tanks flows to this pumphouse and is pumped by centrifugal pumps to the sludge storage tank.

6. Sludge Storage Tank and Road Tanker

During the design stage it was intended to provide for two-stage design digestion of the sludge and indeed a provisional contract was placed for the necessary equipment.

Following negotiations with Glasgow Corporation it was decided to abandon this proposal and instead, convey untreated sludge to Glasgow for disposal at sea.

The Town Council therefore purchased a 3,000 gallon road tanker and a sludge holding tank capable of holding about a fortnight's capacity (100,000 gallons) was constructed.

The administration block contains a garage, main switch room, office, laboratory, machine room, mess room and shower.

The estimated cost of the work is 150,000.

The Consulting Engineers were Messr E Crouch and Hogg and the main Contractor Wm Tawse Ltd, Aberdeen.

Provost John M Buchanan
Convenor of Cleansing and Public Health, Senior Magistrate Bailie John M Gardner J.P.

A dwelling house was constructed on the site of the sewage purification for the works supervisor, the contract was placed with the John Lawrence Construction Company and built with brick and mortar in the space of six days, a record for this type of work.

Milngavie's £160, 000 Sewage Works Opened

Opened by Provost John M Buchanan, Tuesday 23rd April 1968 at 7.15pm. Bailie John M Gardner, Convenor of the Cleansing and Public Health Committee, the driving force behind building of the sewage works spoke to the assembled Councillors, Ex Provosts and visiting dignitaries on the new addition to Milngavie.

Author and Mr J Lawrence JP; Receiving key to house built in 6 days by Lawrence Construction Ltd.

and sports accommodation. In fact it was just like a cruise ship. It usually returned to Shieldhall Quay around 6pm.

It was further suggested that all Presidents and Dignitaries in connection with the trade in Scotland be invited, with a band in attendance.

My wife and Miss .McNaughton, Matron of the Royal Samaritan Hospital in Glasgow (a close friend of the family) were in attendance. There must have been approximately 150 persons on board. It was midsummer and a beautiful day. As one of the directors, I was given a very important job by Mr McDougal, the President. My duty would suit me fine as I was, as he said, the man for the job of looking after the refreshments in the Purser's Office, with a small window to hand out drinks, the drinks being free for the day. My instructions were don't give anyone more than one glass of whiskey and he showed me quite a large glass. The reason I was selected, according to him, was that I was one of the few people on board who was a non-alcoholic. That being the case apparently I was giving out much bigger glasses of whisky than I should have been, and within a few hours it was reckoned we had everyone jolly. It was thereafter known throughout Scotland by those in the trade as the most remarkable and enjoyable outing on record and I was the culprit. I never saw so many comedians in one day.

As a member of the Parks and Halls, and to improve the environment, a new paddling pool with a water spray was installed at Lennox Park. Also the drainage of Oakburn Park was carried out. Having now been a member of the Electrical Consultative Council, Clyde Area, I attended meetings at the S.S.E.B. in Glasgow. This consisted mostly of domestic affairs such as complaints from customers, accounts and finance, also new works such as Hunterston "B" Station, at that time being constructed. Also being a member of Streets and Lighting, this was mostly extensions of lighting for the new roads being constructed owing to the growth and expansion of Milngavie. In general including improvement of lighting on existing roads with modern equipment.

As Convenor of the Dean of Guild Court I was much involved in the passing of plans for new buildings, extension of buildings and industry, and also control of building and housing. I was now covering a considerable amount of ground due to demolishing of older tenements and slum clearance. I was also made a Bailie in 1966 and sat in Court as a Magistrate, becoming a Senior Bailie in 1969.

It was about this time I was becoming rather annoyed at the slow progress, being made especially in slum clearance, and began to make my presence felt in a number of places, due to the unnecessary legal jargon going on and the accumulation of litter. Plans had been afoot for several years to redevelop the centre of Milngavie; as chaos reigned in the centre of the town with traffic problems, it was essential to preserve the village atmosphere.

At a meeting held in October 1976 the heading in a local paper was

TAKE IT DOWN, IT'S ILLEGAL

It was at the above meeting of the Bearsden and Milngavie Councils' Planning Committee, the convenor Bailie John M Gardner expressed his concern at the amount of time being wasted in committee by hearings.

The hearings were brought about after planning and building officials had discovered that certain building work in the district was being carried out without either the necessary planning permission or building warrants.

People who had not obtained the necessary permission were then asked to appear before the committee and explain their reasons for not doing so.

After the hearings Bailie Gardner said "We are tired of hearing the various excuses time and time again."

This week Bailie Gardner said "From my experience I would advise any person who is contemplating any civil engineering or building works, to get in touch with the local planning and building control officials who are there for the purpose of advising and co-operating with applicants.

In my opinion, it would save a great deal of time and expense, because it is impossible for the ordinary individual to study the rules and regulations now applicable to the Planning and Building Control Standards as they exist today. Before most works commence it is necessary to have planning permission and a warrant to build, this is most important because it protects the applicant and allows any objector to be heard.

Having received the warrant to build and after starting to build, perhaps due to unforeseen circumstances, it may be necessary to alter the existing plans. In a case like this a fresh application should be made for the proposed amendment.

Should any unauthorised building take place without having complied with the regulations, the District Council may require the operations to cease and be reinstated to the original position before operations may be started. This is quoted as unauthorised building operations and could result in considerable unnecessary expense.

"It must always be remembered that regulations and standards are laid down not only for the public at large, but for the protection of the applicant as well."

Mr Gardner also stated that if applicants co- operate with the officials concerned they could save time, money and embarrassment, and in conclusion he said "No one derives any pleasure from refusing to grant permission, but officials have a job to do and the elected representatives are there to see justice is done."

Mr Walter Hemfrey, the Districts' Chief Planning Officer, said this week "I would endorse what Bailie Gardner has said and make it clear that the onus is on the applicant to make sure that the necessary permissions have been obtained before starting work." He also suggested that, if an applicant has an agent or architect dealing with the application, it is important for the applicant to make sure that the correct permissions have been obtained and that everything is in order. The same applies to the Building Control Officer for the building warrants, the public should read these carefully.

Invasion by Rodentia

When convenor of Public Health and Cleansing, I was chairman at a meeting held in November 1967 and was somewhat amazed at a statement made by Bailie Neil Baxter a member of my committee.

He suggested I should take a walk down the main street in Milngavie at 11.30pm some night and I would see a phenomenon. It was like birds in the air flying in formation to another climate the only difference being it was dozens of rats in true formation marching up the street approximately six abreast as if going to war, and others marching in the opposite direction down the street, when they met a fight would take place. The eyes of the rats could be seen like small lights in the darkness, after a time they scattered about leaving some badly injured rats. It was all rather frightening.

I did do as he suggested and found the war to be rather an exaggeration, what I did discover was there did appear to be rats coming up from the Allander Water and others coming down from the domestic side of the street.

I went back in daylight when it was a different kettle of fish, they appeared to be coming from the slum property and from pollution of the river.

I did some research on the lives of rats and gave a short lecture at the next meeting of the Town Council, before doing so I made the following statement.

Slums are breeding grounds for rats

Slums in Milngavie are nothing more then breeding grounds for rats and should be demolished immediately, Bailie John M Gardner said this at the last meeting of the Town Council. He said that excuses did not count in this case, and that slum sites could be used as temporary car parks until rebuilding could take place.

He told Councillors that he had, in fact, caught a rat near the Civil Defence (Decontamination) Centre. It was a brown rat which, he claims, is a good mover and eater, and can carry disease, it may attack if cornered.

Said Bailie Gardner "After recent press reports about rats in property at Main Street, the County Council's Rodent Destruction Officer acted on his own initiative and laid bait with the exception of one area in Main Street. On a later inspection this proved to be clear.

Bailie Gardner added "The rodent officer reports that one shop has been a source of infestation for many years and the problem has not lessened to any great extent. He has asked Milngavie Town Councils ' co-operation to clear up these premises. Property in Stewart Street will be inspected and the necessary action taken.

Bailie Neil Baxter who had originally brought the matter to the Councils' attention stated Mr & Mrs McDonald of 29 Sinclair Street can hardly sleep at night for the noise of rats moving behind the walls."

Said Bailie Gardner "The brown rat exists in Milngavie because it is fed from shops at night and sleeps in the walls of the slum property by day."

The problem could be solved, he maintained, by the provision of proper containers for shops and houses and the removal of slum buildings which are defective and dangerous. He gave as example Mains Street.

Herewith is a short statement on Rodentia

There are two species, the brown rat and the black rat. The brown rat originated in Norway, of the two species it is distinguished by its large size, brownish gray colour, short tail and ears.

It is fierce and cunning and overcomes all allied species with which it is brought in contact. Its original home would seem to be some part of Central Asia, thence it has spread over much of the world, driving out the house haunting species, as in England, all but exterminating the black rat, it is believed to have reached Great Britain in 1730.

The black rat is smaller in size than the brown rat, with longer ears and is common especially in southern lands. It frequents ships and on them has reached most parts of the world. It is more common and more widespread in the tropics than the brown rat, which in these climes is often restricted to the coast or to ports.

This long tailed rat, originally a native of southern Asia, first penetrated to all parts of the world, in many places nearly exterminated the indigenous rats, after this followed the advance of the more powerful brown rat.

The black rat first reached Europe in the 13th century. The Isle of Dogs and Yarmouth in Norfolk are chief English strongholds of the black rat. It is this species that is the chief disseminator of bubonic plague. Both species agree in their predaceous habits, omnivorous diet and great fecundity, they bear four or five times in the year from four to ten blind and naked young which in their turn are able to breed at an age of six months, the time of gestation being 20 days.

The Environment

As convenor of Planning and Parks what I am about to write gives me no pleasure at all.

Bearsden resident destroys 30 trees

If the Bearsden and Milngavie District Council do not take some legal action against a Bearsden businessman who destroyed nearly 30 trees at

Whistlefield, Bearsden, they would be "failing in their duty".

One Councillor described the action which the man had taken as "pure massacre" another said it was appalling that one man could cause such a mess and another said that it was vandalism of the first order.

The fact that these trees had been felled without the authorisation of the Planning Committee of the Bearsden and Milngavie District Council was brought up at last Tuesdays meeting of the committee at Boclair Bearsden.

30 years old

The members of the committee were told by convenor Bailie John Gardner, that 25 to 30 year-old trees had been felled at the side of St Germain's Loch.

The felled trees had since been burned and some of the branches had been thrown into the loch.

Bailie Gardner had visited the site and had been appalled at the mess which had been left.

Many of the residents at the Whistlefield Development had seen men felling the trees, but they thought that the work was being carried out officially.

Police Called

The matter was reported to the police by the chief planning officer Mr Walter Hemfrey and a detective from Milngavie police station was sent to investigate.

It was said at the meeting that a Bearsden man had admitted to felling the trees and had hired a group of men to carry this out.

There was no reason given as to why he wanted the trees removed. The Planning Committee reached a unanimous decision that the man should be prosecuted under section 88 (part 1) of the 1972 Planning Act.

This could mean that any guilty party might have to pay up to £400 for every tree felled.

Police are investigating the matter.

Opinion Vandalism

The following appeared in the opinion column of the Local Press.

We have heard of vandalism and vandalism but the mind boggles a bit at this story. Its the first time we've heard of someone actually hiring men and machines to deprive the area of trees. We're so used to the more common practice of lads breaking off a young sapling as they walk past in the park.
But at least the residents in the St Germaine Loch district will see where their rates go at times - up in smoke.

Corporation of Glasgow (Parks Department)
Inspector of Parks

As Convenor of Parks, Invitation to Inspection of Parks by The Convenor Councillor W M Hutcheson and Members of the Parks Committee request the pleasure of your company at the Inspection of Parks on Wednesday 9th September 1970.

It gave me great pleasure to accept.

Itinerarv

09.30	Leave City Chambers
09.45	Pollock Park - Coffee
11.15-11.45	Hartstone Road Playground
12.30-14.30	Lunch in City Chambers
14.55-15.25	Provan Hall
15.45-16.05	Blairtummock House
16.30-17.00	Tollcross Park
17.30	City Chambers - Tea

Walkways River Cart - Levern Water, River Kelvin - Victoria Park, Bailie Marshall Hutchison and Director of Parks Mr S. A, J. Oldham and myself had previous meetings regarding the proposed West Highland Way from Kelvingrove Park to Milngavie and thence to Fort William.

The West Highland Walk Way has already been put in hand there has been a delay in completing the Way to Kelvingrove Park, Glasgow.

I was therefore interested in the Glasgow Walkways already completed and officially opened during European Conservation Year 1970. These four walkways constitute an integral part of the ultimate parkland trunk route system approved on principal by the Corporation in 1967, bringing the countryside within the city for the enjoyment of the public.

I found the Inspection most interesting and informative.

Highland Gateway

Craigend Regional Park, the name given by a commission that produced the Clyde Valley Regional Plan in 1946 under the chairmanship of Sir Patrick Abercrombie, among those sitting on the commission was Professor Robert Grieve who later gained fame as the Chairman of the Highlands and Islands Development Board and who has on several occasions expressed his fondness for the area, including the north of Milngavie. He is now Sir Robert Grieve.

It is not my intention to make any remarks on that Clyde Valley Regional Plan of 1946, which was very extensive. I can only relate my own experience as Convenor of Planning and Building Control in Milngavie Town Council also a member of Dumbarton County Council, a member of Roads and Planning Committee, a representative on the Scottish National Housing and Planning, having been appointed to serve on the Councils new Executive Committee.

Mr Frank A B Preston, one time Burgh Surveyor of Milngavie had just been appointed Honorary President of the Scottish National Housing and Town Planning Committee, in attendance were Mr John Lawrence, his architect and surveyor, to discuss in general a feasibility study made by Professor A S Travis of the chair of planning Heriot-Watt University, Edinburgh, as to its suitability to comply with the rules and regulations as is necessary for planning permission.

Preface to Study

The idea of a luxury hotel and country club facilities arose out of Mr John Lawrence's desire to provide facilities for the young executives, and their families, who have to be encouraged to live and work in the new and developing Scotland.

From that early concept, it was a short step to progressing from country club facilities to a championship standard golf course, an indoor recreation hall, and an exhibition hall. And, one must remember, all of these attractions would be only 25 minutes from central Glasgow and yet on the doorstep of

underground well. Up to the surface of the pond it was called Gallows Hill, in earlier times gallows were erected on the hill on a piece of flat ground and used for hanging purposes.

At the time I refer to the castle it was occupied by Sir Harold Yarrow, the Clyde shipbuilder, After the Second World War, Sir Harold removed to live in Kilmacolm, the estate was left vacant for a time and re-opened as a zoo with all kinds of animals. It was not a success and after a time it lay vacant for a number of years. In fact the estate never recovered, it was purchased by Mr John Lawrence. Recently I visited the estate to find the castle a ruin. What a tragedy ! From the place I knew as a young man, will the roedeer ever return?

Mugdock Castle and Craigend Castle United

Mugdock Castle estate then the property of Lord Fraser of Allander, Craigend Castle estate then the property of Mr John Lawrence plus Drumclog Moor and Allander Park the property of Milngavie Town Council.

Owing to, I suppose the untimely deaths of both Lord Fraser and Mr Lawrence, the outcome was, with formal negotiations of all the responsible authorities and trusts, that agreement was reached and the formation of Mugdock Country Park took place. There is now a warden service and work is now being carried out. All things being equal it could be one of the finest parks in Scotland.

Dougalston Estate and Mansion House

The place originally formed part of the Barony of Mugdock. The name appears to have been taken from Dugald, Son of Alwin, second son of the Earl of Lennox. For many generations it was in possession of the Grahams from the Mugdock Grahams, being leading merchants, and one was Dean of Guild in 1650.

In 1707 John Graham built a new home in the same place as the existing one. John Glassford, a Paisley man from a wealthy family, purchased Dougalston. He was in the tobacco trade and was one of the "Tobacco Lords". It was he who planted trees, formed lakes and gardens, also a banqueting house and greatly added to the old house making it a magnificent mansion. A fire destroyed the house and for a long time the policies stood neglected and forlorn.

Now a change has taken place under a new laird Mr Ripley Kerr, a tea merchant. The house has been rebuilt from the ashes of the old mansion, with a beautiful house and grounds. Unfortunately Mr Kerr lost a fortune at Monte Carlo only to regain it the following year.

The estate and mansion was sold later to Mr Connell, a shipbuilder from the Clyde. I was fortunate to know both Mr Kerr and Mr Connell, doing business with both of them.

Mr Connell died after World War II. His widow lived there until she died. It was purchased by Mr Reo Stakis, hotel owner. The mansion house being demolished to make way for a golf course.

It was at this time, being Convenor of Planning and Building Control, I had a number of meetings with Mr Stakis and his architects under the name of Ravenstone Securities Ltd., 21 Woodside Terrace, Glasgow.

I had met Mr Stakis some time previous to this in other matters of planning, one being when he took over a property in Mugdock Road, Milngavie with what was known as the Woodlands Bar for which I obtained a license for Mr Stakis. Dougalston Estate was now to be transformed.

Messers I.M. Miller and Partners, Chartered Architects, 19 Royal Crescent, Glasgow, prepared a scheme for the building of dwelling houses and a leisure centre of quite large proportions, including a large hotel and golf course. A comprehensive report was made out and forwarded to the Scottish Tourist Board with details of Leisure Motel Dougalston. Here are a few details of that report.

Description of the Leisure Motel, Dougalston

The three hundred acres at Dougalston were formerly part of the Montrose land holding. When the estate was taken over, the intention was to create a major hotel and recreation centre, attracting tourist traffic both from within Scotland and from England and overseas. The original concept was of a standard hotel with the associated golf and sporting facilities, providing not less than 25 twin bedrooms.

Since the initial concept in 1970, the market for such facilities has altered with the emphasis moving more towards shorter period stays in the hotel accommodation and with a growing emphasis on lower cost self-catering holidays. Accordingly, the Dougalston project has been amended to suit the market.

Although the area is ideally located for tourist traffic going north and south, there is a considerable shortage of bedroom space. The two existing hotels in the area provide a combined room capacity of forty-two beds. The new motel would cater to tourists travelling to and from the Clyde waterway, Loch Lomondside, The Trossachs, Stirling, and, indeed the entire Western Highlands.

As is well known, Glasgow is an important staging point for tourist traffic in Scotland and, although there is a substantial provision of bedroom space for businessmen in the city itself there is an opportunity for something new to amplify and enhance the tourist facilities within easy travelling distance.

An important factor, too, in assessing the potential value of the new project was the changed pattern in holiday spending. During 1974, it was estimated that £310 Million was spent by visitors to Scotland, with only 80 Million coming from overseas tourists. With the increased emphasis on domestic holidays throughout the U.K. (because of the economic problems of the country), the new motel will be excellently located to serve this largely road-transported tourist flow.

Every effort, however, would be made to promote the new motel on an international basis. With its comprehensive facilities, and particularly the superb golf course, it will be of special interest to sporting holiday-makers from abroad. Again, the location is extremely good and lends itself to international exploitation, Glasgow Airport is thirty minutes away, Prestwick Intercontinental Airport another 30 minutes more, and Edinburgh Airport is little more than an hours drive. For rail travellers, the main rail terminals for the fast services from the south and north are an easy drive away.

In establishing the size and standard of the motel and its associated facilities, careful consideration has been taken of the changed pattern in holiday demands. While it is intended to provide a high standard of accommodation - each twin room will have private bathroom, shower, 'T.V., radio, telephone and facilities for making tea and coffee - the motel will not be a luxury project. A large number of people look on an annual holiday as an essential part of life and they expect a high standard; But can they afford, however, luxury prices.

In addition, careful thought has been given to the growing interest in self-catering accommodation (the Chairman of the Scottish Tourist Board has said that already 43 per cent of holidays in Scotland are spent in self-catering accommodation). Accordingly, the motel bedrooms have been designed as larger than standard to allow for longer than average stays by family groups. Throughout the estate, sites have been selected for chalet-type units which can be erected as trading develops.

Such individual units - as has been shown by numerous American developments - can blend excellently into a golf course environment. And the course at Dougalston is particularly suitable because of the amount of natural parkland that has been retained. This lends itself also to the provision for rambling, riding and picknicking around the estate. Already horse trails have been established and, with the motel development, there will be ample car parking for walkers, birdwatchers and day visitors.

Already there has been considerable acclaim for the quality of the golf course, designed by the international consultant Commander John D Harris. There is every reason to be confident therefore, that demand will be strong not only from U.K. visitors, but from abroad, for the course. It is intended that promotion will be directed at encouraging golfing parties from America, Japan, and other countries. The complex, for example, lends itself to Eurogolf type promotions.

Based on the golf course, there will be an unusual golf club. Open to local enthusiasts and day outings, it will have special levels of membership for motel and self-catering residents, and for regular overseas visitors. All the other sporting facilities associated with the motel would be available for a booking charge. Rambling, riding and picknicking facilities would be provided, of course, at no charge to the public.

Submission of drawings and plans were duly received by Milngavie Town Council for Planning Authority and after a number of meetings with all the rules and regulations required as to services, there were a great deal of complications which had to be overcome, such as alterations to plans to meet all the different authorities concerned, before a final agreement for the first stage was granted.

1 The golf course had to be constructed before any housing took place. The Golf Course started construction in June 1972.

2 The hotel submitted was cancelled meantime.

3 As the Woodland Bar Property had been removed for a new development the Licensing Court allowed the license of Reo Stakis be transferred to Dougalston at the temporary building of a restaurant and lounge bar.

4. No trees unless marked had to be felled.

The Chairman and Directors of Dougalston Leisure Estates (Glasgow) Ltd announced the opening of Dougalston Lounge Bar with a buffet luncheon on Friday 29th October 1976 to special guests.

Guests were invited to play golf thereafter before Monday lst November.

In the meantime work was continuing with the building of the houses as laid down by the Building Control. At a later date a private club was started and appears to be quite successful.

This is now 29th August 1986 and having been retired ten years from all Local Authority business I have just been told that an application by the Stakis Organisation for a further development costing £7.5 million has been refused, so much for the environment.

Here is a short story of a discussion I had with Mr Reo Stakis a few days before the opening of the golf course in 1976.

Someone had informed him that I had been a scratch golfer at one time which was perfectly true, he telephoned me to ask me, if in view of our previous meetings would I meet him at Dougalston and tell him about golf as he did not know very much about it, this I did, and sat in his white Rolls Royce car at the outside of the lounge bar for six hours. We talked about golf with a short break for lunch, we had quite a heart to heart talk and he was most grateful; Before leaving he told me how he arrived in Glasgow.

That his mother and family lived on an Island not far from Cyprus and he knew all about hens, his mother did lace work and he was despatched to Glasgow with two cases of lace work to sell.

After having sold the Lace around Partick in Glasgow he rented a small chip shop and later a small Ice Cream shop, and finished by telling me if you can't make money in Glasgow you will not make money anywhere. Eventually he made me an Honorary Member of the Club, what an experience.

Corner of Stewart Street and Main Street

Corbie Hall

St. Lukes Church

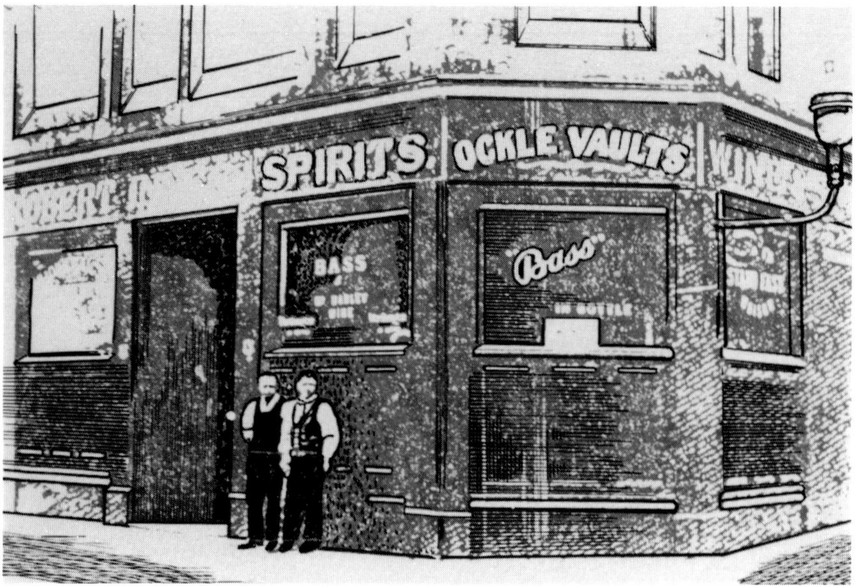

Talbot Arms, (Author born on first floor above, 1907)

Milngavie Week 1966

It is now over 20 years since Milngavie Week started and the 21st Anniversary has been celebrated for which I was invited to attend.

I accepted the invitation with pleasure and it brought back so many happy memories for me. I am now the proud owner of a lovely "Pennant Award" with the inscription 1966-1986 Milngavie Week Award.

In 1966 in a message from Provost John Buchanan it stated - while the idea of holding such a week originated from the Town Council, it has all along been my view that the effort must come from the people of Milngavie themselves - it must not be superimposed from above - and so it has proved.

The present day way of living, both in our work and in our recreation, tends to segregate people from each other and one is inclined to gyrate in one's own small circle within the community. It is hoped that a week of activity in the Burgh in all spheres - social, cultural, sporting and pleasure - would attract all interests and would, as a result, allow the people of Milngavie to mix to meet their fellow citizens and to enjoy a broader friendship and acquaintanceship in the Burgh. To Councillor Angus Chapman as Convener of the "Milngavie Week" and to his band of willing helpers the thanks of all folk in Milngavie are due, and these can best be expressed by all in the Burgh giving full support to the project and, by so doing, making it a success.

John M Buchanan
Provost of Milngavie
Chairman Angus M Chapman
Vice-Chairman D W Blackwood
Secretary Donald Bark
Treasurer John McPherson

Committee

G P Anderson
R Barnes
Mrs M Blackock
R B Climie
Miss M Dickson
John M Gardner
M M McDougall

Jas McGill
Mrs C McLaren
James Meggat
Bert L Mellis
I D R Smith
J R Thomson
Mrs E S Whatley

I will now reveal for the first time how and why it happened. In 1965 I had been given some inside information about certain trophies and a sum of money in storage, in a local bank, I followed this information up and found it to be true, but with some complications attached. There were only two trustees now living, one being ex-Provost John McPherson and the other a Mr McDougall, both of which had now retired. The trophies belonged to the trust of a now defunct Highland Games Association for some time. I withheld my information until after the next meeting of the full Town Council.

My first thoughts were to attempt to resume the Milngavie Highland Games which were very popular just after the war. Unfortunately I was outvoted, because the Provost had the idea of forming a pipe band.

However, at the next full Council Meeting I had another idea to start a "Milngavie Week", you may wonder why I now angled for this, and here is the answer. Being the Councillor for Ward No 1, Barloch, an estate that had recently been built, I discovered people who had lived there for two years, did not know the people next door, this seemed rather unfortunate because in Milngavie in general people were very friendly.

At the following full meeting I again brought forward my idea of a Milngavie Week and in so doing, engendering a greater communal spirit within the Burgh, also I had been promised funds from a source that did not want their name revealed, all this plus the trophies I had already mentioned. I was now on more solid ground since it was one of my aims to try and bring together the people of the community, new and old. To my surprise and pleasure it was unanimously carried. I made it clear with the load of work already on my shoulders it was not possible for me to be convener, but I was prepared to serve as a member of committee to see the idea off the ground.

Mr Angus Chapman, one of the councillors was then elected Chairman. He had all the qualifications to make it a success.

In the meantime I was asked to interview Mr McDougall regarding the trophies, as we already had permission from ex-Provost McPherson, who was willing to let us have them. I arranged an interview with Mr McDougall at his house after giving him my reasons for the interview. He was quite adamant that so long as he lived the trophies would be kept in memory of the original trust, so that was that.

I reported the matter to the Council, so they decided not to bother with him any more as we would have enough funds to start Milngavie Week. This they did, and before long they had forty four items in their first Souvenir Programme for 1966 Week 25th June to 2nd July.

Herewith are the items referred to:-

Old Milngavie Exhibition
Handicrafts
"Guiding"
Miniature Garden Competition
Childrens Art Competition
Cricket Bowls
Decorated Car Parade
Scout Regatta
Milngavie Players
Youth Athletics
Golf
Inter School Sports
Any Questions
Badminton
Cycle Road Race
Children' s Talent Contest
Weight Lifting
Church Organ Recital
Childrens Pet Show
Madrigal Concert
Youth Dance
Floral Art
Milngavie Art Club
Baking and Preserves Competition
Childrens Essay Competition
Childrens Flower Painting Competition
Tennis
Choir Concerts
Football
Open Air Dance and Barbecue
Open Air Religious Service
Community Centre
Coffee Mornings
Speech Contest
Table Tennis
Bridge
Folk Song Concert
Amateur International Wrestling
Gymnastics
Open Air Sing Song
Childrens Fancy Dress Parade
Gala Ball
Crossword Competition

The response to the above was magnificent with Prizes and Trophies.

After a short time Mr McDougall passed on, and we received all the trophies and money left in storage from the Bank concerned.

Milngavie Week has now been in progress for 21 years.

REFUSE DISPOSAL

One of the last duties I had as Convenor of Cleansing and Public Health was to solve the acute problem facing Milngavie regarding arrangement of a new Refuse Disposal Tip. This is not easy due to the type of modern refuse to be disposed off. Most of the sites suitable for this had all been used, this is applicable to Bearsden as well, plus the cost of a new disposal plant to work in conjunction with land reclaimation.

At a recent conference on public health I had a talk with the Burgh Surveyor of Bishopbriggs and like ourselves they had the same problem of cost and land reclaimation. In the company of Mr Arthur Millar, late surveyor of Milngavie, we visited a site at Cadder Estate and found what we thought would be an excellent site, a meeting was arranged with the Burghs of Bishopbriggs, Bearsden and Milngavie, who were quite agreeable provided arrangements could be made with the owners of the ground, as it would be more economical for the three Councils.

After some protracted negotiations an agreement was reached by all parties concerned, which has been most satisfactory.

This was most convenient for ourselves as we were involved in slum clearance and had been bothered by rodentia. With the supply of proper domestic receptacles a very difficult situation was overcome for quite a number of years. I understand some of the ground reclaimed is now part of a golf course.

During this period I was Chairman of New Kilpatrick Cemetery and Boclair Cemetery. This was more or less routine, but a problem will arise in due course as the ground available is becoming scarce at both places.

PLANNING

My next experience was to be of considerable importance to me and the community in general. It was most fortunate that during my student days at the Royal Technical College in Glasgow in Session 1931-32, I studied town planning under Professor G Moncur and F.A.B. Preston, two of the most distinguished town planners of our time and obtained First Class Honours.

In Session 1932-33 I studied building superintendence and professional practice under Professor T Harold Hughes and obtained First Class Honours. This then, together with my previous qualifications as already described seemed suited to the assignment given to me as Convener of Planning, with future development and Building Control of Milngavie District, at the same time becoming a menber of Dumbarton County Council being on Planning, Roads, and Police Committees, later to become an executive of the Scottish National Housing and Town Planning. That as may be, let us go back to the Town of Milngavie.

It is not my intention to go back into the history of town planning other than to state cities have been planned for one purpose or another from the time men first came together in closely built communities, and replanned after congestion, blight, poor housing, inadequate sanitation and other less tangible drawbacks were contested as inevitable consequences of urban living.

Although it is not improbable that planned cities existed prior to 3000 BC, that date marks the first example of authentic record, the Egyptian city of Kahun, built as a housing project for the men who worked on the Illaheen pyramid. From the builders point of view, Kahun was undoubtedly an economical city in which to provide bare shelter for the labourers.

The streets were straight and laid out in rectangular blocks and the houses were small and crowded on the land. Sanitary facilities appear to have been good, by 500 BC, city planning was not unusual procedure in Western Asia.

Modern Times in Planning

After World War Two with the rebuilding of towns and the events leading up to the mechanical age of the motor car many changes in evolution had taken place. If we take Milngavie for instance around the late fifties chaos caused by parking of motor cars, slum clearance, new housing schemes public and private, extension to roads and sewers, decentralisation of Glasgow, people wanted away from the city to live in the suburbs causing additional problems that never existed before, so that some form of Central Area Redevelopment had to take place.

It was in 1960 the Town Council decided that the time was ripe for a planned development of the centre of Milngavie and there then began an experiment in small town planning, unique and to some extent pioneering.

A planning consultant was employed and he in co-operation with a landscape architect, traffic engineers, geographers, and not least county planning officials, has produced a development plan for the town centre, a plan basically simple and well worthy of Milngavie.

Once this plan is finally approved by the Secretary of State for Scotland, it will serve as a guide for the future development of Milngavie. A model of the plan is on permanent show in the Lillie Art Gallery. This happened in 1966. The report was prepared by Jack Holmes and Partners, Architects and Town Planners in collaboration with Arthur A Millar, Milngavie Burgh Surveyor, Jamieson and Mackay, Traffic Engineers and others.

I should explain how Local Government works in preparation of redevelopment. The Local Town Council prepare a report of the requirements necessary. It is then forwarded to the County Council for verification and onward transmission to the Secretary of State for Scotland. It is then studied by his advisers in Edinburgh as a feasibility and the purpose of financial borrowing consents. This can be all very complicated as I will unfortunately have to explain later.

The Structure Plan by the Council and the County should work in the form of a dialogue between Council and County with a proposal, reactions to that proposal and, on occasions a counter proposal, for example the changes necessary on the road systems.

There will always be a wide variety of different types of local plans, typical subjects for local plans might be:-

A town centre scheme, incorporating changes in the road pattern and a new bypass ;

A plan for the expansion of a small town;

A plan for the rehabilitation of an area of older housing where the quality of the environment needs improvement;

A plan for a city aimed at producing better open space provision for recreation and leisure;

A plan for a new township on the edge of a city incorporating a new district shopping centre;

A plan for a Country Park in a rural area.

It will be seen from the above brief description of the new planning system, it is very important that co- operation between Council and County is imperative.

Milngavie Central Area Redevelopment

It was in 1960 the then town Council raised the question of a Central Development Area for Milngavie. This had been brought about mainly by traffic congestion owing to the expansion of Milngavie as a popular place to live in. It was evident the existing streets were being choked by traffic and a state of chaos existed. Various schemes were put forward, there was also the question of the Slum Clearance Property Act. The streets most affected were Station Road, Main Street, Douglas Street, Mugdock Road and Park Road.

It was decided to have a no parking area and to provide car parks as quickly as possible. This was helped by the removal of slum property and the sites used as car parks. "No Waiting" were brought into force, this did not suit everyone as the existing shops had to be serviced, however with the assistance of traffic wardens and the provision of temporary car parks it seemed a sensible thing to do at the time until a proper report was forthcoming. It was with this in mind that the Town Council in 1961 appointed Jack Holmes and Partners to produce such a report. The report was presented to the Town Council in 1966, at this time I had been elected to the Town Council for two years in 1964 and had gained considerable knowledge of the affairs of our Town Council. My business was situated in the centre of Milngavie and my business experience of the building and civil engineering industry together with my associations in the town over the years could be of value to the important projects under contemplation so that when I found myself elected as Convenor of Planning and Future Development and later a member of Dunbarton County Council. How fortunate I was to be an Independent member of the Town Council.

The Holmes and Partners Report 1966

As you will appreciate this is a document of considerable detail. I will not bore you with some of the detail as it is purely hypothetical and of little value. In my opinion, here we have a situation of a town centre requiring redevelopment, incorporating changes in the road pattern and a new bypass road, retaining the village atmosphere and yet cope with modern development of traffic.

I will state in my opinion, the main points for consideration in a project of planning a town centre from a village to a town such as our own.

The Place:- Milngavie, situated on the banks of the Allander Water from early times. It would be agricultural having a small farming community working for the local Baron or Earl of Lennox. It is quite possible that the Grain Mill was built at this period, as the farm at Millbrae as it was called, was the centre for the farms rented out by the Earl and would be a convenient spot for the harvest to be ground into meal and its usefulness came from the power of the Allander. Later it would be handed over or sold to Davie Guy later bleaching and dyeing of cloth for which Scotland became famous.

Assets:- The fortunes of Milngavie for some time depended on the Grain Mill of Mr Guy and the Allander Water, but while the town was progressing from agriculture to an industrial economy, capital was being invested in roads, bridges and services. The railway arrived to serve town and mill and later Glasgow trams brought many Glaswegians out from the smoke to enjoy a walk on the moors. Milngavie has a great asset in its natural beauty, a most attractive place for the city worker to live in.

Landscape:- The protection offered by the Kilpatrick Hills to the west and the Campsie foothills to the north and east, offers to the Milngavie area unusually good conditions for plant growth. This is demonstrated by the density and condition of vegetation at present growing in the area, which contributes largely to the pleasant and sophisticated character of the Burgh.

There had, however, been little planting of any significance carried out over the past 50 years and it must be realised that any character which is present relies on a mature or semi-mature growth pattern which is in immediate need of rejuvenation. This is regarded as being essential to the successful development of the general environment, Milngavie is a nice place and should not be spoiled.

Shopping:- The potentialities of Milngavie have not been ignored and many finance houses have expressed their interest in them. In 1962 a survey by shopping consultants regarding spending in Milngavie shops and confirmed by a later publication of the Census of Distribution, strongly suggest that there is no case for a large new shopping development.

Speculation about the possibility of attracting most or even a large number of the residents in Bearsden are discounted for two reasons.

1. In the absence of a good shopping centre nearby, people tend to travel towards the city rather than away from it, in search of the service.

2. There is a strong probability that despite setbacks Bearsden will eventually have a shopping centre of its own anyway.

Milngavie itself will not wish to completely replace the existing shops with new development. On the other hand, some new development can be expected and should be allowed for two reasons.

1. To serve the gradually increasing population since 1962.

2. To allow the normal opportunities for competition and replacement of obsolete premises.

It is expected that the population will grow as a result of natural increase and some immigration to the town from 9, 0 00 to 18, 000 in the next twenty years.

An essential part of planning for shops is adequate car parking, the general principle is that the area for parking cars will be equal to the area of the shops.

Traffic Planning:-

Experience in traffic control, like evolution, does not stand still, over the years varied so much. The speed by which traffic volume has increased putting more and more pressure on road construction and safety standards. Shortly after the Buchanan Report the danger being between the slow and vulnerable pedestrian and the fast and dangerous vehicle. The ideal answer would be for the pedestrian to use a completed system, but as we do not live in an ideal world, we deal first with situations where inconvenience and danger caused by the mixing of vehicles and pedestrians are greatest, and we deal last, if at all, with the situations where they are least.

The Buchanan Report came out at a time when the consultants were midway through the report. The Buchanan Report having been given its blessing by the Government, the Planning Authorities were asked to take a second look at development plans. The County Planning Officer suggested to ourselves and to the County Road Surveyor, that a more wholesale pedestrianisation of the centre of Milngavie should be attempted by altering the line of the main road to by-pass the main shopping streets altogether on the South.

It was found necessary to employ traffic engineers to assist the planning group and the firm of Messrs Jamieson and Mackay were commissioned by the Council to prepare further studies also they were permitted by the County Road Surveyor to direct that part of the County Survey which most closely affected Milngavie. This means co-operation with the main regional network.

Briefly the outcome of the traffic studies are as follows -

The new road, designed as a four lane dual- carriageway along the southern part of Main Street, bend north eastward at the old Grain Mill to rejoin Station Road as a single carriageway at Buchanan Street. This is the first of the primary roads of the network and it continues via Strathblane Road to join the regional by-pass at Craigmaddie.

The second primary road branches from the first at a reorganised junction with Park Road and continues to serve the west by Craigdhu Road. The third primary road is Clober Road starting at Craigdhu Road and serves the north west area to Drymen Road. These routes provide arterial penetration to the central area from the south, south west, north west, and north east allowing movement around the town.

The areas which lie between these primaries are themselves divided and served by the next category of roads known as distributors.

The designation of distributor roads is a nice balance between their present efficiency in serving the areas as they are at present and their adaptability to a greater ultimate capacity.

There is very little new road making involved in the distributor road pattern except in the central area where another of the most important changes in the plan of Milngavie is affected.

By using the track of the railway which once served the Paper Mill as a road the main primary is connected to Mugdock Road and underpasses the shopping centre.

I have now covered the main proposals as laid down in the report of the Central Area Redevelopment of the Burgh of Milngavie of January 1966 and submitted to the Secretary of State for Scotland in April 1967, in which I was much involved in Milngavie Town Council and Dunbarton County Council level.

As Convenor of Planning and Future Development I was given a copy of the C.D.A., No 5 Milngavie.

Diversion of Route B8030 Historical Summary of Events, that was to become very important in my future dealings from 1960 to 1973, with a personal request for a meeting with Mr Younger then Under Secretary of State on the miss management between officials at Saint Andrews House and officials of Dunbarton County Council regarding hold up of progress. This was granted with very satisfactory results.

Diversion of Route B8030 Historical Summary of Events

Historical Summary

1960 - Town Council raised question of C.D.A. for Milngavie

1961 - Town Council appointed Messrs Jack Holmes & Partners to produce a report.

1964 - Proposed internal by-pass road first mooted. Town Council appointed Jamieson & Mackay as traffic consultants.

April, 1967 - Milngavie C.D.A. proposals and C.P.O. Submitted to the Secretary of State.

August, 1968 - Public inquiry at which traffic consultants' report was a production.

July, 1969 - C.D.A. proposals approved by Secretary of State including by-pass road of obvious dual carriageway width.

March, 1970 - C.P.O. Confirmed by Secretary of State.
29th Dec. 1972 - Letter received from Mr Griffith (S.D.D. Roads) - this contains further historical summary.

19th Jan. 1973 - Request for meeting with Mr Younger.

5th Feb. 1973 - County Clerks reply to letter of 29/12/72.

Feb. 1973 - Tender documents ready for issue.

Early 1973 - Town Council's new Mugdock Road improvement completed (This is to lead from the internal by-pass road).

It was at this stage I became very disgruntled in the progress being made, and I had no alternative but to let myself be heard in matters between the County Council and the Chief Roads Surveyor at Saint Andrews House, Edinburgh.

My contention was the C.D.A. proposals were approved by the Secretary of State including by-pass road for obvious dual carriageway width in July 1969.

I discovered considerable unnecessary correspondence between the Chief Road Surveyor for Scotland and officials of the Roads Department in Dunbarton County Council had been going on for a period of approximately three years and a state of chaos existed caused mostly by the width of the new by-pass road as proposed and accepted by the Secretary of State in 1969.

Herewith is a statement I made at a full meeting of Dunbarton County Council and reported in the Scottish Sunday Express as follows:-

£80,000 Road Goes Nowhere

> Delays by Dunbarton County Council in building a ring road at Milngavie left the local town Council with an £80,000 new road that goes nowhere.
>
> Now Milngavie convenor of planning and future development, Bailie John Gardner, wanted an inquiry by the Scots Secretary Mr Gordon Campbell into why a project first envisaged 11 years ago, given permission in 1968, is still not under way.
>
> The half-mile of the new Mugdock Road follows the path of an old railway line.
>
> Peters Out
>
> It should have linked up with a new ringroad, but at that time just petered out at the old railway. Said Bailie Gardner: "The County

Council were given £100,000 to start the new ring road, which was to be the key factor to pedestrianisation of Milngavie town centre.

"But more than four years later not a shovel has been put to the proposed road and the costs are now estimated to have doubled to £750,000.

"Meanwhile we are left with a perfect new road complete with kerbside that runs to nowhere. "

Having stated my case to a full meeting of Dunbartonshire County Council which was well received, it was not long before a meeting with the Under Secretary of State was arranged, in this I was assisted by Mr Williamson, Chairman of Dunbarton County Council, who arranged the meeting by telephone with the Under Secretary Mr George Younger, to the effect that I would lead the delegation with the Convenor Mr Denny of planning in the County along with the chief surveyor Mr Hynd, our representatives being Provost Breckenridge, Mr Dudgeon, Surveyor, and myself.

The meeting with Mr George Younger took place in April 1973 at Saint Andrews House in Edinburgh in the presence of approximately twenty officials including Mr Griffiths the Chief Road Surveyor for Scotland.

We were welcomed by the Under Secretary Mr Younger who enquired who would put forward the case, Provost Breckenridge introduced myself to the Under Secretary and advised him that since I had full knowledge of the circumstances and being Convenor of Planning, should commence the discussion. I explained to Mr Minister and the officials why the meeting was necessary.

It took a little time to explain about Milngavie and the historical background to the Central Area Redevelopment, why it was so necessary and the reason it was so urgent. The fact of the case was that about 90% of the redevelopment had been carried out and a state of chaos existed in our town despite the fact that the Secretary of State had given his blessing to the C.D.A. proposals in 1969, including the by-pass road, four years waiting was a long time and not a shovel had been put to the proposed road and the costs are now considerable.

It was at this stage Mr Minister enquired "Bailie Gardner, you have given a very good stated case, but what was this likely to cost." I suggested in the region of 3/4 million would now be a realistic figure. He explained he had only a certain sum for the whole of Scotland to be shared out from the

Government. My reply was, then someone must have been given our share a long time ago. After further discussion with the officials and the delegation, it was agreed that something should be done to ease the situation.

The Minister thanked the delegation for their forthright manner in the explanations required and promised to do something immediately. His request was that the County Surveyor and Council Surveyor remain after lunch and work with his officials for a settlement, the remainder of the delegation could go home now, if he could have a word with me before I left. He escorted me to the passage outside the room and asked me if he could phone me at 4pm, I gave him my phone number.

At 4pm Mr Minister, Under Secretary of State Mr George Younger was on the telephone to me advising that a settlement with the officials had taken place. The money would be made available by the Scottish Development Department. There would be a shortfall of some £50,000, but that would be made up next quarter, since this was for the Corn Mill Car Park it could wait, and allow the by-pass road to go ahead. I thanked him for what he had done and that I was delighted with the outcome.

I asked if the local press could publish the news, his reply was wait seven days, and if you do not hear from me, go ahead.

My final question was when will it start, he suggested six months or earlier if possible. The outcome was it was started in three months time.

Yes, it had been a good day for Milngavie.

Events were now travelling fast, within a fortnight the following appeared in the local press.

Go-Ahead for By-Pass Road

Milngavie's "road to nowhere", which runs under Douglas Street at the Templeton's supermarket, will soon have somewhere to go . . . . . .at last.

The Scottish Development Department have given the go-ahead for both Dunbarton County Council and Milngavie Town Council to borrow the necessary cash . . . £856,569, to build the town centre by-pass.

Of this, Milngavie will find £281,253, the remainder being provided by the County Council.

The contract has gone to the firm of Balfour Beattie and Company Limited, the lowest of three bidders.

Asked this week about the start of the work on the town centre by-pass, a spokesman for the S.D.D.Edinburgh, said "This is entirely up to the County Council. The ball is now in their court. "

He said that the County Council will be responsible for the roadworks and that the Town Council will see to the "ancillary services" like car parks, landscaping and the like.

Milngavie Town Council have already provided some of these, like the Mill Square car park and the new bridge parapet currently being built at the Douglas Street site over the already completed "road to nowhere" at Templeton's.

Extract form the Milngavie, Bearsden Herald

Delighted

The man who has fought as fiercely as anyone to gain the go-ahead permission is Bailie John Gardner, Milngavie' s Senior Magistrate, and the Town Council's convenor of Streets and Lighting.

He said, when he heard the good news "At last... after all these years.... I am delighted, it has meant a great deal of hard work, a lot of heartache and a great amount of urging, cajoling, and persuasion to get things done, I'm really delighted to be able to tell the people of Milngavie that their by-pass is almost with us. Now we can concentrate on pedestrianisation of the town centre..... and the resulting safety of our burgh's residents."

The borrowing consent came from the Scottish Development Department last week following a visit to St Andrews House in Edinburgh by representatives of Milngavie Town Council and Dunbarton County Council, when the case for Milngavie was put in strong terms and a speedy conclusion urged by the local councillors and officials.

During the past week the building which had to go to make way for the entrance to the by-pass the old "Ristorante" fish and chip shop, has been demolished, and surveyors are out and about in the vicinity of the new road with their theodilites and levelling-instruments.

By the way, when the new by-pass road is completed it will be called "Woodburn Way", in memory of a former builder who built many stone built houses such as Heathfield Drive, Tannoch Drive, Strathblane Road and Glasgow Road, known by local people as part of the new town, around 1900.

Pedestrianisation

Having got over the main obstacle of the by-pass road successfully, it was now possible to go ahead at greater speed with what I would call the central problems. The factors which complicate traffic planning are the speeds and types of traffic.

All traffic planning is for the convenience and safety of people, and there is an obvious distinction between the slow and vulnerable pedestrian and the fast and dangerous vehicle.

The ideal answer would be for the pedestrian to use a completely separate system, but we do not live in an ideal world, we deal first with situations where inconvenience and danger caused by the mixing of vehicles and pedestrians are greatest and we deal last if at all, with the situations where they are least, the problem was the shopping centre and car parking.

Here is a quote from the local press of one of the first situations to occur at our planning meeting.

Bridge Place, the burned-out eyesore

Bridge Place, the burned-out eyesore, the fire started by vandals. Now it is to be removed to make way for redevelopment of the "backlands" behind the Station Road shops.

One of Milngavie's less salubrious sights was soon to disappear... the old tenements that form Bridge Place, the narrow lane at the junction of Douglas Street and Station Road.

A report on the derelict buildings was given to the Town Council's Planning Committee on Monday night, when the councillors discussed a letter on the buildings from the Milngavie Civic Trust.

The Trust members asked the Town Council to consider the removal of the tenements so that a better and more pleasant view could be had from the town centre and from the new by-pass road when it is built. The Civic Trust said the rear of the Station Road shops and houses would not be seen if the old Bridge Place buildings remained.

The Burgh Surveyor Mr William Dudgeon, told the councillors that there had been "one or two" serious fires in the old buildings recently, with several of the floors burned away entirely.

"Now we are at the tenders stage for pricing the removal of the buildings, " he said, "and I agree that the amount of money that would be required to renovate the block far outweighs the benefits of keeping it."

Bailie John Gardner, Chairing the meeting as convener of the Planning Committee, said that it would be best to clear the site now.

"Better to scarify than re-build," is how he put it. " When Councillor Ralph Black asked what was proposed for the site, the Burgh Surveyor told him that it contained a car park, and a service area for the Station Road shops. "There is a tremendous drop in the ground levels there and this will have to be filled in. The height of the service area will be the height of a platform lorry. " He also promised that the site would be landscaped.

This was carried out to a satisfactory conclusion and improvement to the area, the car park has been a great boon.

Here is another example of what can happen when it comes to Houses v Cars.

A Re-Think on Losing "Whisky Row"

Residents of Milngavie' s "Whisky Row", threatened with demolition to make way for a car park access, turned up in force to hear last week's debate on the issue by the burgh' s Planning and Development Committee, and they heard an argument so finely balanced that the committee' s chairman Bailie John Gardner had to give his casting vote in favour of continuing the matter for further discussion by his committee.

Councillor Ralph Black told of a meeting of residents in one of the houses in Clober Road (Numbers 2 to 22), known locally as Whisky Row, because most of them were one time occupied by workers at the old Tambowie Distillery off Stockiemuir Road.

"The meeting, " said the councillor, "had been long and detailed, and not merely a protest meeting. " But we all felt that the "houses were worth preserving," he said.

Listing the points which had led to this agreement Councillor Black said that these were:

a) Internally, they were in good condition and a fair amount of money had been spent on the interiors by both the council and the tenants.

b) Externally, most people found them to be of a very pleasing character.

c) The residents felt there was merit in being able to live so close to the town centre.

He continued "We all know there is a chronic need for parking space in the town centre, but I would move that we preserve the eight houses and build a brick wall between the proposed car park and the houses for the sake of privacy. As for access to the car park, I move this amendment that the houses be preserved and that we seek some other access to the car park from Claremont or Douglas Street. " He was seconded by Councillor Neil Baxter, who suggested that the Burgh Surveyor, Mr Wm D Dudgeon, prepare some alternative plan for access to the car park.

Bailie Alexander Buchanan stepped in at this point with, "I move the opposite. We have gone into this in great detail in this council. The car park has to be near the shops or the town centre will die. As for the rehousing of the "Whisky Row" tenants, this is provided by the mill site development. "

Dealing with the external appearance of the houses, Bailie Buchanan said that the houses backed on to the car park and it was the rear of the houses which were most seen by the passing public, and this detracted from the appearance. Because of the age of the houses the demolition could be carried out without financial loss to the Town Council tenants elsewhere, for example Claremont Gardens had to face up to the same thing.

Asked the bailie "Why spoil a good development and the pedestrianisation of the town centre for eight houses?" Treasurer Robert W M Kennedy said that he felt that the Town Council were being asked to decide the question without knowing where they were going. The houses formed West End Terrace, the name he thought they were officially called, and they had been built for £400 each on a 40 year loan which ended in May next year. But the neighbouring Claremont Gardens had been scheduled for housing only. He urged that the Planning and Development Committee remit to their sub-committee the argument before them so that they might consider both arguments " put forward that evening. "This is a human problem:', said Mr Kennedy, "and I think the sub-committee could come up with other ideas of how to get into the car park. "

Provost John G Breckenridge admitted that he himself was perturbed at the thought of the houses being demolished. This was like losing part of Milngavie.

"Let us have another look at this, " he suggested "There could be some way to get into the car park without disturbing the houses. Let's investigate this before we have motions and amendments. I do not say that the Town Council of that time were wrong in their decision, but we have a new council now who might see this differently. "

Councillor Alex McLaren who was Planning Convener at the time, said that the plans had been made up with a view for what Milngavie would look like in the future in reference to the number of cars and so on that would use the town. It had been envisaged that by the time Claremont Gardens would have come to the end of their life and "Whisky Row" was planned to go too.

As to the access to the car park he said, "There is nothing to stop us making an access.... but where. These are worthwhile and attractive houses and we should preserve them. We should decide not to demolish them immediately. The time at which they were to be demolished has never been stated by the Council. "

Treasurer Kennedy agreed that a date for demolition had never been mentioned. Said Bailie Buchanan, "The motion before us in the Planning and

Development Committee is that the houses be demolished. "

Then Bailie, Mrs Mary Blacklock, came into the debate with, "I agree that we continue this and seek an alternative access. This has been sprung on us and we have not been able to study this in depth. "

Bailie John Gardner said, "This is a question of houses versus the car, I think we should be given a little more time to consider this. It's the first time it has been before this committee. "

When put to the vote five plumped for the move to take the issue back to a sub-committee for complete examination. Then five voted for no demolition at all, with an alternative car park access being sought.

The casting vote was therefore sought from Bailie Gardner who sided with the continuation for re-examination.

On further examination it was decided that an access be made from Douglas Street and the Whisky Row be left as at present. This has been carried out and it has been found to be a very convenient car park in close proximity to the shopping centre.

After all, it was part of our policy to preserve the village atmosphere and yet cope with the modern development of traffic.

A NEW ADVENTURE 1975

In 1975 I was Senior Bailie, a Justice of the Peace, Convener of Planning and Development, Member of the Police Court, Member of the Licensing Court, Member of a Joint Committee on a proposed swimming pool for Milngavie and Bearsden, Member of Dunbarton County Council on Roads, Planning, Police and General Purposes, Executive on the Scottish National Housing and Town Planning, and Court of Appeal, having served on every department of Local Government and never known defeat in any Election.

It was at this time that Central Government decided on a complete new alteration to County and Town Councils with the result that Lord Wheatley had been given the job to reorganise the whole structure of Local Government.

The position was the County and Council would cease to exist after 1975 and that Bearsden and Milngavie District would be formed as a District Council, it was then I had to decide on retirement or stand for election in 1975 and become a founder member.

After considerable thought and requests from many quarters to stand again, and the completion of the Central Area Redevelopment, I decided to seek a district place with an announcement in the local Milngavie Herald as follows:-

<u>Senior Bailie Seeks a District Place</u>

Milngavie's Senior Bailie Magistrate, Mr John M Gardner, announced this week that he intends to stand for election to Ward One in Milngavie for a seat on the coming District Council. Bailie Gardner, a magistrate for eight years and a prominent businessman in the town, can boast family connections with Milngavie since 1888 and claims to be a real "local boy" having been born and bred in the burgh.

In sport, as in business, he has always been prominent, having played for the old Milngavie Juniors on the football field and as a keen and proficient golfer with both the Clober and Milngavie Golf Club and was at one time Captain at Clober and Milngavie Golf Clubs.

He is now in his second term as Senior Bailie and is convener of the Burgh's Planning and Development Committee. In this capacity he has played a large part in the formation of the coming by-pass road which will lead to the pedestrianisation of Milngavie, indeed, for many years he has harassed both Dunbarton County Council and the Secretary of State's office for greater speed in building the road.

Bailie Gardner joined the Town Council in 1964 and has always maintained his Independent label, for he thinks a local councillor should have no party whip to tell him what to say in the council chamber.

The Bailie's concern for development of the burgh led to his appointment to the County Councils Planning Committee, but he also serves on the county's Roads, Police, and General Purposes Committees.

Active also with the Milngavie Week proceedings, he serves as their sports co-ordinator.

The forgotten Tambowie Distillery, staff and dray

Whisky Row and The Forgotten Distillery

In a wet and boggy field about two miles from Milngavie there are some grassy humps. Nothing special you might think if you noticed them at all, but they are part of the heritage of Milngavie.

The humps are all that remain of what was once a thriving local concern:- the Tambowie Distillery, which in 1885 was producing 48,000 gallons of malt whisky annually.

The remains stand on a small hill surrounded by marsh, just off the Stockiemuir Road before Craigton School. Water was brought from the Tambowie Hills into the works and the stream provided an ample supply for driving power and distilling.

Apart from the state of the ground, there is little sign of the stream today. It was probably diverted to the distillery and has long since gone back to its old course.

A deep ditch runs parallel to the ruins and Stockiemuir Road. It could have been a run off for excess water, although this is uncertain, "Probably a tail race."

The distillery was old fashioned even in 1885 and any alterations were made with the intention of preserving the original design of the building as far as possible. Consequently it was smaller than would have been expected.

There were two warehouses for the storage of whisky, one of them a cave cut out of solid rock, and it is said that this was used by smugglers for illicit distillery in the days of Rob Roy.

Now however no sign remains of it although it must have been fairly large, for casks were ranged along its walls and in a central stack along the floor.

The proprietor at Tambowie in 1885 was a Mr David Chrystal and working under him was a manager whose surname was Watt.

The entire labour force of the distillery was not much in excess of ten and some of the men were seasonal workers who did other jobs at different times of the year. Above the distillery on a hill at the rear were the barley barns which were capable of storing 125 tons of grain.

Only Morayshire barley was considered good enough by Mr Chrystal, who gained his experience of distilling at Camlachie and Benmore Distilleries.

There were several other buildings necessary to whisky production and these are known as kiln, the malt house, the mash house, the grist loft and of course, the still house.

Equipment included rollers to bruise the malt, and a mash tun which included stirring gear and was six feet deep and 12 feet in diameter. There was also a vat which contained about 1,900 gallons of spirit, and the distillery also had its own cooperage.

Eventually the business was destroyed by fire during the First World War and the burnt out shells of the buildings were demolished in the early 1920's. The rubble was removed and used as foundation material for building roads in Milngavie.

During the fire, the Excise man who lived just along the road at Garlogie House, split open the casks and the precious spirit ran into the burn and was carried in the direction of Milngavie, where it is said that local worthies attempted to "rescue" some of it before the flow of water carried it away.

In 1887 the government collected more than £14 million in duty from the whisky distilling industry.

At that time it was the largest revenue from any single industry, for Scotland was producing 18 million gallons of whisky each year.

Tambowie's part in the production of that river spirit was very small and there is little to show today, that it ever played a part. There is even less evidence of the cave where illicit distilling was carried on.

How these days have gone.....

My father who was responsible for transporting the whisky into Glasgow told me the story of how one day the stable door for the horses happened to be left open. Being a two part door, behind one of the doors a pail of pure whisky was always kept, for a quiet nibble by the men. There were some pigs and hens kept at the distillery and they got the wind of this, with the result that when my father arrived home from Glasgow, to his amazement the pigs and chickens must have been in the stables and were all intoxicated wandering all over the Stockiemuir Road.

Had it been in modern times, I am afraid that there would not have been many of the pigs or chickens alive, so much for evolution.

The cost of whisky in those days was "Tuppence a Gill". I have two pictures in my possession given to me by my father showing the transport and staff of Tambowie Distillery also one when he had a temporary job at Milngavie station as porter. 1901.

Gardners, Chemists

Railway staff and Police at Milngavie Station, 1901. (My Father bottom row-far left)

President of the Glasgow and West of Scotland Plumbers and Domestic Engineers' (Employers) Association

Corporation of Glasgow Parks Inspection

RE-ORGANISATION OF LOCAL GOVERNMENT 1975

The formation of Regions, District Councils and Community Councils

Strathclyde Regional Council assumed responsibility for providing major local authority services, headquarters being in Glasgow as follows:-

The region embraces the county of the City of Glasgow, the counties of Ayr, Bute, Dunbarton, Lanark and Renfrew, most of Argyll and a small part of Stirling County, the services being:-

Assessor:- The Assessor and Electoral Registration Department, Chemist and Analyst. The Department offers an analytical and scientific service to other regional and district departments.

Consumer Protection:- The Consumer Protection Department is based loosely on the former Weights and Measures Department.

Education:- The biggest public education service in the United Kingdom is run by Strathclyde Regional Council Department of Education.

Fire Brigade:- Strathclyde Fire Brigade was formed by the amalgamation of the former Glasgow, Lanarkshire, and Western Area Brigades, along with most of the South Western Area and half the Central Area Brigades.

Industrial Development Unit:- The main objectives of the Industrial Development Unit are to encourage the expansion of indigenous industry, and to attract new companies into Strathclyde, the unit is attached to the Department of Physical Planning.

Leisure and Recreation:- Leisure, recreation, and tourism is a function of both the region and district authorities. The main responsibilities of the regions Department of Leisure and Recreation are to provide a strategy for the service.

Physical Planning:- Strategic planning for growth and change in Strathclyde's towns and the City of Glasgow, and for the development of the region's countryside and coast, is the responsibility of the Department of Physical Planning.

Police:- Strathclyde Police Force is the largest in Scotland. Headquarters are at 173 Pitt Street, Glasgow.

Roads: - The Roads Department is responsible to the Highways and Transportation Committee for forward planning, design, construction maintenance and management of all public highways, car parks and lighting installations, ferry terminals and airstrips run by former local authorities.

Transport:- The Highways and Transportation Committee is responsible for the operations of the Greater Glasgow Passenger Transport Executive, who are now agents for public transport.

Sewerage:- Sewers - equal to the distance from Glasgow to Detroit - the responsibility of the Department of Sewage. There are 130 sewerage works and 100 pumping stations. In large modern works like Dalmarnock, a flow equivalent to that of a small river is continuously being purified, the sludge is dumped at sea, south of the Island of Bute by the department's sludge vessels, and also by spraying on agricultural land.

Social Work:- Social Work services for families, children, the old, the handicapped, those who are ill, in difficulty or in trouble are the responsibility of the Social Work Department. Child care, welfare, mental health, probation and after care, prison welfare and hospital social work services.

Water:- Four water boards - Argyll, Ayrshire and Bute, Lanarkshire and the Lower Clyde Water Board - were absorbed by Strathclyde Regional Council. Nearly all existing supplies of water are from upland sources. There are about 170 reservoirs under the control of the Department of Water. There is also a bulk supply from the Loch Lomond source of the Central Scotland Water Development Board.

Bearsden and Milngavie District Council

There are 19 District Councils in Strathclyde Region, one of which is Bearsden and Milngavie District Council. The area will consist of Bearsden, Milngavie, High Craigton and Windyhill. The District Services will be:-

Local Planning and Industrial Development
Building Control
Housing
Environmental Health
Refuse Collection and Disposal, Street Cleansing
Food Hygiene
Clean Air
Cemeteries etc
Shops Acts, Offices, Shops and Railway Premises Act

Health and Safety at Work Act Provisions
Parks, Recreation, etc
Libraries and Art Gallery
Licensing Functions (Liquor, Betting and Gaming)
and Miscellaneous

Into the future with Bearsden and Milngavie District

In 1974, the new District Council was elected and during the last year have met regularly in Milngavie and Bearsden.

A year is a short time in which to build up a new administration, but as the great majority of officials and staff of the new District are drawn from Bearsden and Milngavie Town Councils, the transition from Burgh to District Authority has taken place, smoothly, efficiently, and economically.

The new District extends well beyond the old burgh boundaries, to the bridge over the Allander Water at Carbeth and to Windyhill in the west.

Bearsden and Milngavie District is fortunate that within its area it encompasses towns, small rural communities, farms, attractive hills and open countryside and it is extremely important this desirable balance be maintained in the future.

Chief Officials in Bearsden and Milngavie District Council

Chief Executive:- A R Rae M.A., L.L.B.

Educated at Hamilton Academy and Glasgow University. Town Clerk of Milngavie 1965-1975, with previous local government service in Inverness, Perth and Hamilton. Hobbies crosswords and music. Unfulfilled ambitions: to playgolf and the piano.

Director of Administration: David L Cuthbert M.A., L.L.B., F.R.V.A., N.P.

Educated at High School of Glasgow, and Glasgow University. The first and only Town Clerk of Bearsden 1958-1975. Assisted in gaining burgh status for Bearsden, East Kilbride, Bishopbriggs and Cumbernauld. Was awarded Freedom of Burgh of Bearsden in 1974. Married with three children. Sports and hobbies - golf and caravanning.

Director of Technical Services:- William W Dudgeon, M.A.P.L.E., M.R.S.A.

Educated at Knox Academy, Haddington, and Heriot-Watt College, Edinburgh. Burgh Surveyor of Milngavie 1966-1975 and held similar posts in Galashiels, Fife and Haddington. Married with three children. Other interests include rugby, squash and hill walking.

Director of Finance:- John M Hornby, F.C.C.A., A.T. I. I., F.R.V.A.

Educated at George Watson's Boys College, Edinburgh. Accountancy experience and training obtained in professional accountants offices in Edinburgh. Burgh Chamberlain of Milngavie 1968-1975, with previous service as Town Chamberlain of Haddington. Married with two daughters. Elder of Cairns Church, Milngavie, and interests include caravanning and walking. Unfulfilled ambition - to bid and make a Grand Slam!

Bearsden and Milngavie District Council. First Ward Barloch:- Councillor J M Gardner, J.P.

Member of Milngavie Town Council 1964-1975. Served as Convenor of Public Health and Cleansing, Convenor of Parks and Halls. Convener of

Planning, was Dean of Guild, and served two terms as Senior Bailie, Member of Dunbarton County Council, Convenor of Planning and Building Control of Milngavie and Bearsden District Council. Spare time is spent playing golf to a very respectable handicap.

Chief Librarian:- Mrs S. V. Peters, F.L.A.

Educated at Shawlands Academy, Glasgow, and University of Strathclyde. Previous local government service in Paisley Burgh and Clydebank Burgh. Sport - showjumping.

Mrs S.V. Peters, Chief Librarian

Community Councils

The community council is not intended to be a "third tier" of the new system. Unlike the existing district or small burgh councils, it has not been given duties prescribed by statute. This lack of statutory functions could be one of its main advantages. Whereas a local authority can only do the things which law authorises, community councils can do anything which the law does not expressly forbid. The community council is seen by some people as a "marriage" between a voluntary organisation and a statutory authority.

The Under-Secretary of State described the government's attitude during the parliamentary debate: - "In other words we are looking for the best of both worlds - the freedom of a voluntary association combined with the unquestioned status of the representative body for the neighbourhood."

The community council is free to establish itself and to act along the lines desired by the community: on the other hand, its status and its views will have some recognition by the statutory authorities.

Having given some idea of the formation of the new re-organisation of Local Government 1975, the run down of Dunbarton County Council and Milngavie Town Council, I will automatically retire from County and Town Councils on demise so that it will cease to exist on 16th May 1975.

The new Bearsden and Milngavie District Council having been elected in May 1974, only two of the original Milngavie Town Council were re-elected. In ward No 1 Barloch, Senior Bailie, Councillor J M Gardner J.P.. The other Councillors retired or were defeated including the Provost of one year Mr Blacklock, who was defeated in the Second Ward, Keystone, by Councillor Wm Hamilton J.P.

For historical purposes I herewith give some details for the last year of the Statutory Meetings of the Town Council, Milngavie 10th May, 1974.

Last Statutory Meeting of Town Council
Milngavie, 10th May, 1974

At the Statutory Meeting of the Provost, Magistrates and Councillors of the Burgh of Milngavie held in accordance with the provisions of the Local Government (Scotland Act 1947).

Present:

Bailies Gardner, Mr Blacklock and Buchanan.
Councillors: Breckenridge, Baxter, Black, Conway, Kennedy, McAlpine, Mrs McAlpine, McLaren, and Ryan.
Attending: The Town Clerk, Burgh Chamberlain & Burgh Surveyor.

Bailie J M Gardner, as Acting Chief Magistrate, presides over the Meeting

Provost - Election:- Bailie Gardner called for nominations for election to the vacant office of Provost.

Councillor Breckenridge having terminated office at midnight on 6th May, 1974, and the following were duly proposed and seconded, viz: -

Bailie Mrs Blacklock - Proposed by Bailie Alexander F Buchanan, 57 Braehead Avenue, Milngavie
Seconded by Councillor Alexander McAlpine, 34 Tannoch Drive, Milngavie

Bailie Gardner - Proposed by Bailie Baxter, 55 Carbeth Road, Milngavie
Seconded by Bailie Ralph E Black, 18 Buchanan Street, Milngavie

Voting took place and, those voting for Bailie Mrs Blacklock

1 Independent Bailie Alexander F Buchanan
2 Conservative Councillor Alexander McAlpine
3 Independent Councillor R H M Kennedy
4 Conservative Councillor Mrs Jean A McAlpine
5 Labour Councillor John Ryan
6 **Independent Bailie Mrs Blacklock**

Total Six Votes

Voting for Bailie John M Gardner

1 Labour Bailie Neil Baxter
2 Labour Bailie Ralph E Black
3 Labour Councillor Hugh Conway
4 Labour Councillor Alexander S. McLaren,
5 **Independent Bailie John M Gardner**

Total Five Votes

Absent from the Council Chamber while voting took place Councillor John G Breckenridge.

Bailie Mrs Blacklock having the majority of one vote was then duly elected Provost for one year and signed the formal Declaration of Acceptance of Office and the Judicial Oath.

Bailie Gardner thereupon vacated the Chair and the Provost presided.

10th May 1974

Roll of Town Councillors:-

In terms of the Local Government (Scotland Act) 1973, the Town Council will cease to exist on 16th May, 1975, and all members of the Town Council will consequently retire from office on that date. The following is the Roll of Town Councillors for the year 1974/75.

Provost Mrs Mary L H Blacklock, 27 Keystone Quadrant, Milngavie
Bailie John M Gardner, 2 North Campbell Avenue, Milngavie
Bailie Alexander F Buchanan, 57 Braehead Avenue, Milngavie
Bailie Neil Baxter, 55 Carbeth Road, Milngavie
Bailie Ralph E Black, 18 Buchanan Street, Milngavie
Honorary Treasurer, R H M Kennedy, 7 Craigton Avenue, Milngavie
Dean of Guild, Alexander McAlpine, 34 Tannoch Drive, Milngavie
Councillor Hugh Conway, 26 Galbraith Drive, Milngavie
Councillor Mrs Jean A McAlpine, 34 Tannoch Drive, Milngavie
Councillor Alexander S McLaren, 6 Glassford Street, Milngavie
Councillor John Ryan, 12 Claremont Gardens, Milngavie

The final Demise of Burgh Police Court 30th April 1975

Bailie J M Gardner, 2 North Campbell Avenue, Milngavie

Dear Bailie Gardner,

Burgh Police Court

I have to remind you that you are due to preside at a sitting of the Burgh Police Court on Wednesday 7th May 1975 at 9.15 am.

As this is the final sitting of the Court it may be that all the Magistrates wish to be present. This could perhaps be decided on Monday.

Yours faithfully,

A Ronald Rae,

Town Clerk.

Cases: 2 Ordinary, 1 Trial, 1 Sentence Deferred, 3 Continued.

Demise of County Planning Department, Dunbarton

County Council Offices
Dumbarton
15th May 1975

Wm C A Storrie M.R.T.P.I.
County Planning Officer

Dear John

In this, the last letter which I will write as County Planning Officer, I want to thank you for the pleasant memories of our association throughout the years.

The Planning Department Staff of Seventeen Persons join me in wishing you good fortune and happiness in the future.

Wm Storrie,
County Planning Officer.

Evolution

It is with some regret the demise of the County and local Councils ceased to exist on 16th May 1975. I had made many friends and have pleasant memories of my time spent on the various projects on behalf of Milngavie my home town and Dunbarton County.

Most of the major projects I was involved with were nearing completion such as the Central Area Redevelopment and by-pass road, leaving only environmental improvements. If I had one regret it is that the paving of the streets advised by the consultant at the time, and of which I had no part, have in my opinion been unsatisfactory and should be re-instated at some time, otherwise the project has been very satisfactory and well worthwhile doing, after all, evolution is inevitable, you either go forward or backward and sometimes we have no choice.

In my association with the County Police under the Control of Chief Constable William Kerr O.B.E., Q.P.M., D.L. and Commander Chief Superintendent James Hutchison, who was a nephew of mine, I have happy memories. The following appeared in the press shortly after the demise of the County Council.

First, and Last 15th October 1976

> The first, and only Commander of the Strathclyde Regional Police Force, whose headquarters are in Milngavie, is to retire at the end of the month.
>
> Chief Superintendent James Hutchison first worked in Milngavie after the reorganisation of the Strathclyde Police Force in 1975 when "M" Division was first realised.
>
> His retiral day Saturday October 3Oth, is the day when "M" Division is to be absorbed by "C" Division.
>
> Born in Bearsden, Mr Hutchison started his career in the RAF. During the Second World War he trained as a pilot in the U.S.A. After this time he was commissioned and served in India and Burma.
>
> After the war he joined Dumbarton police force in September 1947. He served in uniform and in the C.I.D. From the rank of constable, Mr Hutchison rose to the rank of Commander (Special-

ist Services) in Dumbarton. During this time at Dumbarton he served under such officers as Mr William Kerr O.B.E., Q.P.M., D.L. and Mr R McNeil Q.P.M.

In May 1975 when Strathclyde Police were undergoing reorganisation he became Commander "M" Division.

While in Milngavie he has served under the Chief Constable of Strathclyde Police, Mr David McNee.

Vice-president of the Association of Scottish Police Superintendents, Chairman of Strathclyde Police Benevolent Fund and member of the British Institute of Managers, Commander Hutchison has led an active and varied career.

"I have had a wonderful career in the R.A.F. followed by an equally wonderful career in the police. I have always tried to be helpful to the community and to deal fairly with the many problems which arise daily," said Mr Hutchison this week. "But retirement does not mean an end to this full and interesting career for this Milngavie policeman." "On November 1st, I am to become the organiser for the Citizens Advice Bureau in Glasgow. I know that my 30 years of experience in the police force and my dealings with people in that time will enable me to cope with most of the problems which may arise in my new career."

A keen golfer at Milngavie Golf Club, and whose hobby is gardening, Mr Hutchison can boast a father who was constable in the then village of Bearsden many years ago.

Although Mr Hutchison will be working in Glasgow next month, he will still reside in the Bearsden and Milngavie District with his wife Joane.

His son, Iain, is at present teaching chemistry at St Ninian's High School in Kirkintilloch. He is also studying for a Master's Degree in Bio-Engineering at the University of Strathclyde, to add to his B.Sc. Honours Degree.

Balanced Communities

I was not long in the District Council of Bearsden and Milngavie, when the arrival of the new Strathclyde Regional Report for 1976 came out.

I remember at the next meeting of the full council of Bearsden and Milngavie District, being part of the Region, I made the suggestion that Glasgow should be a more balanced community as this was the future of modern planning and in so doing build more houses of a private nature for sale even in the central area, instead of having so many council houses for renting, since the Smoke Control Act had made it a much better place to live in.

However the following week Regional Councillor Charles Gray, chairman of the Region's Physical Planning and Development Committee sent a letter to the local press objecting to my remarks, by stating that Glasgow might have been more balanced as a community if the inclusion of the Districts of Bearsden and Milngavie, Eastwood, and the inclusion of Bishopbriggs had been made. This of course was quite out of order.

I had no alternative but to defend myself at the next meeting of the full Council. The following appeared in the local press:-.

> At the outset of reorganisation the people of Bearsden and Milngavie had wanted to become a District and were successful, and here Mr Gardner referred to a statement by Mr Gray that he, Mr Gray "..... might still consider a wager that these areas (Bearsden and Milngavie and the others mentioned above) will go into the City District next time the Boundaries Commission review the position."
>
> Councillor Gardner, at one time Milngavie Bailie and Planning Convenor, said at this point, "Did it ever occur to Councillor Gray that what would happen would be that the Strathclyde Region's boundaries could be completely altered?"
>
> Continued the Independent Milngavie Councillor, "Over the years I have been fortunate to be able to study town planning and, during the past ten years, I've been connected with the central re-development in that part of the District called Milngavie. I can do no better than invite Mr Gray to Milngavie, which is part of the Region, so that he can see for himself a practical demonstration of what can be done in the making of a balanced

community."

And he added, "My telephone number is 956 1680 Mr Gray ..... you will be made most welcome."

Councillor Gray sees for Himself a Balanced Community

The recent invitation sent to Regional Councillor Charles Gray, Chairman of the Regions Physical Planning and Development Committee, was taken up last week when he came to the district to see for himself what the district councillors were talking about when they criticised the Region at a recent meeting.

The invitation was issued to Councillor Gray by District Councillor John M Gardner, the local Planning Committee convenor. He, with others in the district council, had severely criticised Councillor Gray, who later replied through this paper in a lengthy letter.

Mr Gardner acted as host on the tour of Milngavie and although the time at the disposal of the party was short, Mr Gray was shown various parts of the town, which have in the past caused concern to the district councillors.

Cross Roads

Included on the tour was a special point of interest, and acute disappointment to Councillor Gardner, who has fought for years to have traffic lights installed at the Park Road, Douglas Street cross-roads.

Mr Gardner told his guest that in no way would the rehabilitation of Glasgow District be paid for by the people of the Bearsden and Milngavie District.

But Councillor Gardner later stated that the short visit had proved quite informative and to the mutual advantage of the two authorities.

Topics touched upon included transportation, education, housing and the environment in general. Among the party was Provost Bill Hamilton, who also thought the visit of great use to both councils. He said this week:-

"Councillor Gray's visit proved very valuable especially from the planning point of view. In the long term it will be especially valuable in maintain-

Sir James Miller; Mr A Ronald Rae and author at handover of sheltered houses to the District Council

IN RETIREMENT

Having retired from business and public life and having a little more time to reflect on some of my experiences on life so far, I sometimes wonder how I managed to cope. Being the youngest of a working family of seven, my father was a hard working man although in later years my mother proved to have a business brain on buying property.

When I had to leave school, I did not have a job for nine months. I was lucky to get a job as an apprentice plumber and sanitary engineer, the wage per week being nine shillings for a 48 hour week and an allowance of one shilling pocket money, little did I know then what life was all about.

I had a fair record at Milngavie Public School, but when I won a King's Badge in the Boys Brigade being the highest honour a boy could achieve I started to assert myself to gain further honours where possible. There was always an urge to do something better. I wanted to get on in life and it became clear to me, you had to be good at your job and learn as much as you could practical and theory. With this in mind I attended evening classes at the Stow College in Glasgow. Having achieved excellent results, the head teacher Mr Cunningham suggested I should raise my sights to be like himself, a sanitary inspector or even a surveyor of works.

I certainly had the confidence to go ahead. There was no turning back. Having gained all the necessary qualifications there was some difficulty in obtaining a post owing to the depression at the time. In the meantime I was gaining experience in the building and civil engineering side of the business. Just as it appeared I was getting somewhere the Second World War broke out which changed my whole life. Later I started a business of my own and reached the top of my profession as Guild President and on to other things like Local Government and to meet many distinguished people. As a senior magistrate I had to learn there are always two sides to a story. I have known great happiness and great tragedy, but evolution takes place, having been given a wonderful world, man sometimes is his own worst enemy, yet we survive somehow.

Reflections

There is no doubt I feel most fortunate to have been born and bred in Milngavie. It is only natural I should feel very proud of the place they call Mulguy. With the exception of the war years I have been more or less connected with the place most of my life growing up in surroundings such as we have. A gateway to the North, yes, as a village I have seen many changes take place over the years to what is now a nice town and a lovely place to live in.

It has been a great honour and privilege to serve the community in business and public life. I did so sincerely and used any qualifications or gifts I may have been endowed with for a greater communal spirit within the community. It was not always hard work I was given a great deal of pleasure in many instances. It was with pleasure the Town Council adopted my idea of a "Milngavie Week" over twenty years ago.

I do not forget my first trip to Edinburgh as a delegate to Saint Andrews House on behalf of the County Council and Town Council, the purpose being to meet the Secretary of State Mr George Younger to gain borrowing consent for 3/4 Million Pounds for construction of the by-pass road. After a debate with Mr Minister and his officials I was successful. A good day for Milngavie.

To continue with the lighter side of life. Here is my rendering of Milngavie as I saw it:

Good Old Mulgy

When you're feeling fed up
And your world seems wrong
In your heart there's no place
For a joke or a song.
Dear friend let me tell you
You will feel nimble and spry
If you just spend an hour around "Bonnie Mulguy"

Your clouds will dissolve
Your sun will shine through
And you will say to yourself
"I've been a silly "Ba-Boo"
To sit down and grumble
Heave many a sigh
When I could be happy around "Bonnie Mulguy"

There lies Craigallion Loch
And Blane Valley to
The sweet hills of Campsie
In their mid summer hue
You can see Old Ben Lomond
Point its peak very high
If you just take a
stroll around "Bonnie Mulguy"

'tis a beautiful spot
Which cannot be beat
For the scenery around
Is one perfect treat
I'm sure you will praise it
Right up to the sky
If you just take a run out to "Bonnie Mulguy"

John M Gardner

HOLIDAYS

Ca'n Pastilla, Spain

Continuing with the brighter side of life; my first experience abroad on holiday was at a place just outside Palma called Ca'n Pastilla. The hotel which my family and myself had been booked for was unfortunately not available owing to a mix up in booking arrangements, so we were despatched to a new hotel not far away called the Mirraflorus Hotel. At this time we found an English lady and gentleman in the same situation as ourselves and quickly made friends with them. They were a Mr and Mrs Regie Bowater from Halesowen making a party of six. Although we had never been to Spain before we quite quickly fell into the routine. Not far from the beach we did the usual swimming, tours etc, as laid on from the hotel with the help of a courier who was very helpful. We enjoyed the bullfights, visiting the wine manufacturers exhibitions, and porcelain factories, plus the usual gift shops, and did some short evening cruises, all very enjoyable.

However, for some unknown reason when I arrived for meals, it appeared as in my case special treatment was given to me by the chief waiter. This was quite noticeable to the other members of the party until after three or four days at my arrival for dinner a little late one evening, with its usual performance of special treatment, the waiter tapped me on the shoulder and whispered in my ear "Sir you are quite like General Franco." Thereafter I was not very sure whether to sit still or make a run for it. However, he continued to see my shirts were washed, special attention given to footwear etc. Later I noticed he was drawing the attention of some of the residents to my table until

I began feeling rather important, I must say, with the attention I was given. It turned out to be quite a remarkable holiday despite our unfortunate arrival. It was rather a joke. I was then being introduced to friends we met on the beach as "Sir John", especially when one of them turned out to be a reporter for a London newspaper. Dear me, what a start to my first holiday abroad.

Lido de Jessolo, Near Venice, Italy

One of the more eventful and amusing holidays I spent with Evelyn my elder daughter, and with Edith and Reg Bowater from Halesowen with whom we met at Ca'n-Pastilla near Palma on our first holiday abroad. It was a place called Lido-de-Jessolo a few miles from Venice. On arrival at Venice airport we were met by a lady courier and escorted to a small bus to Lido-de-Jessolo, approximately half way to the Roma Hotel where we were booked in. We were advised that two double bedrooms had been booked, one for the Bowaters and one for the Gardners'.

I informed the courier that it was not usual for my daughter and myself to sleep in the same room, as we had booked for two single rooms with separate bathrooms, only to be advised this was not unusual in Italy for a family to sleep in one room.

So I had to advise the courier it was not done in Scotland where we came from and if the apartments for which we were booked and paid for were not forthcoming I should like to return to the airport in Venice to return home. However, after further explanation and consultations with the staff at the Roma Hotel it was another case of the hotel being overbooked, having had previous treatment at Ca'n-Pastilla I was having no nonsense.

It was then discovered there was only one double room available for the four of us in the hotel, I then suggested the four of us go back home and reclaim all expenses caused so unnecessary. After a great deal of argument it was arranged that the two ladies would sleep in the double room for the night and that accommodation would be found for the two gents in a new hotel at an approximate distance of five miles. After seeing the ladies settled in, Reg and myself were taken by taxi to this new posh hotel five miles away, only to find the only apartment available was the honeymoon suite. It was quite palatial, but only for one night.

After dinner we were just settling in nicely when Reg Bowater had a telephone call from his wife Edith stating someone had put on a fire below and their room was being filled with smoke by a pipe outside. She appeared to be in some distress, and we were requested to go back to the Roma Hotel. No taxi was available, but a shop near our hotel would supply us with two push cycles for the five miles straight road to the Roma Hotel.

We also bought some fruit as an offering for the ladies. Although I was used to cycling Reg had not been on a cycle for years with the result on the way he fell off the bike and lost the gift to the children who picked up the fruit and ran off.

Eventually we arrived at the hotel and further arguments. We settled the ladies in another compartment for the night and we returned to our honey-moon suite. Next morning at breakfast Reg suggested we try and arrange to live in this new hotel and get accommodation for the ladies as well.

However, it was not to be. A taxi arrived for us from the original hotel and we had to return to the Roma and were duly given what we had booked for, in fact we spent a very nice holiday and became quite friendly with the management, spending some of our time in Venice with all its history, sight seeing, and shopping. In fact, what started off as a disaster finished up as a splendid holiday.

Island of Jerba, Tunisia (Djerba)

My first visit abroad was to the Island of Jerba not far from the important and historical town of Tunis. I was booked into the Tanit Hotel at the edge of the blue Mediterranean Sea in North Africa. Of modern Islamic design, the ground around was low and sandy shelving slowly into deeper water.

Having booked in on my arrival from Heathrow, London, my first thought was of getting a nice tan from the lovely sunshine, that was my first mistake. After twenty minutes the skin on my nose started to peel. I soon retired to my chalet to await a call for dinner later in the evening. I soon made friends with some English people on holiday and also an Irish couple, Doctor and Mrs O'Brien from Dublin who very kindly showed me around. The doctor did not appear to be interested in the number of camels around, but in the company of Mrs O'Brien I was to learn my first experience of camel riding, which seemed to be the mode of transport. Mrs O'Brien used to call at nine in the morning and we went camel riding each day for one hour. After falling off the camel once or twice I soon got quite used to it and enjoyed it very much. Not far from the Hotel we went to a bay suitable for swimming. This was rather a surprise as it appeared to be near a nudist camp for natives, but no one seemed to be perturbed over the situation.

On one of our outings we came across rather a large piece of ground studded with grape vines, having been put there during the occupation by the Italians in Roman times. The ground seemed to be particularly suited to olive growing and agricultural growth. livestock consisted mainly of cattle, sheep, goats, camels, horses, mules and asses.

Arabic is spoken mainly by the natives and they were either very wealthy or poor.

There was something quite interesting to me just three miles from the hotel. There was a huge mountain of empty food cans, I was advised the food cans had been gathered from a large area and were the remains of what was left after the German occupation during the First World War 1914-1918. They appeared to be in good condition and may have been a type of memorial from a historical point of view. That part of Tunisia seems to have been under Turkish, Roman and French Rule from time to time. Climatic conditions on my visit were remarkable, during the fortnight I was there. While waiting for the plane at the small air terminal I was on two occasions asked if I was the airport manager. I do not know why, perhaps because I was on my own.

Famagusta, Cyprus, Holiday 1973.

In company with my two friends from Halesowen, Worcestershire, England, Mr and Mrs Fred Bowater, we duly booked for ourselves a holiday for a fortnight at Famagusta on the island of Cyprus which I understand to be the third largest island in the Mediterranean, 60 miles west of Syria and 40 miles south of Turkey. I travelled alone from Glasgow to London (Heathrow) and from London to Nicosia Airport. Accommodation had been reserved at the Constantia Hotel in Famagusta, room 65 Second Floor as follows, "One single bedded room with private shower/balcony/Harbour view for 14 nights." It all appeared very simple. On my arrival at Heathrow Airport the Glasgow plane was late with the result I had only a few minutes to catch the plane for Nicosia. It was not helped when I was detained by a lady of ill repute, if I had not been helped by a steward I would have lost the plane as the engines had just started for off. However, I managed somehow by being pulled aboard, everything appeared to be normal until I was advised that my luggage had been left at Heathrow Airport.

On arrival at Nicosia I was met by a courier and explained my situation. After some delay by the filling up of a form called (P.I.R.) Property Irregularity Report for B.E.A., I was allowed to go to the arrival gate to show my passport. I was questioned on my luggage and was asked to stand aside, after a few minutes the arrival of two police officers asked to see my passport as I appeared to have been around a few countries, which I could not deny, and was I a Jew. After a few Glasgow words had been spoken by myself, which I am sure they did not understand except one word "Escosia", I was let through.

Waiting outside was a taxi-driver to take me to Famagusta, the time was now 3am in the morning.

We were only on the road about four minutes when we passed a police station on fire. I then asked if there was a war on, "Oh no, me take you encore round mountains. "By this time I was exhausted and soon was asleep in the Taxi only to be awakened in about two hours time in Constantia Hotel, Famagusta.

On reporting at the office of the hotel I was shown to a room along a long passage to a room with no services other than a bed and advised a lavatory was 20 yards down the passage.

I nearly exploded and demanded to see the manager of the hotel or I would sleep down at the main entrance of the hotel.

The manager was duly awakened and after what now appeared the usual row I was given the manager's room until my baggage arrived from London two days later. Which was then left in some other persons room. What a start to another holiday.

On meeting the Bowaters next day, eventually all was settled and I had a lovely room with a double bed and all domestic conveniences, just one more experience of a holiday abroad. I was becoming educated.

Cyprus is of course very historical. There was the Bronze Age or Early Cypriot Age, which could have been of Greek origin. There was influence from Egypt for minerals during the Iron Age with an influx of Christians, due to persecution from the mainland, with the result of Jewish settlements by the Cypriot Jews.

Moslems arrived and an Arab garrison was established. Italian merchants from Genoa and Venice assumed some political control. For a period of time there was also a Turkish administration.

On June 4 1878, Great Britain by treaty with the Sultan, who was assured of British assistance against Russian encroachment on Turkey' s eastern provinces, took over the occupation and administration of Cyprus; it remained nominally Ottoman territory.

Cyprus was annexed to the British crown in Nov 1914, when war with Turkey broke out. The British Government offered the island to Greece upon the latter aiding Serbia from Bulgaria. The offer lapsed when Greece declined. Turkey formally recognised the British annexation under the treaty of Lausanne, ratified in 1924, and in the following year Cypress was made a crown colony.

After World War II, Archbishop Makarios emerged as leader with support of various political groups with considerable discontent. British, Greek, and Turkish foreign ministers failed to agree on a solution to the problem and a Governor was appointed. Makarios was deported to the Seychelles, but later released. It lead to an improvement with the Greeks, but the Turks declared partition of the island between Turkey and Greece was in their opinion the only solution to the problem, since then a type of partition has taken place.

My own education on the island was greatly enhanced by a friend of mine who spent a considerable time in Cyprus, General J Macfie, Chief of the Medical Services in Cyprus, who lived near me in Milngavie. When he retired he gave me a copy of a lecture he delivered on Cyprus, which I found most informative, so that when I went on holiday I was able to enjoy the importance and history of the island. Herewith is a copy of that lecture on Cyprus.

CYPRUS

The youngest of the British Crown Colonies, Cyprus has a political and cultural history longer than any other part of the Commonwealth - longer than that of Malta, of India or of Ceylon. In area the island is about half the size of Wales and it has always been within the circle of the world's civilization, the meeting place of the races of the three old world continents.

It's renown was sung in classical times as the place where Astarte was reborn as Aphrodite from the froth of the sea and her temple at Paphos became one of the most popular places of pilgrimage in the old world. Cyprus is said to have been offered to a Ptolomy by Julius Caesar and to have been given to Cleopatra by Mark Anthony; it was sold by Coeur de Lion to the Knights Templar and then assigned to Guy de Lusignan; it was offered in 1915 by Great Britain to Venezelist Greece, under conditions which King Constantine was not prepared to accept.

For its climate and its scenery it has been famed throughout the Ages. Gilbert Murray has translated for us a song of Euripides:

Where is the Home for me
0 Cyprus set in the sea?
Aphrodite's home in the soft sea foam
Would I could wend to thee;
Where the wings of the Loves are furled
And faint the heart of the World.
Where the rainless meadows smile
With riches rolled from the hundred fold
Mouths of the far off Nile.
O there is Grace, and there is the Heart's Desire
And peace to adore Thee, thou Spirit of Guiding Fire!

It was the first country to be governed by a Christian ruler.

The earliest identifiable inhabitants were of Asia Minor stock with a language whose script is still undeciphered. Throughout the years the race has been influenced predominantly by the Greeks from the west, but also by the Phoenicians and the Cilicians from the north and east and by the Egyptians from the south. A Turkish element, now amounting to about a fifth of the population, was introduced in the sixteenth century.

Ancient Cyprus was divided in to small independent Kingdoms, some Greek in civilization, others Phoenician.

The records begin with Thotmes III of Egypt who conquered the Island about 1415 B.C. Egyptian rule was broken by periods under the Phoenicians and the Assyrians but we have it from Herodotus that in 596 B.C. Cyprus was again under the rule of Egypt (King Amasis) later to pass along with Egypt to the Empire of Cambysis of Persia.

In 502 B.C., the Cypriots, allied with the Ionians, revolted against the Persians, but in 374, Cyprus was again under Persian rule.

Then, in 333 B.C., Cyprus fell to Alexander The Great. Ptolomy I of Egypt tried to seize the island in 306, but was only partly successful until 296 B.C. when he succeeded and, with short intervals of self government, Cyprus belonged to Egypt for two and a half centuries.

In 58 B.C. Cyprus became part of the Roman Empire and remained so for over three hundred years. The fourth Governor during 51-50 B.C. was Cicero.

In A.D. 45 Saint Paul with Barnabas and John Mark landed at Salonis and journeyed to Paphos where they criticised the rites of the temple of Venus.

Saint Paul was bound and beaten here but eventually he overcame the arguments of the local sorcerer and converted Regius Paulus, the Roman Proconsul and founded a Christian community.

In A.D. 116/117 there was a brutal insurrection on behalf of the Jews in which thousands of Greek Cypriots were massacred. It was suppressed with difficulty, all the Jews were expelled and ever since there have been few on the island.

During this Roman occupation, the island became very prosperous and the ruling classes rather notorious for the luxury in which they lived.

In A.D. 395, the Roman Empire was divided and Cyprus fell to the lot of the Emperor in Constantinople under whose rule it remained until 1184.

In 478, the tomb of Barnabas was discovered near Famagusta and in it his translation of the Gospel of Saint Matthew. This was presented to the Emperor Zeno who thereupon confirmed the independence of the Church of Cyprus already recognised by the Council of Ephesus but challenged by Antioch. The Church of Cyprus is one of the oldest autocephalous bodies of the Holy Orthodox Eastern Church, junior only to the four original Patriarchates of Constantinople, Alexandria, Antioch and Jerusalem.

Then came the rise of Islam and its conflict with Byzantium during which there were several invasions of Cyprus with temporary success.

In A.D. 632 Abu Bekr father in law of and successor to the Prophet captured Kition or Larnaca.

In another invasion in 649, led by the first Ommayad Khaliph, a female relative of the Prophet, the lady Umm Haram took part. She landed with the expedition at Larnaca, and, in the words of the Turkish manuscript preserved in her tomb, "was set with all honour on a mule; and on arrival at the place where now her luminous tomb is seen, they were attacked by Genoese infidels, and falling from her beast, she broke her pellucid neck and yielded up her victorious soul, and in that fragrant spot was at once buried." Her tomb became and still is a much venerated Moslem shrine.

In A.D. 965, the Emperor freed the island from Moslem invaders for two centuries of peace, but in 1184 a great nephew of the Emperor Manuel 1, a singularly unattractive tyrant, one Isaac Comnenus arrived in the island with forged Imperial letters, usurped all power and proclaimed himself Holy Emperor of Cyprus.

In 1187, Jerusalem fell to the armies of Saladin and Western Christendom began to organise the Third Crusade.

In 1191, the fleet of Richard of England, on its way from Messina to the Holy Land, was scattered by a storm and three of its ships were driven towards Cyprus. Two of these were wrecked off Limassol and plundered by Isaac Comnenus. The third, on which were travelling Richard's betrothed, Berengaria of Navarre, and his sister Queen Dowager of Sicily, managed to find a safe anchorage but was very rudely received by Isaac and the royal ladies were saved rough usage only by the timely arrival of Richard himself. Richard landed some of his troops and eventually conquered the island. Richard and Berengaria were married in the fortress of Limmasol on the 12th May and Berengaria was crowned Queen of England by the Bishop of Evreux.

When Richard arrived in Syria, he soon found himself short of money to prosecute his Crusade and sold Cyprus to the Knights Templar. They, however, soon found it more trouble than it was worth and Cyprus was handed over to Guy de Lusignan possibly to compensate him for the loss of the Kingdom of Jerusalem.

Cyprus now became the base of the Crusaders' operations in the Holy Land against Islam.

From 1192 until 1489 Cyprus remained under the sovereignty of the Lusignans and played a brilliant and distinguished part in mediaeval civilization. This meant, however, that the native population, mostly Greek speaking and of the Orthodox Church were subjected to a French speaking Roman Catholic feudal aristocracy which subjected the Orthodox Church to the Roman and appropriated most of its property and ecclesiastical appointments.

There were eighteen Lusignan sovereigns of whom one of the most attractive was Peter I who reigned from 1359 to 1369. He travelled across Europe to gather allies and material for a Crusade and was received by Edward III and Queen Philippa and was dined by the Mayor of London along with Edward III of England, David of Scotland, John of France and the Prince of Wales.

In 1291, Acre, the last Christian stronghold on the mainland, fell to Saladin and Cyprus became the forward bastion of Christianity in the Eastern Mediterranean. As a busy port, Famagusta almost rivalled Venice and Genoa.

The last of the Lusignan rulers was Queen Catherine of Cornaro,

Venetian by birth and the widow of James II.

Venetian occupation

By 1488 the Venetians, in their struggle against the Ottoman Turks, had virtually taken possession of Cyprus and they held it for 82 years. It was a military occupation and whereas the Lusignan period left behind it the famous mediaeval castles and Gothic churches the reign of the Venetians is noted for the fortification of some of the towns, especially Nicosia and Famagusta. Trade languished and agriculture was neglected. It was during this Venetian period that there occurred the incident on which Shakespeare based the Tragedy of Othello.

Turkish Occupation

In 1570, the Sultan, Selim II, launched a powerful expedition against Cyprus. After a hard fought siege, Nicosia was captured and in 1571, Famagusta heroically defended by Marcantonio Bragadino for four months, also fell to the Turks. In 1573, the island for long renowned throughout Christendom, became an obscure Ottoman dependency.

But, in many ways, Turkish rule was liberal or perhaps should we say, negligent. The islanders were allowed freedom of religion which they had not previously enjoyed. The supremacy of the Orthodox community was recognised, possession of churches, houses and land was assured, serfdom hitherto common was abolished and the Orthodox Archbishop restored.

Indeed we have the paradox that it was under Islamic rule that during the seventeenth and eighteenth centuries, that the Orthodox Archbishops gained a political authority almost supreme in the island. When the Turks captured Constantinople in 1453, the Sultans granted a measure of autonomy to their non-Moslem subjects which was defined not by race or language, but according to the Ecclesiastic whom they recognised as their spiritual head. Throughout the Ottoman Empire, men were accustomed to being classified according to their denominational affinities.

The heads of the Christian Communities - Orthodox, Armenian, Jacobite and Assyrian and the several uniate Patriarchs with the Archbishop of Cyprus - received the State confirmation of their authority in the form of a Commission from the Sultan. This acknowledged them ecclesiastical Heads of their Churches but also constituted them Civil Heads of their nation, millet or ethnos. They became high dignitaries of the Ottoman Statsand, formed an essential part of the machinery of Government, all conditioned upon unquestioned loyalty and obligation to serve the regime as required.

It is this title and the attributes of Ethnarch, a function peculiar to the Ottoman Empire which Makarios III, the Archbishop elected in 1950 sought to revive long after Ottoman rule had ceased to apply.

The conquest of 1571 introduced a number of Ottoman Turks, partly from the Army, partly by immigration from Anatolia and Rumelia. They remained a separate community retaining their own language and customs but, at the same time, maintained amicable relations with the Greek speaking Cypriots who were heartily glad to see the end of Latin rule.

On attaining power, the Archbishop and the Bishops soon entered in to alliance with the local Turkish officials to enrich themselves at the expense of the peasantry and, at the beginning of the 19th Century, the Archbishop was, in fact, ruling Cyprus through control of its finances. He assessed the amount of the people's contributions and remitted annually the sums for which the Island was farmed out to the Imperial treasury or to the Grand Vizier. Turks and Greeks alike regarded him as the source of real authority and there naturally arose, especially amongst the Turks, a good deal of resentment. There was an outbreak in 1821 during the Greek War of Independence in which the Turkish Governor took strong action, arrested Archbishop Kyrenios Kyprianos, the Bishops of Paphos, Kition and Kyrenia and other leading ecclesiastics and citizens and had most of them executed.

But reforms were also in hand. In 1837, the annual tribute of the Island was fixed and the practice of leasing it to the highest bidder discontinued. The Governor was given a fixed salary and a representative Council of eight members was appointed to assist him.

Second British Occupation

Nine days before the Congress of Berlin which opened in June, 1878 and from which the British delegates, Lords Beaconsfield and Salisbury brought back "Peace with Honour", Dizzy had signed a secret treaty with the Sultan Abdul Hamid II whereby Cyprus was "to be occupied and administered by England" as a base in the Near East under the sovereignty of the Sultan to enable her to support him in the event of further aggression by Russia. In July, Vice-Admiral Lord John Hay hoisted the British flag in Nicosia and ten days later, Sir Garned Wolseley landed with a force of British and Indian troops and became the first British High Commissioner.

This Convention of 1878 remained in force until 1914, when Turkey entered the First World War on the side of Germany, and Cyprus was annexed to the British Crown. Annexation was recognised by Turkey in 1923 and, in 1925, the Island became a Crown Colony.

It may well here be noted that, at the time of the annexation, in 1914, the Archbishop, Cyril II, led the Greek members of the Legislative Council to Government House to "express their satisfaction at the annexation of the Island by Great Britain as they considered this a stage from which it could the more easily return to the Arms of Mother Greece."

It is also to be noted that, in November 1915, when things were going badly for the Allies on the Balkan Front, an offer was made, under strong pressure by the French, of passing the Island to Greece if she came in at once with the Allies against the Bulgarians. Venezelos was all for it, but King Constantine overruled him and the offer lapsed. At this time, again, there was a deputation to Government House, when the High Commissioner pointed out that the offer had not been accepted by Greece and hoped that the Greek speaking Cypriots would now recognise in the fullest manner their obligations as British subjects.

When the British took over in 1978, Cyprus was in an impoverished state, but steady, if unspectacular, progress was made even before the Colonial Development and Welfare Acts originated in 1940. Only by 1907 did revenue exceed £300,000; by 1955 it had risen to £11.5 million. In retrospect, a grave omission was made in failure to establish English schools or even to teach English as a common language. Up to 1914 this omission was based on a possibly misplace policy of unwillingness to Anglicise a population still under nominal Ottoman sovereignty, but, even up to the present day, Cypriot Greek schools are staffed by teachers from Athens who are apostles of Greek nationalism in an extreme form.

In 1956, the estimated population was 520,700 of whom about a fifth were Moslems.

ENOSIS

The idea of Enosis can be detected in a passage of the Iliad, but the only time when Cyprus formed a part of a Greek political organization was that of its inclusion in the Byzantine Empire from which it was detached by Isaac Comnenus, a member of the ruling house of the Empire.

In modern times, Enosis was first mentioned publicly in 1878 by the Bishop of Kition when he welcomed Sir Garnet Wolseley at Larnava; and, although Greece has contributed nothing material to the making of modern Cyprus, the most enduring cultural impression upon the Cypriot Orthodox is undoubtedly Greek.

At the same time, emigration figures are of interest. In 1954, 3688 Cypriots emigrated to Great Britain and the Commonwealth, five to Greece. For the first twelve months of terrorist activities starting in 1955, the figures were over four thousand to one.

As recently as 1931, a leading mukhtar said that eighty per cent of the villagers wished the Island to remain British and would vote against Enosis if free to do so, but this same year there was an outbreak in which the Bishops were heavily implicated and those of Kyrenia and Kition, along with other agitators, were banished from the Island.

Then there was peace, until Makarios, Bishop of Kition, was at the early age of 35, elected Archbishop in 1950.

In the Near and Middle East, men enter monastic life for very diverse motives - either to retire from the world, or to seek a position of power in politics and national affairs. Most of the leaders of the Eastern Churches have been political ethnarchs rather than spiritual fathers and Makarios is one of the majority.

At one time it was assumed that there had grown up with his connivance a political movement which developed into a terrorist organisation he was unable to control. Eventually, it was discovered, that he was not only an abettor of terrorism but its leader.

His claim to the authority and privilege of an ethnarch, an appointment peculiar to the Ottoman Empire, cannot be substantiated. He was not appointed Ethnarch by the Sovereign, he is not a functionary of the Cyprus Government, nor, of course, does he give implicit obedience to the State.

The other Cypriot Faction which is clamouring for union with Greece is the Communist Party and their aims are wholly logical. If they win they become available to reinforce The Party in Greece; if they fail, they have at least stirred up trouble in the Near East.

The Cypriot Turk forms a fifth of the population which is content for British rule to continue. He feels, however, that if there is to be any change, the Island should, on geographical and on historical grounds, revert to Turkey. Indeed the revival of Enosis in 1950 has made the Cypriot Turk more

Turkish minded than he has been for centuries.

Self determination is nowadays regarded by many as a universal "right" and a panacea for all ills. It is difficult to see how it can be made applicable to Cyprus as a whole. No plebiscite can be devised under present conditions, to assess the real wishes of the people; any held would be regimented and meaningless. The Church held a so called plebiscite on Enosis in 1950. The signatures in favour were displayed in every parish church and the penalty for failure to sign was excommunication.

How can self determination be moulded to unite the races of a small island which has never been inhabited by one race only and has, throughout the centuries been the meeting place of nations? It was while I was on holiday in Famagusta that I had a very pleasant experience. The best way to do this is to quote an extract from the local paper Milngavie and Bearsden Herald, given to them on my return home:-

The Coincidences of Bailie Gardner

Senior Bailie John M Gardner of Milngavie had "a most interesting time" when he holidayed on the sunny island of Cyprus.

He returned this week, with a permanent souvenir he will share with his fellow members of the Rotary Club of Allander.

Our picture shows the bailie displaying the official banner of the Rotary Club of Famagusta, given to the Allander Club as a memento of his visit to the Mediterranean isle. He handed it over to his Milngavie and Bearsden colleagues during a short speech at the club's weekly meeting in the Black Bull Hotel last Thursday.

Bailie Gardner also received from the Cyprus Rotarians a very attractive attendance card, on one side of which is a colour picture of the ancient gymnasium of Salamis.

By a remarkable coincidence, when he sat down to the meal, and the meeting of the Famagusta colleagues in the town's Sandy Beach Hotel, the Bailie found himself among a group of Famagusta's district councillors and one of them was his own counterpart .... planning and development, the post Mr Gardner holds on Milngavie Town Council.

Naturally they found themselves with a great deal in common, and their conversation was enhanced by the fact that the Famagusta planning convenor, Mr George Papagophoulos spoke excellent English. Mr Gardner was asked to return for another visit the following week, but had a previously arranged sailing trip on that day.

Surprise

But the Bailie's coincidences did not end there, he made a surprise visit to a Milngavie man and his family!

Mr William S Stobo is a civilian with the Royal Signals branch of the British Army on the island and no one was more astonished than Mr Stobo, (Bill to his friends), when the bailie walked in to see him.

Mr Gardner had been given Bill's office address by Bill's cousin in Milngavie, Mrs Jean Collins, wife of the local joiner Mr Dan Collins.

At the Royal Signals Unit the Regimental Sergeant Major gave the bailie the home address of Bill and his wife Aileen (who is from Lamlash) and their three daughters.

The group had a great two-hour chat about everything under the sun appertaining to Milngavie and Mr Gardner took colour pictures to pass on to the Milngavie relatives who include Bill's brother Jack, the Clober builder, and their sisters who live in Ferguson Avenue, Milngavie.

One bright spot in the bailies visit was when he took the three Stobo youngsters swimming. They had not realised that Senior Magistrates could swim!

And a final coincidence, Aileen Stobo in Cyprus has a brother in the police force, an Inspector, and he lives in Ayr. But where is he working at the moment? In the Milngavie and Bearsden Police Office at Keystone Milngavie!

It is a peculiar thing in life that sometimes one has to have a quarrel or disagreement with someone, and thereafter become great friends, as I did with the manager of the Constantia Hotel in Famagusta and his family, I am pleased to report. Nothing of any importance happened on my return journey home. In the end all very enjoyable and worth while. Just another experience.

Israel Holy Land Tour 1969

This must have been one of the most interesting and best holidays I have had.

The official agents were Davidson, Park and Speed Ltd., 4 Bothwell Street, Glasgow G2, they were most helpful and efficient in every detail.

The passenger list consisted, for the tour, of twenty-one, the Rev. J.M. Ewing from Cromarty being the tour leader. I did not realise until the day before departure that two of the passengers would be a Mr & Mrs A. Dawson of Milngavie, two friends of mine, a well respected family in Milngavie; the remainder being from Glasgow and surrounding district.

Holy Land Tour, Special Departure - 19th July 1969
Itinerary

1st Day Saturday 19th July:

Depart Glasgow by B.E.A. for London.
Continue by B.O.A.C. VC10 for Tel Aviv.
During the flight, lunch will be served, free of charge.
On arrival at Tel Aviv airport we will be met and taken by private car to the Shepherd Hotel, Old Jerusalem, for our stay in Jerusalem.

2nd Day Sunday 20th July:

The morning is free in Jerusalem.
In the afternoon we enter the Old City to visit the Temple Area, the Mosque of Omar (Dome of the Rock), El Aqsa Mosque, Solomon's Stables, the Golden Gate, the Wailing Wall and the Tower of David.

3rd Day Monday 21st July:

In the morning, drive along Mount Scopus to the Mount of Olives from where we get a general view of the Old Walled City of Jerusalem with its domes and minarets.
Visit the Chapel of the Ascension, the Church of the Paternoster and Dominus Flavist, the Garden of Gethsemane, and Basilica of the Agony and the Tomb of the Virgin Mary.

Continue our drive along the Kidron Valley past the Tombs of Absalam, Hezir and Zachariah, the Virgin's Fountain to the Pool of Siloam.
Visit the Palace of the High Priest Caiaphas; Prison of Christ (St Peter in Galancantii), Mount Zion, the Room of the Last Supper, King David's Tomb and the Abbey of Dormition.
Return to the Hotel for lunch.
In the afternoon, enter The Old City by St Stephen's Gate and visit the Church of St Anne, the Pool of Bethesda, Chapel of the Flagellation Sisters of Zion. Pilot's Palace and Judgement Hall, Eco Homo Arch, follow the Way of the Cross up to Calvary and the Church of the Holy Sepulchre, built on the site of the Crucifixion.
Return to our Hotel for dinner.

4th Day Thursday 22nd July:

After breakfast leave Jerusalem by private car for Hebron. Drive past Rachel's Tomb, the pools of Solomon and St Philips Fountain; through olive grove and vineyard country to Hebron and the Mosque of Abraham, where Abraham is buried with his wife Sarah and his sons Isaac and Jacob and their wives Rebecca and Leah. See Abraham's Oak and Mamre.
Resume drive to Bethlehem past the Shepherds' fields and the field of Boaz where Ruth stood amid the corn.
In Bethlehem visit the Church of the Nativity and the Manger. Return to the Hotel in Jerusalem for lunch, the afternoon being for leisure.

5th Day Wednesday 23rd July

After breakfast, an excursion by private car through the Judean Wilderness down to Jericho and the Dead Sea. On the way, stop at Bethany to visit the house of Mary and Martha and the Tomb of Lazarus. Pass the Inn of the Good Samaritan and visit Old Jericho (7000 B.C.), Elisha's Spring, the Mount of Temptation and the tradition of Baptism on the River Jordan.
Continue to the Dead Sea where there will be an opportunity for bathing before returning to Jerusalem for lunch.
For those particularly interested in seeing Quram, where the Dead Sea Scrolls were found quite by chance by a shepherd, a visit on an optional basis will be arranged.

6th Day Thursday 24th July

The day is at leisure in Jerusalem. Masada, Herod's fortress, scene of the Zealots' last stand against the Romans (AD 66-73) has once again sprung into prominence because of the momentous archaeological discoveries made there during the last 5 years. A special visit for those interested could be arranged on one of the free days in Jerusalem.

7th Day Friday 25th July

After breakfast, drive from our hotel through New Jerusalem to Ein Karem, the birthplace of St John the Baptist. Visit the Church of St John and the Church of Visitation, return past Mount Herzyl from where we have a view of the city including the Israel Museum and Hebrew University. Drive past the Church of St Andrew and the Cathedral of St George on our way back to the hotel for lunch. The afternoon for leisure.

8th Day Saturday 26th July

Free in Jerusalem.

9th Day Sunday 27th July

Free in Jerusalem.

Galilee Tour

10th Day Monday 28th July

Morning leave Jerusalem by coach for Nablus (Sheckem) Samaria. On the way, pass Birck where Mary and Joseph missed the Child, and Bethel where Jacob had his dream. Visit Jacob's Well where Jesus spoke to the Women of Samaria. In Nablus visit the Samaritan Synagogue and see the ancient manuscript of the Pentateuch (the first five books of the Bible).
Continue the drive to Sebastich to the Palace of Omri, where Salome danced and tradition says John the Baptist was beheaded.
From the ruins of the Palace we can look across and see the Mediterranean beyond.
Our drive takes us through the Valley of Jezreel to Megiddo (Armageddon) one of the chariot cities of King Solomon.
Lunch at Afula.
From Afula continue to Tiberias past Mount Tabor to the Hartman Hotel, Tiberias for dinner and our stay in Galilee.

11th Day Tuesday 29th July

After breakfast, leave Tiberias for Nazareth to see the Church of Annunciation, Mary's Well, Joseph's Workshop.
On our way we will stop at Cana of Galilee where Jesus performed his first miracle. Return to the Hotel for lunch.
In the afternoon drive along the shores of the sea of Galilee to Capernaum. Pass the ruins of ancient Magdala, birthplace of Mary Magdalene, Kibutz Ginosarr, Minya to Tabgha. Visit the Church of the Multiplication of Loaves and Fishes. Continue to Capernaum and the Mount of the Beatitudes. Return to the Hotel

for dinner.

12th Day Wednesday 30th July

The day is at leisure in Tiberias.

13th Day Thursday 31st July

14th Day Friday 1st August

These two days are free and optional excursions can be arranged to Acre, Haifa and Safad or to the Kibbutz.
Deganya and Ein Gev on the opposite shore of the Sea of Galilee.
Other places of interest nearby are Banias (Caesarea Philippi) and the Beit Shean, site of a Roman Theatre of the 3rd Century A.D., but with a history of 6,000 years.

15th Day Saturday 2nd August

After breakfast leave Tiberias for Tel Aviv (Lod) Airport for the flight, by B.O.A.C. Rolls Royce jet, to London.
Lunch served free of charge during flight. Arrive London Airport in the afternoon. Continue to Glasgow by B.E.A.

I was fortunate enough to cover the ground as mentioned in the itinerary. The first week I found a little heavy going by visiting so many churches. It appeared to me for each historic happening a church had been built on the spot where it happened.

One of my first experiences while living at the Shepherd Hotel in Jerusalem happened on a visit to the "Wailing Wall". One morning a member of our group, Mrs R Boyd, became separated from her husband and got lost in the crowd. They were an elderly couple and Mr Boyd asked me at lunch would I pay a return visit to the "Wailing Wall" to find her.

I immediately returned to the "Wailing Wall" and after some time I found her standing at "The Damascus Gate" and in my company escorted her back to the hotel to a very relieved husband Mr Boyd. Later I was informed Mr Boyd was a retired film director and his wife had been an actress.

To show his appreciation while visiting Ein Karem the birthplace of St John the Baptist, he wrote a thank you poem and gave it to me as follows:

Written By A Wall at Ein Karem

Friday 25th July 1969

To an ancient land so far away
On a Pilgrimage we came one day
To see the Sites our Saviour trod
And listen to the word of God
Like many who have gone before
Our faith renewed for ever more

Then some of us, who came to look
with little knowledge of the "Book"
Received a message, where he taught
A message that we all forgot
But now we know that even today
It's good to meditate and pray

When we return from whence we came
We won't forget His Holy name
T'will lead us to a better life
Amid this world of care and strife
So let peace reign on every hand
Be the message from the Holy Land

R.A. Boyd

My next experience was on an afternoon drive along the shores of the Sea of Galilee to Capernaum passing the ruins of ancient Magdala, birthplace of Mary Magadalene and Tabha to Capernaum and on to exit from the Sea of Galilee of the River Jordan. Where the motor coach stopped to allow the female numbers of our group to obtain water from the Jordan in glass bottles for the purposes of taking home for baptismal purposes. I was authorised to fill the glass bottles with water. Unfortunately one of the members, a lady from Hawick in Scotland, was so anxious to fill her bottle she overstretched and fell into the water carrying me with her.

The depth of the water was about five feet and fairly fast running. Being able to swim I managed to return her to the shore and safety. I did not expect to be baptised in the Jordan like that.

On another excursion by private car through the Judean Wilderness down to Jericho and the Dead Sea, on the way we stopped at Bethany to visit the house of Mary and Martha and the Tomb of Lazarus, past the Inn of the

Good Samaritan, visit Old Jericho (7000 B.C.) Elisha's Spring, the Mount of Temptation and the traditional place of Baptism on the River Jordan, continuing to the Dead Sea where we took the opportunity for bathing.

The Dead Sea is a wonderful place, possibly the lowest spot on earth. The sea is heavy with minerals, so heavy that you can float in it, just lie on your back, stretch out your legs and you will be amazed at the ease with which you can float, completely without effort, even if you have never been able to swim before.

Before taking a dip you are best to make sure that you are near one of the beach showers where you will be able to wash off the salt deposit later. However the bathing huts where we were had the roof blown off by gun fire from the opposite shore about a fortnight before our arrival so we were exposed to the sun. To make matters worse I accidentally took a mouthful of salt water while swimming and I was in distress for some time. However it was an experience I would not like to have missed as the sensation of floating without effort was colossal.

Many of the rocks around the sea are nothing but chunks of salt, no wonder vegetation is scarce.

It was during the Six Day War in June 1967 that the damage was done to the roof of the beach showers. Some 26,100 square miles have come under Israel jurisdiction. The population of Israel in 1967 was approximately three million, made up of Jews, Moslems, Christians, Druze and others.
From an historical point of view I was impressed by:

(1) The Mount of Olives and its historical sites. The Church of Gethsemane at the foot of the Mount and the Garden of Gethsemane where I sat a few times with a peaceful feeling I had never felt before.

(2) Dominus Flevit where Jesus wept over his beloved Jerusalem.

(3) The Garden Tomb, the Lord's Tomb
This Tomb is hewn out of the rock of Calvary.

There are so many important features of the Holy Land it is quite impossible to record even the main points as so much has been written since the beginning of time.

Modern Times

The State of Israel was proclaimed in May 1948 in part of the former British Mandated Territory of Palestine. Israel is a Republic headed by a President who is elected by a 120 member Kneset (Parliament). The Government is headed by the Prime Minister.

Elections to the Knesset are held every four years on a system of proportional representation. All Israel citizens over the age of 18, irrespective of sex, race or religion are entitled to vote in secret balloting for both the Knesset and local government bodies.

Before the Six Day War in June 1967, Israel covered an area of 8,000 square miles, as a result of the Six Day War a further 26,100 square miles have come under Israeli jurisdiction. Hebrew the revived language of the Bible, is the common language of Israel, however many other languages exist such as Arabic, English, French, Yiddish, German, Russian etc. Most people are fluent in two or more languages.

Main Industries and Products

Israel is a vigorous industrial and agricultural country. It is virtually self-supporting in food stuffs and has a large export of out-of-season agricultural produce marketed throughout Europe, although Java citrus fruits continue to be the leading agricultural export.

Israeli industry ranges from the production of steel, motors and a full range of agricultural and other machinery, through highly skilled and other science-based industries, the diamond cutting and polishing, the manufacture of modern synthetic fibres, the processing of the valuable mineral resources of the Dead Sea and Nigev Desert, with a fully developed consumer industry supplying fashion, books, furniture, processed foodstuffs and the majority of modern necessities.

Kibbutz

I was particularly interested in the Kibbutz, a type of small holding, it would appear to be a unique phenomenon. Many of Israel's collective agricultural settlements where the youth of the country have made use of the agricultural education given to them, run many of Israel's settlements and run their own guest-house. The guest-houses are members of the Israel Hotel Association and are subject to the exacting standards of service and cleanliness, as all other Israeli Hotels, and offer complete privacy and excellent country style food. Service is by members of the Kibbutz, though the accommodation and dining room are completely separate from the members quarters.

The guest-houses are situated in various parts of the country - Western and Northern Galilee, the Central area, the Judean hills and the Northern Nigev. Many of them arrange special evening programmes to help guests become acquainted with life on the Kibbutz - film shows, lectures, meetings with members etc.

There is no obligation to participate in any communal activity, nor of course, to work, though if visitors are interested, the management will arrange for them to spend time in the fields or the service branches of the settlement.

This type of small holding agriculture education has served Israel well, when one considers the great expansion in agriculture throughout the land.

Great strides have been made in developing the country, both economically and culturally. Hundreds of thousands of new immigrants have been absorbed into life and the old transitional camps have almost been liquidated. Large areas of land have been reclaimed for agriculture and industry. Yes there is a great future for this country and for those who will arrive during the next decade.

Having now completed the Holy Land Tour, we seem to have covered a considerable amount of ground in the time at our disposal. On my way home all was quite as expected, so much to see, so much to learn, a real joy to have been there, thanks to some nice friends and a well organised tour.

Gibraltar

In the company of my eldest daughter who had just completed her nursing training, we decided on a holiday to this most important place in the history of the British Empire. Connected to the Spanish mainland by a sandy flat, it is approximately three miles long with the greatest breadth nearly one mile. Known generally as "The Rock", it has been a British fortress and crown colony controlling the Strait of Gibraltar for many years and has been the scene of many battles. It has been of great value as a base for Allied navies, especially the United States. I am informed many Spanish refugees sought shelter in the fortress during the civil war of 1936-39.

After Italy entered World War Two in 1940, all women and children were removed from Gibraltar as well as all male civilians except about 3,000 engaged in essential work.

Additional defences were constructed on the land side of the Rock to guard against attack through Spain. Military engineers expanded the interior defences fivefold, the length of tunnelling being increased from 2 miles to 10 miles and a canal was cut across the isthmus.

The repatriation of the 17,000 evacuees in the years following the war created housing and other difficulties. Successive Spanish governments, and especially that of General Franco, stated from time to time Gibraltar was Spanish Territory to which the Spanish people did not renounce their claim - a claim that has never been recognized by the United Kingdom government.

On our arrival at Gibraltar Airport we were very interested in the runway, the control gates and of course the "Rock" itself, a very imposing feature, and how close we were to the town of La Linea on the Spanish mainland, our hotel being The Rock Hotel with all modern conveniences.

I remember the great ocean liner Queen Elizabeth was anchored in the bay at the time. Gibraltar had one tremendous advantage, it is in the sterling area and no language problems. You can relax in the Mediterranean warmth, climb the slopes, explore the caves, dance, swim, sail and fish, and go to concerts and shows.

The barbary Apes roam around on the Upper Rock. One of our excursions took us to Tangier, a fun city, with its Casbah and markets, with the flavour of the Arabian Nights.

On our visit to La Linea, spending the day mostly shopping, the prices for articles for sale seemed very reasonable. On the Rock itself the people were very friendly with lots to do. St Michael's Cave is a must with its natural auditorium used for concerts and other performances. The Cable Car runs from Alamada Parade for a six minute ride, halfway up you can make an optional stop at the famous Apes Den. They are fed at 9am and 4pm at recognised feeding places. The Gibraltar Museum contains many interesting exhibits, a 17th century Spanish gun, and some fine paintings. Altogether a very nice place to visit with the time at your disposal seeming very short. Our flight by B.E.A. to and from Gibraltar was first class.

Costa Del Sol

During the next few years in the company of Mr and Mrs Fred Bowater, we visited Malaga. It is quite a large city and capital of the Costa Del Sol, having a nice sea front, quite historical.

It has a first class shopping centre; Quite a nice place for a holiday. There is a Limadet-ferry from Malaga to Tangier, but like most other resorts of the type, it is a 19th century city which has recently found out what the 20th century is all about; to me, rather artificial.

Torremolinos we found even more artificial and city culture from what appeared to be a one time fishing village into new world of hotels, countless bars, swinging clubs, noisy discotheques, it is the fun-capital of the Costa Del Sol.

Marbella is the jet-set playground of the Costa Del Sol. favoured by the rich, the famous and the titled. A thriving town of luxury hotels, pleasure-craft harbours, and it is right in the heart of golf-land, within easy reach of world class championship courses such as Sotogrande etc. Although very much a part of the Sunny Coast tourist boom, the town of Marbella has retained much of its charm with quite a number of sights to see and of course the Bullring.

Fuengerola If Torremolinos is the fun city, then Fuengerola is considerably quieter and geared to a more leisurely pace. I consider it to be the family town of the Costa Del Sol. Cosmopolitan is the word which describes it. German beer cellars, English tea shops, Danish pastry shops and even a Jewish Kosher restaurant are examples of the internationalism to be found there.

Fuengerola retains elements which have existed for centuries, the big fishing fleet still comes in every morning and is a sight not to be missed, the old Arab castle of Sohoil, wander along the new Pasea Maritimo with its tropical plants, swim on the long sand beach, the beach bars, open air cafes and the mountain village of Mijas on the outskirts. Like the adjacent towns it is reaching skywards to accommodate the influx of vacationers.

We were booked into the Hotel Piramides, a little expensive but with all the facilities, such as swimming pools, tennis courts etc., service was excellent.

Portugal

Our final visit to that area was at a place called Torralta - Algarve. We were booked into the Hotel D. Joao. It was not unlike the towns in Spain, very much artificial with modern hotels, good swimming pools and a lovely beach, tennis courts, table tennis, riding and golf. The only difference was we rented a car and managed to cover a considerable amount of ground and of course the usual amount of sunshine. I suppose we were getting quite used to this type of holiday.

We did have another holiday at two places in Italy-Rimini and Maramaree, where I am told Mussolini used to visit on vacation, plenty of sun, rather artificial.

Canary Islands

On a visit to the Canary Island of Tenerife, at the town of Puerto De La Cruz, we were booked into the Las Vegas Hotel with the usual modern cluster of buildings. The island consisted of mountain peaks, quite picturesque but more volcanic in origin.

On a visit to "Mount Teide" at the top of the mountain, it was scene of a volcanic crater and lava consisting of basalts. Then nearer ground level the dragon tree and shrubby composite plants. The climate in the hottest parts is similar to that of Egypt. There are grown among other plants, the coffee tree, date palm, sugar cane, banana, and orange tree. With lovely black sands along the shore for swimming, the inhabitants are mostly Spanish. There is no doubt it was slightly different from the mainland. Quite a good place for a holiday.

Malta "The George Cross Island Fortress"

After visiting many countries in Europe and Africa over a period of more than twenty years our last holiday abroad was spent on the famous place called Malta.

The Maltese islands are situated between Europe and Africa, in the central channel which connects the eastern and western basins of the Mediterranean Sea. The group belong to the British Commonwealth, Malta being the chief island.

We were booked into the Grand Hotel Verdala Rabat, a lovely hotel on a raised site; a very large hotel with two swimming pools, tennis courts and sports facilities with a splendid view of the Mediterranean Sea.

Malta has a magnificent natural harbour and while we were there the sur was very strong whilst the air was clear and invigorating.

The Maltese people we found very friendly and would invite you into their houses. They loved to hear about Scotland. We also used to visit a small cafe near the hotel for a coffee or ice cream.

I also made friends with a Mr Hargreaves from Chorley, England. He was a member of Rotary as could be seen by the small badges on the lapel of his jacket. We always went swimming together.

From a historical point of view Malta has seen many changes as is shown by megalithic temples and stone antiquities, possibly by the unique position it has in the Mediterranean and the strategic importance in peace and war.

During World War I the Maltese provided a garrison for the island, many seamen for naval ships, as well as labour battalions for service at Gallipoli and Salonica. In addition Maltese did excellent work in hospitals and in 1921 a self governing constitution was set up, debates were conducted in English, Italian or Maltese, but all official entries were in English or Italian. English was declared the official language of the administration during the Nationalist administration. The two sides of the dyarchy worked the constitution with little friction.

After Italy entered World War II in 1940, Malta became subject to ceaseless aerial attacks by both German and Italian bombers from bases in Sicily, within 20 minutes flying time. The island, 1000 miles from the nearest British position, became of the very first importance as a base of operations.

For three years Malta was defended by both the garrison and the people. It was only possible to send aviation gasoline and munitions to Malta by submarine, while additional fighter aircraft of the Royal Air Force were flown to the island from the decks of distant carriers. Food became very scarce but despite hardships, civilian morale stood high.

On April 15th 1942, George VI awarded the George Cross to the Island Fortress of Malta to bear witness to a heroism and devotion that will long be famous in history.

At the time of the British occupation there were about two dozen families bearing titles of nobility granted or recognized by the Grand Masters.

The Maltese are a thrifty and industrious people. Prolific and devoted of their offspring, their religion is mostly Roman Catholic. Malta and the Islands

Valletta, Malta

depended mostly on agriculture and fishing. The new industries, the making of gloves, buttons, plastics, boots and shoes, beer and nylon stockings, the older industries being lace, silver and homespun cloth.

Other than going to the island of Gozo, legendary home of the Calypso, we remained in the town of Malta and Valletta as we had all the services required near the hotel.

I had one very interesting experience in company with my two friends. We made company with about another two dozen English visitors on the terrace outside the hotel where we would meet every day. I was the only Scot in the company and I used to have my leg pulled being the only Scot. However, after being at the hotel about three days and becoming quite tanned from sunbathing and swimming with my friend from Rotary.

One afternoon on coming out of the swimming pool I was accosted by a rather tall distinguished gentleman stating he would like to have a few words with me, remarking that he and his wife had been watching me from the side of the pool, that I was about of an age with himself and they noticed I had taken on a good tan in a short time and appeared to be a good swimmer.

He went on to advise me how the tan I had achieved for the few days I was there, at my age was now not doing me much good, in fact if I continued to take much more I would do myself more harm than good. After telling me in some detail the effect on the corpuscles etc., on my skin, I asked if he was in the profession, yes, he was Sir Sydney Smith consultant in St Thomas Hospital, London. In fact, he was President of the Malta Cross Association and that he and his wife were on a holiday-cum-business trip from London. He was out to present a medal to Sammy Davis the american actor for work he had done in the Middle East. Showing me some photos of the event, he explained that during World War 2 he was with the staff to Earl Mountbatten of Burma.

We then engaged in quite a conversation. I explained to him where I came from, that I was in the building trade as an employer, and gave an account of my own experiences during the war, and experience as a Local Councillor, Senior Magistrate and Justice of the Peace. I was invited to meet his wife Lady Smith who was resting in the shade of an artificial tree just outside the hotel on the lawn. She advised me that she insisted that Sir Sydney should tell me the disadvantage of taking so much sun tan and I thanked her very much.

At this stage my friend Mr Bowater came along to enquire what was wrong, but I assured him everything was alright and that we were having a very nice conversation. I introduced him to Sir Sydney and Lady Smith and he left us to continue our conversation with a titled couple at the side of the pool. The upshot of the affair was I was invited to have breakfast with them next morning in the hotel and I agreed to do so.

In the meantime my friends got to hear of my exploit and of my intention to have breakfast with my new titled friends, with the result the next morning as I was coming from my bedroom down the main stairway to have breakfast all my English friends were lining the stairway with the words "Good Morning Sir John", that was all I got for the remainder of the holiday. However it was all very good fun. I enjoyed myself very much and quite sad when we had to leave on our return journey home, a very worthwhile holiday. I did not realize at the time that the advice given to me regarding the effect of the sun and the fact I was now reaching the age of seventy, was the last journey I would make abroad as I retired at the age of seventy three. I think very wisely taking my holidays in Scotland where I had a boat in Loch Lomond for the past twenty five years with all the lovely scenery.

Loch Lomond

My first experience with Loch Lomond started in 1959 with a lOft Fibreglass Seamaster Dinghy with a British Seagull Engine 3 H.P. Seabee, until 1962 with an addition of a Seamaster "Iona" Standard 22ft Sloop having a fibreglass hull sleeper de luxe version with 10 H.P. "Sea Farer Engine, mast and rigging with jib and main sails consisting of terylene sheets with all standard fittings to sleep four with inside toilet, sink, stove, and double table dinette. While I managed to handle the engine it took me some considerable time to learn the know how with the sails, however with some patience I became quite proficient in the art of sailing and began to get educated about the loch and its long historical background. There is no better place to be on a summer evening, the scenery itself is one perfect treat.

I located my base for operation on the Loch at Messrs Alex MacFarlane Boatyard, Balmaha, being most convenient to all parts of the area and it was quite a coincidence when in conversation with Mr Alex MacFarlane that he and I found we were born on the same day 1907. We became firm friends and always exchanged birthday cards each year on the 2nd day of October. He gave me some very sound advice on the various islands and conditions attached to Loch Lomond, the most dangerous part being from Rowardennan to Ardlui, where the mountains are high and the depth of water south of Inversnaid being of great depth at one part of over 100 fathoms; At the Balloch end of the Loch it is relatively shallow.

The great attraction is the islands where my family and friends spent so many happy days. There must be over thirty islands in Loch Lomond, a very great selection, the principal ones being Inchmurrin, Incheailloch, Inchfad, Inchmoan, Incheruin, Inchtavanach, Inchlonaig, and Ross Isles. The small islands off Luss called the Luss Straits are very lovely and suitable for picnics, the larger islands being suitable for walks and nature trails.

From an historical point of view it is very obvious quite a large number of people must have lived or frequented the islands, for instance Inchmurrin contains an hotel and a fairly large farm, Inchcailloch also has had a farm, the remains of building can be seen today. There are also remains of a 12th century church with quite a number of tombstones, a nice sandy beach, it contains a number of trees from large oaks to firs, flowering plants and ferns all giving a clue to former human activity and land use. This applies to most of the islands.

On the shores round the loch there are many buildings including mansions and remains of castles. The once remote fastness of Macgregors, Macfarlanes, Buchanans, Colquhouns, and Grahams, is within an easy day' s tour from Glasgow by road or rail and steamer, an unspoilt sanctuary except at one or two spots since Rob Roy first trod here upon his native heath, and today The West Highland Way runs from Milngavie (Mulguy) to Fort William, although the signposting for this Way is a disgrace.

The acquisition of Balloch Castle estate by the Corporation of Glasgow in 1915 as a public park still further popularised the neighbourhood, so that today on a public holiday the scene is greatly changed. Crowds pour thither by train from Glasgow to Balloch, touring coaches, private motor cars from distant places which gives the added pleasure and interest of seeing so many people, mostly young and free from care so innocently and whole- heartedly enjoying themselves.

Where the loch narrows at Balloch to become the river Leven there are dozens of houseboats anchored along the banks with motor boats, speed boats and rowing boats embarking passengers at the little piers with happy parties moving everywhere on the water. The loch from above the road bridge forms a picture that is not rivalled anywhere in Scotland. The same can be seen at Balmaha and to a lesser degree at Rowardennan. There is the growth of Caravan sites on the shores of the loch with a wild game park near Luss. There are also a few ferries still existing across the loch with the usual paddle steamers from Balloch Pier. The charm of the place has not been spoiled but every now and then people are reminded not to leave litter behind when they depart.

At home, aged 70

Daughter's Evelyn, Freda and Cynthia; Son Iain; with Son-in-Law Leonard

For a period of fourteen years when my family were growing up we enjoyed many happy times on the loch and made many friends. However through marriage, members of my family were leaving home and changes in circumstance meant the boat went out of favour and I reluctantly sold the 22ft sloop, but kept my small fibreglass dinghy.

It was at this period when I was heavily engaged in politics. I experienced an outlet to my life by the purchase of a second caravan and trailer. I found this convenient way to travel north to my relations at Burghead and Elgin area, also it was becoming quite a popular pursuit as a holiday arrangement for touring, it was very modern and easy trailing.

My first tour in the new caravan was with my daughter Freda, her husband Leonard and their twins. It was on the autumn holiday we travelled to Fort William to a caravan site near Ben Nevis for the night and thereafter continued to the Isle of Skye on the second day. I was no stranger to the Misty Isle as I had visited Skye as a boy of seven with my parents and once with my late wife. In the first instance we sailed from Glasgow to a place called Roag where my mother was born, about one mile from Dunvegan. On the second time with my wife we were fortunate to have permission from Dame Flora McLeod to park our caravan in a peninsula at the sea front inside the grounds of the Castle, a lovely spot looking out towards McLeods table top mountain. On this occasion we settled in a caravan park just outside Dunvegan with all the services laid on, it was quite convenient. Unfortunately we were only there for a few days and had to make the most of our time, the weather was in our favour.

Our first visit was to Dunvegan, the MacLeod stronghold, standing on a rock at the head of Loch Dunvegan. Parts of it are said to be of ninth construction, but most of the massive fortification dates from fifteenth to the nineteenth centuries.

Dunvegan is Britain's oldest inhabited castle in the continuous occupation of the same family. It is moated and the walls in places are ten feet thick.

A fifteenth century dungeon is a reminder of ancient cruelties and there are many relics of MacLeod achievements in battle and in hospitality.

These include the two-handed sword of the legendary twelfth chief, Rory Mor, as well as his drinking horn with the capacity of two modern bottles of claret which he is said to have been able to quaff at one draught.

Visitors to Dunvegan are also shown the Fairy Flag, said to possess magical powers and captured by a MacLeod from the Saracens in the

Crusades. You will also be told of the Fairy Bridge bear Waternish at the cross-road. It is a pleasant spot, with a brown peat burn spanned by a good stone bridge where preachings were held. It has been said it was a fairy ground where fairies danced on a green grass triangle and horses always shied at the bridge whether driven, ridden or led across, that as may be.

The Clans of Skye are mainly MacLeod, MacDonald and MacKinnon of which much has been written.

The next experience was to tour the north of the island taking the west coast route and returning by the east coast route to Portree, the capital of the island, and thence back to Dunvegan.

Our first stop was Uig. It is said to have got its name from the Norse "Ogr" (Bay) and lies on a beautiful one. A tweed centre with its hospital, Uig was well in the forefront of the land reform agitation and was one of the places visited by the navy, King Edward VII himself opened the new pier. Whale and seal meat formed an important part of the island diet.

We travelled on to what must be one of the most spectacular places in Skye, "The Quirang", which is obviously the result of natural upheaval. Its famous "Needle Rock", it is an extraordinary feature. The road through the Quirang is very exciting with all its hair-pin bends.

The "Quiraing The Cup" was used as a safe hiding place for cattle in time of trouble, because two or three men could hold the entrance against a force, Baca Ruach at the back of the same range of hills is very dangerous, to be seen is to be believed.

We now came to Flodigarry, a place very closely linked with the island's eighteenth century heroine Flora MacDonald. Whilst the island's clan chiefs were laid low during the 1745 rebellion, she came to the rescue of the fugitive Prince Charles Edward. The Young Pretender and claimant to the British throne, following the defeat of his army at the Battle of Culloden in April 1746.

Flora was on a visit to the Outer Hebridean island of South Uist where she was born, when at the greatest risk to her personal safety, she allowed the prince, who was disguised in a flowered linen gown as an Irish spinning maid Betty Burke, to accompany her in a boat to Skye.

Off the north-west coast of the island they were fired on by English troops but rowed on to Trotternisk, where at Kilbride near the MacDonald home at Kingsburgh the prince took shelter.

It was not long before Flora's role in the affair was discovered. She was arrested and imprisoned, but was pardoned in 1747. Before the Prince left from the safety of her home prior to the next stage in his flight to France he asked Flora to cut off a lock of his hair in remembrance, this she did and gave a portion of it to Mrs MacDonald of Kingsburgh.

Flora MacDonald died on March 3rd 1790, and is buried at Kilmuir, some 20 miles from Portree. A sheet in which Bonnie Prince Charlie slept was her shroud and her grave is marked by a memorial cross 28 feet high.

A short distance from the burial place of Flora MacDonald we visited The Skye Cottage Museum. Apart from exhibits connected with Flora MacDonald, the Museum contains preserved relics of the Island's past, as well as items from Uist, Barra, Mull and the Highland mainland. We returned to Portree where I am informed my grandfather had an office and looked after the McLeod estate as a Master of Works. Thereafter continuing our way across country via Skeabost Bridge and Edinbane to our caravan car cark at Dunvegan.

Next day we made our way back to Fort William where I visited a few friends before returning home, a short but successful tour.

My companion Ex-Police Inspector Graham Henderson

In 1978 I went back to my old love and purchased a second hand fibre Glass 15ft Motor Cruiser, having a 9.5 H.P. Yamaha Engine with remote control. It was two' seasons old, but in very good condition.

Being a widower with my family now removed from home I had been playing bowls and looking forward to my retirement from business and politics, however I met a friend who was an ex-inspector in the Glasgow Police Force while playing bowls. He too was a widower and lived with a married daughter only 200 yards from my own house. Like myself, he was interested in boating and we struck up a very nice partnership and became firm friends, in fact he was my partner in a few bowling competitions we had played in, his name was Graham Henderson and he had just recently retired, being about an age with myself.

My son Iain was by now running the family business and I was easing out of politics so I had more time to myself. My life seemed to be taking a new shape, so I had more time for the sports side of bowls, golf and sailing. It was usual for me to play bowls during the week, golf on a Saturday and cruising on a Sunday. Although I was still quite active it was more recreation than business.

We were fortunate to get a nice berth at Messrs McFarlane, Balmaha and most suitable for cruising the boat with remote control and a splendid canopy. It was very comfortable, with my past experiences of Loch Lomond it was quite easy to navigate the islands.

It was usual for us to leave home on a Sunday at 9am and did not return until 9pm, having taken enough food and stores, having a gas cooker aboard. It was not unusual to picnic on one of the islands.

So now we had a caravan, a boat, bowls and golf, not bad for a couple of senior citizens. We were the best of pals, quite suited for each other.

However, at the end of 1979 after a sailing season, for the first time in my life I had to go into hospital for an operation, having a strangulated hernia. It was in December and was quite a good time of the year for me. The operation was carried out in the Western Infirmary in Glasgow and was a complete success, and with the coming of spring I was once again in good health.

During the next year we decided to do our sailing and have a caravan tour, coupled with a bowling expedition, going up the west coast to Skye and across country to the north east, returning by the east coast to Milngavie of three weeks duration.

The boating season starts in the middle of April so we did May, June, July sailing, August and September caravan touring, taking us into the autumn.

We had a mixed bag for weather at the beginning of the season, but the weather became much better later during our cruising period of May, June and July. It was very enjoyable as we were prepared for any kind of weather going over all the old haunts. It was first class, the only snag was the increased number of speed boats on the loch making it a little more dangerous, plus the additional caravan sites and smaller craft, also water-skiing.

During August we set off on our caravan touring and bowling exercise, the first stop being Fort William in a caravan site at Corpach on the edge of Loch Linnhe and the entrance to Loch Eil, with excellent services, for a few days.

We contacted the local bowling club and were made very welcome by the members. We did a long walk up Glen Nevis and a run in the car to Glenfinnan to see the Prince Charlie Monument. I was able to show Mr Henderson the local sights as I was stationed in Fort William for a period during the war and met some old friends. We were made temporary members of the bowling club and given a club badge in remembrance of our visit.

Our next stop was Kyle of Lochalsh, had lunch and on to Portree, had a game of bowls spent some time shopping in town and continued to Dunvegan to the camping site I had been in on an earlier visit, no bowling, but managed to find a relation of my mother a shepherd by the name of McLeod. We were very well received and I was given the history of my mother's family and obtained a photograph of the original house, now a ruin, where my mother was born at Roag, and we had a visit to Dunvegan Castle but as we were only there for overnight and one day, it was all we could do. Off we went across country to Nairn to quite a large caravan site. I knew Nairn from a previous visit and Graham Henderson had been there on holiday with his late wife. It was a nice place to visit and we lived there for a week. He knew some members of the bowling green and it was not long before the members were having us play in their competitions. We were both fairly proficient at the game and won one or two prizes.

Next to the bowling green was the Church of Scotland, quite an architectural building of some size. It was on an imposing corner site. The Minister was a Mr Donald MacDonald, who previously was the Minister of St Pauls Church of Scotland in Milngavie, of which I was a member, and knew him quite well, unfortunately he was away from home on a weeks holiday.

However it so happened that the second day on the bowling green I was playing in the same rink as the beadle of the church. I mentioned the fact to him of my acquaintance with his minister, he told me he would be on the telephone to Mr MacDonald that evening and he would mention that I had been playing with him.

Next morning the beadle advised me with a smile on his face "Oh yes, Mr MacDonald knew me alright", but he added John Gardner must be an old man now, his reply was, Mr Gardner may be over seventy but you should see him running up and down the bowling green after the bowls.

When Graham Henderson heard of this he thought this a great joke and thereafter at every opportunity he would say "poor John that old man". It was all good fun. The only way I got my own back was to walk so quickly he could not keep up with me.

However for the next week we were constantly on the bowling green, here again we were made temporary members and given a Nairn Badge in remembrance of our visit with an invitation back to the bowling green at any time.

We did not get a great deal of time for sightseeing as we had made so many friends and we were due to leave for our next stop at Elgin.

On arrival at Elgin the caravan site at the river side was ideal and very suitable to our requirements. Our first visit was again to the bowling green. The circumstances here were rather different, my partner discovered the secretary of the club was an ex-policeman from Glasgow, who knew him also, also, my brother from Elgin was quite well known to the members.

They would not allow us to pay any fees and were made guests and allowed to play at any time. We further discovered the secretary of the club had attended the same police school as a nephew of mine, it was now like a home from home.

During the next fortnight we enjoyed ourselves very much and were even selected to play for Elgin against Buckie, rather an honour. We managed to win our games and received a gift of a bowl carrier made from part of a fishing net, it was most useful.

One of our day outings was to Lossiemouth where my partner had already visited on holiday. We visited a friend of his and finished up playing on the Lossie bowling green.

Another outing was to Craigellachie, where my youngest married daughter lived and after spending most of the day, we were taken to Aberlour in the evening and had our usual game of bowls.

We also had to visit my family relations in both Elgin and Burghead, do our shopping and sightseeing. The time seemed to go in so fast. It was time to go on to our next stop at Grantown and leave Elgin, where we had made so many friends.

At Grantown we were only passing through, but had one game of bowls and carried on to Aviemore, booked in overnight, and spent the next day exploring the vicinity including the Aviemore Centre. We arrived home slightly tired, just another experience in the life of two senior citizens.

The following year in 1981 we did another caravan holiday going direct to Elgin caravan park off Oakwood Road by the river side. It had a shop and all the services. This time the weather was excellent, it was more of a restful holiday instead of touring. We very quickly made contact with our bowling friends and usually played in the evening or sometimes in the afternoon.

We spent more time with our friends at Craigellachie, Burghead, Findhorn, Lossiemouth and one day at Inverness, plus one day at Forres on the golf course. The coastline in the north east has some lovely sand beaches, so between paddling in the sea, making meals in the caravan or eating out, we spent a high old time, and it was with regret after a fortnight with real holiday weather we packed our bags and returned home.

For the next two years most of our time we spent on the lovely islands in Loch Lomond. Unfortunately Mr Henderson was failing in health, in 1984 he died of cancer after six years of a very happy partnership.

During the latter part of 1984 I found myself having severe pain in the lower muscle of my left leg until I was unable to walk any distance at all.

I was taken into Gartnavel General Hospital for an X-ray in the Vascular Ward, where it was discovered a blockage above the knee in the main artery of the leg. This was the second visit to a hospital, so I had a little more knowledge of the routine. By now I was seventy seven years of age and had been retired from business five years. It was an experience I am not likely to forget. There can be a funny side to what happens in a hospital too.

Before my X-ray I was examined by a doctor who asked me my age, his immediate reply when told was - "you won't have an operation anyway" - so I asked what they would do, the reply was, "you will be given jags and drugs", my reply was "you can jag away, but I don't want drugs". He was rather annoyed and said "we will see about that" and walked out the room.

Later, when lying on the X-ray table awaiting the return of the plates, I asked the doctor operating the machine is it true I cannot have an operation because of my age. He had two sisters assisting him, they smiled rather broadly and the reply from the Doctor was, "it is a long time since we have seen a more fit man at seventy seven, you will have an operation, but the boss will let you know later", the boss being the chief surgeon, a Mr McKay. When I was back in the ward the chief gave me a visit, explained the situation and told me that I would be having an operation and what is known as a by-pass done, I was very relieved.

Later that evening he called again and asked me if I ever had varicose veins. My reply was, "no never", he then asked to see the leg affected. The vein next to the artery was ideal. In a short time later another surgeon asked me the same question and looked at the leg with the same reply, without hesitation I said "it is not my vein it is the artery where the obstruction is". It was at this point he explained the idea was to cut out a section of the vein and redirect the flow of the vein so that it could be grafted into the artery.

My immediate reply was I did not know that could be done. It was then he advised me they had been doing this type of operation for the last eighteen months and they had never lost a patient yet.

The outcome of the operation was a complete success.

I was out of hospital within eight days. When it was time to leave the chief surgeon Mr McKay of the vascular ward gave some instruction on how to behave for about a month during my convalescence. My final question to him was "I am not natural anymore", his reply, "no John, you're bionic".

It is wonderful what the advancement of medical science can do. Now, three years later, I will shortly be 80 years of age and in first class health, in fact I have been given a new lease of life.

My caravan was presented to my daughter Cynthia, in Craigellachie, as they live in a lovely part of the country near the River Spey and are making good use of it. I have recently disposed of the 15ft fibreglass cruiser so I am now back to where I started many years ago, but still manage to play outdoor and indoor bowls, along with my golf. I have been most fortunate, and pace myself as necessary.

Classroom group and woodwork class in 1918

MY RETURN TO MILNGAVIE SCHOOL

The schoolboy returns over 70 years later

My return to Milngavie School

One of the nice things to happen recently was when I was introduced to Mrs Reid, head teacher of Milngavie Primary School, Hillhead Street, Milngavie. She advised that for some time she had been on the look out for someone to give a lecture on the history of the school, then she discovered I had been born, brought up and educated at Milngavie Public School. With my background and experience of local conditions it would be nice if I would visit the school for the purpose of giving a lecture to the pupils.

This indeed was a very great honour for me to return to the school where I had obtained my very early education and to which I had so many happy memories. From five years to fifteen years of age is a very important time in your life.

The idea was for the teacher of the class in this instance, with the co-operation of the pupils, would put down a series of questions for me to answer, herewith are a number of the questions put down and my reply to them.

1. Can you describe the classroom and its furniture in 1913?

   Reply:- The classroom was quite spacious, approximately 24ft x 24ft. One half consisted of a flat wood floor. Each desk was suited for two pupils rising in tiers to the rear of the classroom with a passage between desks, capacity for pupils about 45 places. There were large windows giving plenty of light with the usual blackboard, with 4ins cast iron pipes for heating. The teacher had her special desk and a cupboard to hold books etc.

2. Were school meals available? If so, what were they like and where were they eaten?

   Reply:- No school meals were available at first, later a place they called "The Laundry" in the basement of the school was turned into a type of canteen suitable for country pupils or others who wished it, but most of the pupils were allowed 1 1/2hrs to go home for dinner.

   It was usually one plate of soup, with bread, potatoes with mince, semolina or rice for a sweet, one cup of tea. There was a very small charge for the cost of the meal.

3. Was there corporal punishment? If so, what form did it take.

Reply:- Depending on the offence, the teacher kept a leather belt or tawse used to strap the hand of the pupil as necessary or the other punishment writing out 100 lines of verse or poetry.

4. At what age did you start school? Was it 5 like us?
At what age could you leave school?

Reply:- It was 5, like you, and we had to leave school at 15 years.

5. What sort of school outings did you have?

Reply:- The only outings of note was an occasional Saturday morning to the Glasgow Art Galleries for the purpose of painting an object in colour or black and white pencil. The winner for the best object usually got a prize of a book.

6. About how many pupils in each class?

Reply:- Approximately 40 to 45 pupils.

7. Did the less able pupils have to repeat a class? Was there any special remedial class for them?

Reply:- The less able pupils did have a repeat class for one year. No special remedial class was available.

8. Did you have an exam for Secondary school?

Reply:- We had a Qualifying exam at 12 years old, thereafter supplementary classes, one, two, and three at 15 years of age you left school.

9. What sort of games did you play in the playground?

Reply:- The girls had skipping ropes and ball games called beds marked out with chalk. The boys played football with a small tennis ball or in season 'chestnut breaking' by a string attached to the chestnut, this was called conkers.

10. What sort of clothes did you wear to school?

Reply:- I had in my possession photographs of previous classes showing clothing worn, no special uniforms were in vogue in our day. Later a uniform jacket with cap or hat was introduced.

11. Was school milk available?

Reply:- No.

12. Were there toilet facilities in the playground?

Reply:- Yes, there were outside toilets situated in the bottom playground against an outer wall built with white enamelled brick having a communal fireclay trough with separate compartments, one section for boys and the other for girls. They were sometimes frozen in wintertime, later they were discarded for inside toilets with the invention of modern sanitary science.

Having completed the stated questions, one boy asked the teacher if I would answer another question, to which she agreed. His question was:- What was my opinion of video?

My reply was, in my time it was the gramophone or wireless, now replaced by radio and television. My experience with video was not very great, but I was quite sure there would be a place for video in the home as with other modern inventions.

Hereafter I gave a general description of the Lower School being erected in 1875. It was of sound construction being stone with slated roof and spacious classrooms, having six rooms and a hall, used mostly for gymnastics. Later one of the rooms became a dentist surgery. At the time of building it was known as Milngavie Public School, but with the increasing population of Milngavie it became necessary to build a much larger school around 1905. It was a two storey building unlike the lower and smaller school of one storey, which by now became the Infant School. The larger or top school was again of stone construction with a basement and two storeys with twelve classrooms. The basement was laid out with a laundry fully equipped and a pottery for ceramics etc. There was quite a large sized hall, in the class rooms there was a Science Room, Music Room, the remainder being the usual classrooms with two smaller rooms for the teaching staff, one for ladies and the other for gents, the schoolmaster' s room at the boys entrance. An annex building was built on the opposite side of the street to house, two classes, one for Cookery ground floor and Woodwork on the top floor.

When Douglas Academy was built at Mains Estate, the school became known as Milngavie Primary School as it exists today. The annex building was surplus to requirements and was demolished. A considerable number of pupils still attend the existing school today.

A few days after my visit to the school I met Mrs Reid the head teacher and Mrs Leslie the assistant head teacher and was invited to attend the end of term assembly in the Milngavie Town Hall to present the prizes at the ceremony with a short speech, this was an additional honour I could not refuse.

On the 17th June 1985 I received the following letter from Mrs Reid, head teacher:-

Dear Mr Gardner,

Firstly let me thank you most sincerely for the time you have spent in the school enchanting and entertaining the Primary 7's with your wealth of information not only about the school but about Milngavie in general.

I am writing to give you the final arrangements for Thursday 20th June, our end of term assembly in the Town Hall. We would be most grateful if you could be there before 1.30pm. You will be sitting on the platform with one of our school chaplains and myself.

I look forward to seeing you then.

yours sincerely,
Christine Reid,
Head Teacher.

I duly attended the term assembly in the Town Hall. It was quite an occasion. The hall appeared to be at full capacity with parents and pupils. After I had made the presentation of prizes, giving me great pleasure and happy memories of my schoolboy days, I gave a short address to the pupils under the heading of first health, second education, third self discipline, fourth finance. The audience were most attentive and the reception quite extraordinary at the finish. I was presented with a lovely copper plate picture of my business premises in Station Road by one of the senior pupils. That now has a prominent position in my dwelling house, a great honour indeed.

In 1987 I was again involved with the pupils in what was called a "Milngavie Study". My discussion on this occasion was a general run down of old Milngavie and the necessity for a Central Area Pedestrianisation Scheme or Precinct, the pupils were Primary 5.

"Before my retirement from the Bearsden and Milngavie District Council I was Convenor of Planning and Building Control. Also, my job was made more simple by the fact I was born in Milngavie.

The main reason for Pedestrianisation is traffic congestion, that being the case a by-pass road was called for as it was not an economical proposition to attempt to widen the existing Station Road, in addition it was beneficial to use the track of the railway which once served the Paper Mill as a road. The main Primary is connected to Mugdock Road and the underpasses the shopping centre. The existing buildings on the shopping area could remain, they are much less entangled one with another than they would have been if sweeping changes had been proposed and pedestrian shopping much simpler. It was very much easier to construct car parking with some minor alterations. The final design proposals were submitted to the Secretary of State Mr George Younger for approval.

Approval for the design was passed, but some delay in the financial arrangements took place, and I was delegated along with the District Burgh Surveyor and County Surveyor to have an interview with the Secretary of State after a full explanation was given to the Minister."

Having answered some questions from the pupils they seemed satisfied with my visit.

Within the next week I received a letter from all the pupils in their own writing as follows, it was very amusing and very kind:-

Milngavie Primary School
Hillhead Street
Milngavie
Glasgow G62 8AG

Friday 13th March 1987

Dear Mr Gardner,

Thank you very much for coming to see us on Wednesday. We really enjoyed what you had to say about old Milngavie.

The most interesting thing you told me was the Railway Inn. I never knew about it, or how the band used to play outside it.

Also I have always wondered how Milngavie got its name and so has my aunt.

I was very interested in the opening of the waterworld because My Great Grandfather was the caretaker of Mugdock Reservoir so my Grandfather was brought up in the Reservoir House, and he has sat on the Chair that Queen

Victoria sat on to open the waterworks.

What you said about Gavins Mill Wheel which powered the machinery interested me the most, I had not heard of that before.

I liked the part when you told our class about you as a baby, and how one of your older brothers left you in Lennox Park.

I thought that everything you said was interesting especially the part about Mansefield. I live in Baljaffray where you said there used to be a coal mine, and they used to walk down to Highland Road.

I was very interested in the Chemist which used to be an Inn, and the square patch outside the Chemist was where the band sat and played to the people who came off the train.

It was very interesting how the building across the road was used for cooking classes for the girls and woodwork for the boys.

I was very interested especially in the building of the precinct because my grandfather was the Provost at that time and he helped with it as well.

I was interested in the rings of the Black Bull being used for tying up horses. I've often wondered why they were there.

The most interesting thing you told us was how Milngavie got its name, also my Dad is thinking of taking the ginger beer bottle to the Lillie Art Gallery for the Milngavie Exhibition.

I enjoyed hearing about the oldest buildings and what they were, also I was dying to know what Milngavie was like before it was pedestrianised, now I know.

You told me a lot I did not know about Milngavie it was interesting to know about the buildings that used to be in the village, also I did not realise how recent cars are.

We all liked hearing about the letter to Mrs Thatcher to tell her about the conditions of Lennox Hospital, and how she <u>did</u> do something about the conditions.

It was very good of you to come even when you had to say a speech later on at night. I hope you will come and see us again.

Thank you again.

Yours sincerely,

All the boys and girls of P5.

Herewith is my reply to the boys and girls of Class P5.

"Clavie"
2 North Campbell Avenue
Milngavie

21/3/87

<u>To the Boys and Girls of Class P5</u>

Dear Friends,

I am in receipt of your lovely letter to me dated Friday 13th March 1987, it was very kind of you and I thank you most sincerely, it was a pleasure for me to come back to my old school room where I was taught so many years ago.

Our discussion appears to have been quite successful, according to what you write, you have been most attentive, and did not miss much of what I was saying, therefore I must compliment you on the questions raised, we did cover quite a lot of ground with the time ai our disposal.

Should there be any further questions you would like to ask, give a note to your teacher and she will convey them to me, you are very fortunate to have a teacher like Mrs Millar.

Yours sincerely,

John M Gardner.
<u>M.I.B.E., R.P., M.I.P., J.P.</u>

Dear Mrs Reid and Mrs Leslie,

Just a short note to state how much I enjoyed being back to have a discussion with the pupils of P5 and the nice letter I received from the Boys and Girls, I thought it was wonderful.

Enclosed is a reply for the pupils which I hope will be in order, they are very lucky to have a teaching staff like yourselves.

Wishing you all the best.

Yours sincerely,

John M Gardner.

9th April 1987

Milngavie Primary School

Dear Mr Gardner,

As you are aware the pupils of Milngavie Primary School P1-P7 have been studying many aspects of Milngavie, past and present, over the past few weeks. You, with other members of our community, have contributed generously of your time and expertise in either visiting the School, allowing the children to visit you or providing resources.

This is the first time this type of study in this form has been attempted and for the first effort we are pleased with the work produced. Displays from each class will be on view in our G.P. room in the upper school on the afternoon of Thursday 9th April at 2.30pm.

You are warmly invited to attend our celebration "cutting of cake", on that day you will again have the opportunity to speak with the class teacher.

It is our intention to have a large photograph taken to mark the occasion, so should it be that you are unable to attend in person, we would be grateful if you could arrange for a substitute to come along to represent the help which you gave.

Yours sincerely,

Christine Reid,
Head Teacher.

LETTER TO MRS MARGARET THATCHER

I now turn to an important matter that happened during 1986. It was with much concern I found it necessary to communicate direct to Mrs Margaret Thatcher, Prime Minister on 26th June 1986, as follows:-

The Right Hon Mrs Margaret Thatcher M.P. Prime Minister
No 10 Downing Street London.

Dear Prime Minister,

Enclosed please find a short report drawing attention to a very vexed question in this large area, if only something could be done it would be appreciated by a large number of people in the community.

I am not sure if the information given by me should be private and confidential for yourself or not, you will know best how to deal with it.

Yours faithfully,

J M Gardner.

John M Gardner J.P.
"Clavie" 2 North Campbell Avenue
Milngavie
Dunbartonshire
Thursday 26th June 1986.

Report with enclosure on separate page overleaf

The Rt Hon Mrs Margaret Thatcher M.P.
Prime Minister,
No 10 Downing Street London.

Dear Prime Minister,

Lennox Castle Mental Handicap Hospital Stirlingshire
Subject:- Hut No 3 Female Accommodation

May I be allowed to draw attention to the following, Hut No 3 was built in 1941 as temporary accommodation for soldiers, it consists of wood with asbestos cladding, at present there are 28 Patients, the toilet and washing facilities are very much below standard, the clothing supplied either by the hospital or some from the relations of

Milngavie Town Council would show.

Here is another situation caused by yours truly on a different subject and much more pleasant.

Milngavie Weeks 21st Birthday

It all started with another simple question by Bailie Gardner, lets have a "Milngavie Week". I have already given details of how it happened in 1966 and now we have just celebrated 21 years on, how time goes by for which I had a special invitation during the final night and enjoyed it very much.

I herewith quote a message given by Provost R W Robinson for the occasion.

Milngavie Weeks 21st Birthday

Happy 21st Birthday
Its Milngavie Week time again
That is good news
The event that all in the District should mark in their diaries. As you can see by the programme a varied number of events have been arranged by the hard working Milngavie Week Committee for your enjoyment. Everything from Aero-modelling through the alphabet to Youths Variety Show. Old favourites and new ideas. Something for everyone. Show your support by attending your Week "Milngavie Week" and enjoy yourselves and make it a very happy 21st.

R W Robinson

Message from Mr Ian Galloway. Chairman Milngavie Week Committee.

Dear Reader,

Frequently, when I'm out and about in business or pleasure, people ask me where I live. When I say "Milngavie" I get the usual, "Where's that?" or "Spell it" remarks, but often the response is "Oh, its a lovely place - "its kept its village atmosphere". At times like that I realise how easy it is to take our "good life" for granted.

This year we celebrate 21 years of Milngavie Week and I hope you will enjoy the events that have been paid on for your entertainment and enjoyment. I hope you will be able to renew old friendships and possibly make new ones. We hope to bring a little comfort to those much less fortunate than ourselves, struggling for existence in the drought and famine stricken areas of the world. Our newest event is a "Knit-In" and you will find details of the project later in the programme. I'm sure that our community effort will set a precedent that others will gladly try to match.

MILNGAVIE ART CLUB AND LILLIE ART GALLERY

The Art Club goes back to the First World War. The building of the Robert Lillie Art Gallery provided the opportunity for the development of the Club' activities under the Presidency of A Gordon Thomas, R.S.W. My interest in art started in 1917 when as a pupil under Mr Hannah, our school art teacher, we were given the necessary instruction in painting with colour and black and white.

I used to sit next to Mr Hannah's son Andrew, who later in life was responsible for the Burrell Collection in Glasgow. We were allowed to visit the Kelvingrove Art Galleries in Glasgow on Saturdays to do drawings of various objects, it was most enjoyable.

At the age of seventeen when I was serving my apprenticeship in the building trade, my firm was doing an alteration to a mansion house at Bardowie called "Robinsfield", at that time owned and occupied by a well known artist called Mr McAuley Stevenson, he was a brother of Mr Stevenson a Lord Provost of Glasgow.

For some reason I became quite friendly with this famous artist, he would give me money to buy cigarettes in Milngavie for him for which I received quite a good tip. However one day, he asked me if I knew about art, and I related to him my experience in drawing at Kelvingrove Art Gallery, so he said, "come into my studio and tell me what you think of this oil painting I have just completed, it has been sold and is going to a purchaser in America."

It was quite a large studio, without thinking I walked up to about three yards of the picture and he let me go while he stood some 20 yards away, suddenly he shouted to me "come back boy, you know nothing about art." He asked me what did I see. I was quite honest and said I did not understand the colouring. He took me by the hand to about 15 yards from the painting and said "look now and tell me what you see", Do you know, it was the most beautiful picture I had ever seen. Now he said, "let that be a lesson to you, never go up close to an oil painting again", for which I duly thanked him.

I was most fortunate to meet and discuss art in various forms with local artists during my school days and later through my business.

I shall always remember as a boy in the Boys Brigade, the sketches and lectures given on Sunday mornings at the Bible Class by Mr T.M. Kelly of Dunrowan House, Tannoch Drive, Milngavie, it was captivating. I also had a few conversations with Mr Forrester Wilson of Clober Road, Milngavie.

Mr Campbell Mackie of Buchanan Street Milngavie, an architect and member of The Glasgow School of Art I found a lovely gentleman to discuss both art and architecture with and of course, Mr William and Mrs Mary Armour of Clober Road, Milngavie. It was a pleasure to do business with and discuss various topics, both local teachers and artists were very distinguished. Jean Irwin, Strathblane Road, Milngavie was an artist and hard worker for Milngavie Art Club.

Two gentlemen I shall never forget, Major General J.M. Macfie and Professor A.L. Macfie of Heathfield Drive, Milngavie and Glasgow University. How often I visited their house and the cups of tea I received, they were real friends to me and the picture gallery in the house was quite exquisite. They were great benefactors to the Lillie Art Gallery.

A. Gordon Thomas, President of the Lillie Art Gallery, living at Strathblane Road, Milngavie, presented me with a Water Colour portrait, painted in 1930, of Baldernock Wood and Cottage, to all these people I was most grateful.

I have left the name of Mr Robert Lillie to the last as there is a special story connected with this great man, who lived at Tannoch Loch, Heathfield Drive, Milngavie, with his family of sisters and brothers. Although I knew the family through business, it was also through my late wife in 1949 whilst as a sister at Cloberfield Nursing Home in Milngavie. She nursed Robert Lillie in his final illness and he presented her with a black and white portrait "Near Milngavie" signed with the artists complements and best wishes, showing Dumgoyne and Ben Lomond in the distance. This portrait now hangs in a very prominent position in my dwelling house. All this happened one week before he died.

Another more pleasant experience I had was when as a Local Councillor in Milngavie Town Council. In my younger days I was employed by Mr Currie, the local plumbing, electrical and heating engineer. He had an adopted daughter, Miss Cathie Currie, who later became a Mrs Sheran and lived in Aberdeen. One day I received a telephone call from her aunt in Clober Road, Milngavie, stating that I would shortly be receiving a portrait in oils painted by Robert Lillie of Cathie Currie nee Sheran and would I present it to the Town Council for onward transmission to the Lillie Art Gallery. This indeed was a great pleasure for me to do and it is now in the Gallery's collection.

Herewith is a short extract taken from the 25th Anniversary of the Lillie Art Gallery, 1987.

Robert Lillie

Robert Lillie, the eldest in a family of nine, was born in Edinburgh in 1867. When Robert was five the family moved to Glasgow where he was educated and where somewhat reluctantly he followed his father's profession and entered the British Linen Bank in 1882. He remained with the bank until 1925, when he retired after 43 years service.

At the same time as he started work in the bank Robert Lillie began attending evening classes for art and after passing the examinations for Art Class Teachers and the Masters Certificate of South Kensington, he joined the life class of Glasgow School of Art under Fra Newberry. He taught at evening classes for several years until his work at the bank became too demanding.

As well as teaching, he exhibited regularly at the Royal Glasgow Institute of Fine Arts, the Royal Scottish Academy, Greenock and Paisley Art Clubs. When he retired he devoted his time to painting and in his studio at the family home "Spouston" in Tannoch Drive, Milngavie, he produced many oils, watercolours and etching of mainly landscape subjects. His interest in art led him to become one of the founders of Milngavie Art Club, along with such distinguished artists as Willie and Mary Armour.

When Robert Lillie died in 1949 he left, apart from small bequests to members of the family, the bulk of his estate and his collection of paintings to the Burgh of Milngavie to be used to erect an art gallery for the benefit of the citizens of the town.

The Lillie Art Gallery which is situated in the centre of the old burgh of Milngavie and is adjacent to the new town hall is now part of the district of Bearsden and Milngavie. The Gallery was built in 1962 with a bequest of £23,000 left by Robert Lillie plus a large collection of his own paintings. These paintings formed the nucleus of a permanent collection which was later transformed into an important collection of 20th Century Scottish Art. This was achieved by the annual purchase grant made available by the Burgh Council, who took over the running of the new Gallery, and also by the gifts of some notable local benefactors.

From its humble beginning in 1962, this collection has grown steadily and now consists of over 280 items. Its scope has broadened to include a small collection of glass, ceramics and sculpture. The emphasis of the collection is on 20th century and contemporary Scottish works of art.

The Gallery has from the beginning been extremely fortunate in its benefactors who have gifted a number of notable paintings to the collection.

A fine example of work by the Scottish Colourists is "The Studio" by F C B Caddell, which was presented to the Gallery by Gilbert Innes. Most of the works in the collection by the Glasgow Boys were the result of the generosity of Professor A L MacFie and his brother Major General J M MacFie, who between them did much to enhance and strengthen the growing permanent collection.

More recently the gift of 59 working drawings by the late Joan Eardley from Mrs P M Black, has not only considerably increased the Gallery's collection of works by this distinguished artist, but also established a good study collection as an adjunct to the paintings on display.

The purchasing policy of the Gallery has been such that it now has a good representation of work by 2Oth century Scottish Artists and tries wherever possible to fill gaps in the existing collection. Notable purchases have included "Inconostases" by Sir Robin Philipson, "Magic Picture No 68" by Alan Davie, "Summer Bouquet" by Sir William McTaggart and "White Flowers in a Bowl" by Anne Redpath.

More recent attempts have been made to strengthen the print collection with purchases of works by Adrian Wisniewski, Peter Howson and Bruce McLean. The continuing generosity of Mr W Bowie has made it possible to add to the collection work by Elizabeth Blackadder. The growth and development of the collection in its first twenty-five years has been impressive. It is to be hoped that Robert Lillie would feel very proud of this achievement and that the Lillie Art Gallery can continue to develop its objective of providing the residents of the District with a place for the study and enjoyment of art well into the 2lst century.

CONTINUAL GROWTH AND DEVELOPMENT

With continual growth and development within the Burgh, I found it necessary to engender a greater communal spirit, to bring together the people of the community new and old.

I made an attempt to resuscitate the original Milngavie Highland Games. I was not successful for the reason that at that time the then Provost was John M. Buchanan, my role being that of Senior Magistrate. It was evident to me that he wanted to start a Milngavie Pipe Band as he himself was a keen piper; needless to state he got his pipe band started.

However not to be outdone, I came up with the idea of having a "Milngavie Week". Further, I was prepared to put my money where my mouth was and contribute a certain amount of my own money if the Council would also make a contribution, provided the amount I would make would be kept a secret and not disclosed. To my great pleasure the Council agreed to the terms and a "Milngavie Week" started in 1966 under the Chairmanship of Councillor Angus Chapman, I was a member of the committee that first year.

The following year I was made Convener of Planning and Future Development in the Council and with the Central Re-Development of Milngavie going on I was unable to remain on the committee, but it was in the very capable hands of the Chairman, Angus M Chapman. While it started off as an experiment and exercise in community co-operation, it is now over 21 years and still going strong, thanks to the people of Milngavie themselves.

Milngavie Week 21st Birthday

It all started with another simple question by Bailie Gardner, "lets have a "Milngavie Week". "I have already given details of how it hppened in 1966 and now we have just celebrated 21 years on, how time goes by for which I had a special invitation during the final night and enjoyed it very much.

I herewith quote a message given by Provost R W Robinson for the occasion.

Milngavie Weeks 21st Birthday

Happy 21st Birthday
Its Milngavie Week time again
That is good news

The event that all in the District should mark in their diaries. As you can see by the programme a varied number of events have beeen arranged by the hard working Milngavie Week Committee for your enjoyment. Everything from areo-modelling through the alphabet to Youths Variety Show. Old favourits and new ideas. Something for everyone. Show your support by attending your "Milngavie Week" and enjoy yourselves and make it a very happy 21st.

R W Robinson

<u>Message from Mr Ian Galloway. Chairman Milngavie Week Committee.</u>

Dear Reader,

Frequently, when I'm out and about in business or pleasure, people ask me where I live. When I say "Milngavie" I get the usual, "Where's that?" or "Spell it" remarks, but often the response is "Oh, its a lovely place - "its kept its village atmosphere". At times like that I realise how easy it is to take our "good life" for granted.

This year we celebrate 21 years of Milngavie Week and I hope you will enjoy the events that have been laid on for your entertainment and enjoyment. I hope you will be able to renew old friendships and possibly make new ones. We hope to bring a little comfort to those much less fortunate than ourselves, struggling for existence in the drought and famine stricken areas of the world. Our newest event is a "knit-in" and you will find details of the project later in the programme. I'm sure that our community effort will set a precdent that others will gladly try to match.

This year we have tried to capture the spirit of earlier Milngavie Weeks by reviving some events from "weeks" gone by, and by reproducing some snippets from previous programmes that we hoped you will find interesting.

May I extend my thanks to a hard working committee, to our various sponsors, Strathclyde Regional Council, Bearsden and Milngavie District Council and Council staff members, our advertisers, and the many individuals, who all help to make Milngavie Week possible. We have "done our bit", now it's up to you to enjoy.

Yours,

Ian Galloway,
Chairman Milngavie Week Committee.

I am now the proud owner of a cloth manuscript presented to me by Mr Ian Galloway as Chairman of the Milngavie Week Committee in 1986 as follows "1966-1986 Milngavie Week Award", which now hangs in the hall of my house, along with other momentos of honours achieved during my period of association with all the other activities I was interested in.

Casket

Before going further there is one item of interest in connection with the building of the new town hall in case it may be overlooked.

On laying the foundations of the Town Hall, a small compartment in the concrete was made and in this compartment a casket containing all types of coins, small articles made locally and a copy of local newspapers etc., are contained therein, so that future generations will be in a position to acquire knowledge of the past.

This was done on the instructions of Mr Arthur Millar the then Burgh Surveyor and Sanitary Inspector for whom I had the greatest respect.

GEORGE BENNIE RAILPLANE

As a young boy I used to visit a factory site at Burnbrae on the Milngavie Road called the Turkey Red Bleaching Company and admire the large overhead steam pipes that crossed over the road. It was one of the number of Bleaching Companies around the Burgh of Milngavie in the early days of steam, however most of the trade was being transferred to England and the closure of the factory was inevitable. The site had an old railway siding and it was here a rather unique feat of structural steel engineering took place and Milngavie became known nationally and even internationally in 1923 with the advent of the "George Bennie Railplane". The design of the coach was similar to a train bullet in appearance and slightly longer than a train coach. At each end it had blades like an aircraft with wheels in the formation of a bogie. It travelled overhead on a rail and gave the utmost security and safety. The advanced system meant no interference with the permanent way underneath the railplane. The air screws of this revolutionary invention could be driven by an internal combustion engine or electricity, giving rapid acceleration combined with high speed with safety.

The interior of the railplane was in the luxury class, much above the standard set by first class rail coaches. Seating was of the armchair type with round tables adorned with reading lamps. The windows were curtained and the central aisle carpeted.

Each car could carry fifty or one hundred passengers, running singly or as a complete train, truly a magnificent invention. For a fee of one shilling anyone could go to Burnbrae, sit in the coach and enjoy the trial run. The track was 426 yards long, it was out of this world. It was designed for speeds of up to 150 mph, but for the growth of commercial aviation something might have come of this project, and one still hears of successful monorails inspired by the Bennie experiment in Germany and Japan. Like a lot of other Scottish inventions due to a depression and lack of capital it foundered. There is no doubt Bennie was far ahead of his time. From time to time this must have been discussed by railway executives when assessing the cost of electrification in the United Kingdom and realising that this was an opportunity missed.

As the years went by, the residents still watched to see when this engineering wonder would take off. No one doubted that the project had to be abandoned and dismantled for scrap in 1957, it was a wonder of the age.

The company which built the railplane, had also built the record-breaking airship R.34. Yes, indeed, the world can be a cruel place at times. Evolution can be wonderful, unfortunately sometimes we go forward, at other times backward.

Storm Damage, January 20th, 1984

Storms and Snow bring chaos and confusion to area

The storms of last week followed by near blizzard conditions this week have caused widespread damage and confusion throughout Milngavie, Bearsden and districts.

Last week Bearsden and Milngavie District Councils workmen were working overtime to repair damage to roofs, chimneys, skylights and windows.

In addition, all 500 plants in the stock at Mayholme Nursery were destroyed as frost attacked them through broken panes of glass, and plants were also lost at the Crossveggate Nursery.

The workmen were also called out to repair a cupola at Kilmardinny House and 15 headstones were blown over in the New Kilpatrick Cemetery, Hillfoot.

The main problem this week was the snow which meant repairs on outstanding storm damage could not be carried out and any roof work was deemed too dangerous.

According to Mr Bill Dudgeon, Director of Technical Services for the District, the damage is as bad as during the severe winter of two years ago. However, he said, the damage was not enough to drive people out of their houses as is happening in other parts of the country.

Accidents:- Milngavie police reported there had been five accidents in the area over the weekend, but none of them were serious and only one person was slightly injured, and there was a word of praise for the local drivers for taking heed of the warnings of the dangerous conditions.

However, Balfron police criticised drivers for abandoning their cars unnecessarily, particularly around Queen's View on the Stockiemuir Road, where cars had blocked one lane of the road as their drivers skied on the hills.

They asked drivers to have a "little thought" before leaving their cars. The abandoned cars made it difficult for buses to pass, they also hindered snow-clearing operations.

Trees:- While gritters have been out they have found it especially difficult to keep the roads clear as the blizzards continue and the operations have been made additionally difficult as the storms have blown trees down over the roads.

Trees were blown down on the A875 road between Balfron and Killearn, the A81 at the Glengoyne Distillery, and at Weavers Winnel at Balfron, all of which blocked the road for some time. All over the area children were being sent home early to avoid the worst of the weather conditions.

Gales:- The gales of last week caused much destruction, but none in the district proved as spectacular as the "misplaced" garage roof which ended up 15ft up a tree at North Campbell Avenue, Milngavie.

The roof of the garage was perched precariously on top of a garden hut belonging to former councillor Mr John M. Gardner, and the sides of the garage, which were blown from a neighbours garden was seen lying on top of Mr Gardner's boat.

The Milngavie area was blocked out as a power cut stopped the electricity supply to 150,000 consumers throughout the north-east of Glasgow. At 3.02 the lights went out after a main transmission line was damaged and it was not until 4.35 that power was restored.

A spokesman for the South of Scotland Electricity Board blamed the weather for the failure, saying that they were investigating the possibilities of lightning or slush being the cause.

While the cut went on for just over one-and-a-half hours, commuters were virtually unaffected. A spokesman for British Rail said "The effect of the cut was minimal on rail services".

AN INVENTION

"An Improved Aluminium Solder"

During 1940 I did research work on an improved aluminium solder with some very satisfactory results. Having achieved this I found it necessary to employ a chartered patent agent, being J. Alfred Brewer, 58 St. Vincent Street, Glasgow, who were very interested and forwarded a complete specification for Patent Rights to the Patent office London as follows.

Patents and Designs Act, 1907 to 1940
Aluminium Solder No 8842, 12th July 1941.

Complete Specification
"An improved aluminium solder"

I, John Mitchell Gardner, A British Subject, of 16 Duncraig Street, Inverness, formerly of 7 Strathblane Road, Milngavie, Glasgow, do hereby declare the nature of this invention and in what manner the same is to be performed, to be particularly described and ascertained in and by the following statement:-

Difficulty has been experienced in effectively soldering aluminium. It appears that a film develops very rapidly on the surface of the aluminium and hinders proper adhesion, and, moreover, soldered joints in aluminium, although they may appear to be good, rapidly deteriorate and disintegrate when exposed to the atmosphere. Various more or less complicated soldering processes and materials have been evolved without much success.

The present invention refers to an improved aluminium solder which can be simply applied.

According to the invention, an aluminium solder is used which is made by melting together and mixing in sheet form and block tin, ie commercially pure tin. Some variation may be made in the proportions of zinc and tin but in general it is found that the proportions of two parts by weight of zinc to three parts of tin give an effective solder.

With this or approximately this proportion of tin, the optimum tinning action of the solder on the aluminium seems to be obtained, in conjunction with satisfactory hardness. If the zinc content is higher, a harder joint is obtained, but the adhesion is not so good. If the tin content is increased, good adhesion can be obtained, but the joint tends to be too soft.

Using the solder described above no flux is required and the operation of soldering can be performed with an ordinary soldering bolt.

In carrying the invention into practice, each of the aluminium parts to be joined is scraped or rubbed until the bare metal is exposed. The bare metal part is quickly tinned with the solder, using an ordinary copper or iron soldering bolt, heated somewhat higher than is used for ordinary soldering. The two tinned surfaces in contact and a heated soldering bolt is applied to fuse the tinning, more solder is applied if necessary. For soldering sheet aluminium, it is not generally necessary to use a blow lamp with the improved solder, but for heavier material the use of a blow lamp may be desirable.

Having now particularly described and ascertained the nature of my said invention and in what manner the same is to be performed, I declare that what I claim is:-

The manufacture of aluminium solder by melting together and mixing zinc in sheet form and block tin i.e. commercially pure tin.

The manufacture of aluminium solder according to Claim 1, characterised by the proportion of zinc to tin used being about two parts by weight of zinc to three parts of tin.

Aluminium solder when made in accordance with Claim 1 or 2.

Dated this 6th day of August 1942.

<u>An Invention. Improved Aluminium Solder</u>

<u>To the Director of Scientific Research</u>
<u>Ministry of Supply, Great Westminster House, London SW1</u>
<u>for onward transmission to the Minister of Aircraft Production.</u>

Sir,

I take the liberty of writing to you on the subject of soldering aluminium.

In the first place, I may state that I am a master plumber by trade and well versed in the trade both the theoretical and the practical points of view.

It is generally accepted that aluminium is a difficult metal solder. I know that various proposals have been made regarding aluminium solder, but as far as I know these are either too elaborate for ordinary use or are not satisfactory in practice. Besides the difficulty in obtaining proper adhesion of the solder, even if this is obtained the joint tends to disintegrate under atmospheric and other influences, often very quickly.

I have experimented in the production of an aluminium solder and have evolved a solder which is very simply applied. Enclosed are two samples of soldered joints. As you will see, the adhesion is very strong. Moreover, I have tested the durability of the jointing by exposing the jointed metal in a wet condition to the atmosphere, by immersing it in water for a time, and by wetting it and keeping it wet with a solution of washing soda. I have applied for a patent for the solder and I am writing to enquire whether your department is interested i.e. whether to your knowledge there is a need for a really satisfactory aluminium solder.

If you are interested, I shall be glad to supply you with particulars.

Thanking you in anticipation of an early reply.

Yours faithfully,
John M Gardner

7 Strathblane Road,
Milngavie,
Glasgow.
23/7/1941.

Reply from Ministry of Aircraft Production 13/8/41

Ministry of Aircraft Production, Millbank SW1

Dear Sir,

Your letter dated the 23rd July, on the subject of aluminium solder to the Ministry of Supply, has been forwarded to this department for attention.

In reply, I am to say that as the requirements of the Ministry in this respect are satisfied, it is regretted that advantage cannot be taken of your offer.

Nevertheless, the Department wish to thank you for your interest, and for the trouble you have taken in bringing the matter to notice.

Yours faithfully,
J H Lyle,
for Director of Scientific Research.

J M Gardner,
7 Strathblane Road,
Milngavie, Glasgow.

Commercial Letter to Messers Bulpitt and Sons Ltd.

On the 18th of August 1941 I wrote to Messers Bulpitt and Sons giving them details of my invention, their trade mark being Swan Brand Aluminium hardware, electric kettles, cooking and heating appliances, with samples for inspection and interest, as they are the most important firm in Great Britain in aluminium.

On the 20th of August 1941 I received the following letter from Mr Walter H. Bulpitt, Director.

Mr John M Gardner
7 Strathblane Road
Milngavie
Glasgow

Dear Sir,

We are in receipt of your letter of the 18th instant, and have inspected your samples with interest.

From visual inspection the samples appear to be quite satisfactory and the material has retained its hardness.

We should carry out a number of tests on the samples to satisfy ourselves as to durability and the strength of the soldered joint. We are enclosing you herewith a few sample strips, and would be glad if you would solder them together with 1/4" overlap for this purpose.

We have used aluminium solder of our own manufacture between 25/30 years now, and the only way to ascertain what additional value your patent has would be to carry out the tests referred to.

Will you be good enough to let us know on what basis you are prepared for us to handle your patent in the event of our taking same up?

You are probably aware that the use of aluminium at the present time is prohibited for any articles except for Service requirements, and to these they do apply very stringent tests, and would not allow it to be used without considerable delay to enable them to approve of the method.

However, if you will let us have the details asked for, we shall be pleased to go further into the matter.

yours faithfully,
pp Bulpitt and Sons Ltd.,
Walter H. Bulpitt
Director.

On the 24th December 1942 the situation had become very complicated as I was by that time called to the Services and was stationed at the time at Fort William, Inverness-shire as Chief Technician to the Deputy Commander Royal Engineers, when I received the following letter from J. Alfred Brewer Patent Agents, Glasgow.

J.M. Gardner Esq.
c/o Major T.R. Wray D.C.R.E.
DCRE Office Fort William, Inverness-shire

Dear Sir,

Patent No 8842 dated 12th July 1941

We have received a query from the Patent Office, London. In your specification you speak of the use of sheet zinc. The citations simply refer to zinc. We hardly think it likely that there is any substance in this difference, but we would be interested to know whether there is any distinction. It has also been pointed out it will be a considerable time before a settlement can take place. In the meantime you can keep the recipe of the solder to yourself as far as possible, use the solder in your own practice, and sell it to others, and thus probably reap some advantage, however we would be glad of your observations.

Yours faithfully,
J. Alfred Brewer.

Having considered all the circumstances it was clear to me as I had no facilities to continue, or time to negotiate due to my war service it was impossible to continue until hostilities ceased.

At the end of the War I purchased the business of plumbing, electrical and heating engineers where I served my apprenticeship. My life had changed and I found it was not possible to continue owing to the circumstances in which I found myself. In any case I found out recently someone had found a solution quite near to my own and it would not have been wise to incur further expense in the prosecution of the patent application.

It is quite interesting that I still hold samples of aluminium soldering in my possession today 1988, and they are as good now as when they were carried out in 1941, giving great satisfaction.

My experience with the aluminium industry continued during my war service at the different factories.

No. 1 was the aluminium works at Fort William just on the outskirts of the town. They were all hydro-electric, Fort William being served with a water supply from Loch Treig to a fountain head and thereafter by four huge cast iron pipes into the factory. The tail race being discharged into Loch Linnhe. During hostilities one stick of bombs, four in number, landed near the pipes carrying water into the factory, three never went off and one carried on under the pipes without exploding, a most lucky escape. One of the bombs, when defused, was erected at the entrance to the factory with an opening cut near the apex so that money could be deposited for war purposes for the disabled. This being a very important place during the war, a smoke screen was installed at Loch Treig.

No. 2 was at Kinlochleven near Ballachulish district. It was not so large as Fort William but still very important. It was fed by a water supply, the Blackwater reservoir. Here too a smoke screen was in action. The materials being supplied and taken up the hills to the loch by mules and members of the Indian Detachment.

No. 3 was at a small village on the shores of Loch Ness called Foyers, fed by a water supply from Loch Mhor. It was not so lucky as part was temporary put out of action by a bomb during daylight hours, a very brave action, but the plane was shot down over the Forth. I had to witness the damage. However, the works did carry out an important contribution to the war effort.

The part played by the storage of ammunition and the guns, which if an invasion had taken place in that area, were very well protected. Also to the brave soldiers who trained at Achnacarry, of which a monument stands at Spean Bridge today. Yes, we do have a lot to be thankful for.

MY WORLD OF GOLF

Milngavie Golf Club Clubhouse, in 1914 and more recently

Milngavie Rotary Golf Club Cup won by author

The historical origin of golf is obscure, early spelling goff, gouff or gowff. The last form indicates the old pronunciation, although most historians credit its present form to Scotland.

I understand in the British Museum there is a picture from an illuminated book of hours, made in Bruges early in the 16th century, which shows three players, each with a ball and club, putting at a hole in the ground.

The earliest Scottish reference to golf is in connection with the Fourth Earl of Montrose who lived at Mugdock Castle. He was a quiet country gentleman. He seems to have been much occupied, latterly, with domestic matters, and spent a good deal of his time in golfing and archery; also he was much addicted to tobacco.

Some years ago there were discovered at Kinnaird House the account of James Duncan, who is styled "Burgess of Glasgow Factor of Mugdock", and also the accounts of the Factors of the other estates. Opposite are a few extracts from the account:

We know that golf was played over nine holes at Milngavie since before 1625.

Golf has been known since old times as the "Royal and Ancient" game. James IV is the first who figures formally in the golfing record, followed by James V and by his daughter Mary Stuart who was "seen playing golf and pallmall in the fields of Seton" a few days after the murder of her husband.

James the VI (afterwards James I of England) in 1603 appointed one "William Mayne lower burges of Edinburgh, during all the days of his life time, clubmaster to his Highness".

Associations and Clubs

Golf Clubs began to be founded in the 18th century as follows

The Honourable Company of Edinburgh Golfers	in 1744
The Royal and Ancient Golf Club of St. Andrews	in 1754
The Bruntsfield Links (Edinburgh)	in 1761
The Royal Musselburgh	in 1774
The Royal Aberdeen	in 1780
The Royal Blackheath	in 1787

…of his cousine …ms to have been much occupied …omestic matters, and spent a good deal of his time in golfing and archery, and he was also much addicted to tobacco.

Some years ago there were discovered at Kinnaird House the account of James Duncan, who is styled "Burges of Glasgow, Factor of Mugdok," and also the accounts of the Factors on the other estates. I give here a few extracts—

ITEM given the 12d of Marche, 1625, to Patrik Lytstone for ane dusone goiff balls to my Lord,....................iij lib.

Item to the minister's man that brocht books to my Lord at command....................vj. sh.

Item for iiij unce tobacco to my Lord be the way cumming to Montross from Kincardin, at vij sh. vj d. the unce....................xxx s.

Item given the 14th of Apryle for iij ells ane quarter ell round linning claith to my Lord his black breiks,....................xxiiij sh. vj d.

Item for two dusone tobacco pypes the said day,....................viij. s.

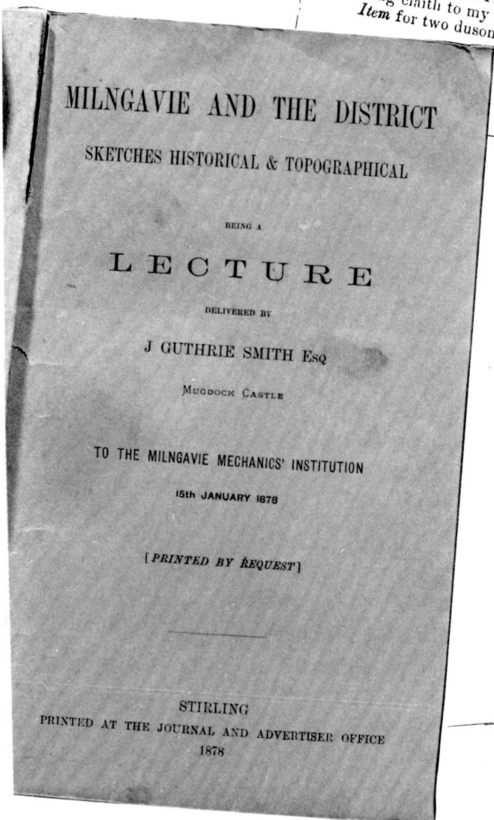
MILNGAVIE AND THE DISTRICT

SKETCHES HISTORICAL & TOPOGRAPHICAL

BEING A

LECTURE

DELIVERED BY

J GUTHRIE SMITH Esq

Mugdock Castle

TO THE MILNGAVIE MECHANICS' INSTITUTION

15th JANUARY 1878

[PRINTED BY REQUEST]

STIRLING

PRINTED AT THE JOURNAL AND ADVERTISER OFFICE

1878

12

Item that day to ane tailzeour that maid ane stand of claiths to my Lord,....................iiij lb.

Item that day for ane pig full of ink to my Lord,....................vij. sh.

Item for half ane pund tobacco sent to the west countrie to my Lord,....................iij lb. viij s. iiij d.

Item for 18 Goff balls to my Lord,....................v lib. viij sh.

Item gevin for tobacco pypes,.....................vj sh.

Item for ane pair of shone to Lord James, the xxvj October, 1623,....................xxvj sh. viij d.

(This "Lord James" was the future "Great Marquis.")

Item for shone to the bairne Beatrix,....................xl sh.

(The "bairne Beatrix" was Lady Beatrix Graham, afterwards Lady Maderty.)

Item on the 29th of September, 1620, for fyve gang of schoone to my Lord's horse before his Lordship raid to Rosedo,....................v lib.

Item for twa gang of schoone to Lord James' *twa* naiges,...xxiiij sh.

We close our extracts with the following letter from Mugdock, … to his Factor at Kincardine:—

Old Manchester	in 1818
The Royal Devon at Westward Ho	in 1864

The were more than a score of clubs at the start of the 19th century, and many of these were still in existence in the middle of the 20th, when there were about 1,800 clubs in the British Isles.

The Royal and Ancient, whose present clubhouse was erected in 1840, is the premier club of the world, with royal personages as captains.

The Royal and Ancient is the supreme authority in golf; it frames and revises the rules, and its decisions are accepted by clubs throughout the world except for the United States, which has its own ruling body. In 1951 the Royal and Ancient and the United States Golf Association agreed upon a uniform code, including the abolition of the stymie. After this the only important difference remaining was the size of the ball: the US ball measures 1.68 inches in diameter, the British 1.62 inches (the weight is constant at 1.62 oz).

The British Open and Amateur championships and the Walker Cup matches, when played in Great Britain, are also under the jurisdiction of the Royal and Ancient.

I suppose like all others matters in life changes take place, especially in the equipment used; Even in my own lifetime the changes from the original feather made golf ball to the later gutty in 1848 to the Heshell rubber ball in 1902 to the modern composition ball. The alteration in golf clubs from the early days from wood to steel shafts, in the manufacture of golf bags in size to hold all the equipment.

Alterations to golf-courses such as putting greens, extended length in courses, clubhouse design, improvement in play.

Golf is now big business with the continuing professional millionaires and sponsorship as other types of sport aided and abetted by television with world wide entertainment. However club golf exists at all levels with so many people able to take part, in my opinion probably the best game in the world. There is no doubt that for myself golf came so much into my life, coming as I did from a working family, if you are prepared to work hard and specialise in any game today, it is possible to reach quite a good standard, with all the pleasure and enjoyment it involves. From my schoolboy days I seem to have overcome considerable difficulties to attain a few honours.

It all started as a small boy when my father took me to see an exhibition golf match at Milngavie Golf Course being played by such famous golfers at that time, consisting of Harry Vardon, James Braid, George Duncan and J.H. Taylor.

The popularity of the game of golf is now more well known and Milngavie and district have no fewer than six courses within bounds.

From a picturesque stand-point, the Milngavie course holds the premier position.

Long ago the line of separation between the Highlands and Lowlands of Scotland was the long chain of hills now known by several names as the Kilpatrick Hills and Campsie Fells.

Dumbarton Castle commanded one extremity and Stirling Castle the other, while here and there the range was pierced by natural passes formed by the river alleys. The central pass, formed by the Stockiemuir and the Allander Valley is of particular interest, for here at the meeting of the north and south, Milngavie Golf Course has been laid out on the lands formerly owned by the Duke of Montrose. At this point the Highlands begin, and here Bailie Nicol Jarvie and young Frank Osbaldistone must have ridden on that memorable tour to the Clachan of Aberfoyle.

From the highest point of the course, aptly termed Mount Zion, there can be obtained a Pisgah view of the broad plain of the Lowlands extending away to the east and south, and a few miles off may be traced the famous Roman vallum which Agricola built to protect the civilisation of the south form the Barbarian hordes of the north.

During alterations on the course some years ago, two ancient urns containing human remains were exhumed. One of the urns is now on exhibition in the Milngavie Club House giving details of the find, the other urn was so badly damaged it was unable to be repaired.

The glamour of romance and historical association are but secondary consideration however to the visitor, this charming, but picturesque upland, along the whole length of the course runs the Allander, a pretty trout stream. Should the player tire of fighting Colonel Bogey, he may find solace in listening to the sermons of the running brook.

The course consists of 18 Holes of the finest ancient turf that has been nibbled and cropped by blackfaced wethers since the days of Rob Roy.

The course was first laid out in 1895, but with the advent of the rubber ball re-arrangement became necessary. After experimenting with various plans the committee, at length, fixed on a permanent course of about 5,000 yds and spent almost £500 in draining and improving the land.

There is a delightful variety of holes, which run from 100 to 460 yds in length, and are abundantly supplied with natural hazards.

The extended course was formally opened by the Marquis of Graham prior to the First World War in 1914, membership being 350, Charles E Cruickshank was secretary and treasurer at that time, John Godley, greenkeeper, the course being 1 1/2 miles from Milngavie Station with the service of a horse and brake from the station to Clober Dam as transport, leaving a few hundred yards to the clubhouse. The entry fee was £7-7/- and annual subscription was £3-3/-.

Monday was recognised as Church Ministers day. It was not unusual for two brake loads consisting of twenty ministers to arrive at the bridge of Clober Pond where the caddies were waiting to carry the golf clubs to the clubhouse and thereafter continue with the clubs round the course. The Ministers were usually from Bearsden or Glasgow.

In fact when I was 15 years of age and had to leave school, employment was not easy and I used to do my caddy occasionally, the fee being in the region of one shilling. It was always something to do.

It was quite an interesting area from the stance at Clober Pond to the Clubhouse. The Pond was made by James Watt, hydraulic engineer and inventor, who married the daughter of Mr Macgregor who lived in Clober House nearby and owned Clober bleachfield.

James Watt planned the water courses and the erection of the machinery for his father-in-law during construction of the bleachfield. He superintended the making of the water courses and erection of machinery which consisted of making a connection to the Allander Water near the Golf Course, leading the supply by a water lode called the long race with sufficient water head to water filters, and from that point to the formation of Clober Pond, the outlet continuing to the works by another lode to a fountain head with control valves. This in turn continued to a water wheel at the level of the works. The water wheel, constructed of buckets, in turn drove the machinery necessary for bleaching, before being discharged back into the Allander Water at a lower level. A very ingenious and economical method of water power, when you consider the law at the time required any water taken from a source of supply must again be discharged into the same source at another point after use.

The works, so long carried on by the late Major Walter Drew, an ex-Provost of the Burgh, under the firm name of Messers James Pender and Sons, have now ceased to exist.

Clober pond became a coup for rubbish by the Milngavie Town Council and the water courses destroyed, in my opinion pure vandalism, something that should have been preserved as a historical monument for all time.

At 16 years of age I was fortunate to acquire a situation to serve an apprenticeship at plumbing and sanitary engineering and did not come in contact with Milngavie Golf Club until 1933. After being a member and Captain of Clober Golf Club, I became a member of Milngavie. My life had changed somewhat and my admission to Milngavie Golf Club turned out to be most fortunate.

It was with some regret I found it necessary to resign from Clober Golf Club as one of the early members of the club where I laid the foundation of my future golf career. I had made many friends, especially the Lyle family. While acting Secretary for a short period I met Mr and Mrs Lyle Senior who originated the course as owner, first as 9 holes and later 18 holes. I had many discussions with Mr Lyle and his wife Bertha - the club was not in a good financial state.

However I did my best to gather in some cash for them by running a stop-watch competition and with some local business people we managed to make ends meet. I also did my best for the Lyle boys who were younger than I was in the playing sense as I was now playing from one of a handicap.

In 1933 with another three trustees I presented the club with their first trophy known as "Silver Trophy". On the 50th Anniversary, being the only trustee now living, the club presented me with a lovely "Silver Salver" in 1984, a great honour indeed.

In 1934, when I left, they were in a better financial state and as a parting gift I was presented with a Westminster chiming clock, it was wonderful.

Time marches on, evolution takes place, I suppose nothing, more or less, remains constant. At the Milngavie Club I received an enthusiastic welcome as I had now become a scratch player. I was allowed to play in the club matches against other clubs, and continued to play for a period of twenty years. Changes were taking place on the course itself and a new clubhouse was being built.

It was at this stage I was asked to become a member of the committee and was appointed Greens Convener. The work consisted of purchasing part of a field from Mr Pirrie, Laighpark Farm, extending the 13th Hole by 150yds, making a new green with sand bunkers. This was a new departure as all the hazards had been natural, plus a few stone dykes crossing the fairways. In fact most of the greens, within the next few years, had sand bunkers installed and new greens made at the 1st, 2nd, 3rd, 6th, 7th, 9th, 10th, alteration at the 4th and 11th (Double green), 10th, 16th, 17th, 18th holes. The last hole,during my time, has been re-made three times due to car parking and lengthening of the hole. Improvement and invention of new machinery, the greens are now larger with wider fairways. In 1988 it was proposed to alter the 6th, 7th and 8th greens, extending the holes as necessary, to upgrade the bogey of the course.

The method used to enable the new clubhouse to be built was as follows. Drumclog Moor was our property, it was sold to the Local Authority for a considerable sum of money, each member paid £100 as a debenture to be repaid. It was a very successful business deal and a lovely new clubhouse was built to replace the existing corrugated and wood structure.

The following statement will clear up any misunderstanding in connection with the sale of courses between Milngavie and Hilton Park Golf Clubs and His Grace the Duke of Montrose of Auldmurroch Estate.

Milngavie Golf Club
"Sale of Golf Course" Joint Negotiations
30th Day of October 1926

His Grace the Duke of Montrose and Auldmurroch Estate
Purchase of Milngavie Golf Course and Proposed North Western also Bankhead by Joint Negotiations
Mr D.K. Michie, Valuator

Auldmurroch and Hilton valued	£1890
Laighpark and Farm	£2520
Milngavie Golf Course	£3250
Drumclog and Farm	£575
Total	£8235

Legal adviser Milngavie Mr Rowley Orr, Solicitor	£4100
Captain Caldwell agreed sum of	
according to original Ratio Acres Milngavie Course 107 acres, Drumclog Farm 100 acres	
purchase from the Duke of Montrose mutually agreed	£4100
Cost of Milngavie Course and Drumclog with Farm	£5150
Cost of Hilton Park and Laighpark with Farm	Total £9250

Payable and Settlement to take place at Whitsunday 15th May 1927

Hon. President Milngavie Golf Club His, Grace the Duke of Montrose
Hon. Vice President Milngavie Golf Club, Lord Alister Graham

The above details were taken from the Milngavie Golf Club Minutes by John M Gardner, J.P., Hon. President of Milngavie Golf Club.

The Sale was duly carried out Dated November 1987

It is also worthy to note on the 10th Day of December 1926, Charles E Cruickshank, secretary and treasurer of Milngavie Golf Club, sent a circular to all members of the club inviting them to a meeting to be held in the Christian Institute, Bothwell Street, Glasgow on the 13th Day of December 1926 for the following reasons:

1. *To consider, and if agreed, resolve, as to the policy the Club should adopt in view of Public advertisement of sale of the Farm of Laighpark, including the Club's Course.*

2. *To decide whether steps should be taken to try and purchase the course, if so resolved.*

3. *To give Committee appropriate instructions and powers. In view of the very great importance of the business I am instructed to ask you if you will make a special effort to be present.*

yours truly,

Chas. E. Cruickshank
Secretary.

The committee were given appropriate instruction and power to negotiate both the sale of the course and Drumclog Farm with the very satisfactory result maintained.

In addition to the Hon. Vice-President, Lord Alister Graham the following were also Hon. Vice Presidents at the time;

Hon. Vice President T. Ripley Ker
" " " Major W. Drew
" " " Chas Ker
" " " J. Rowley Orr (Legal Representative)

I was very fortunate to receive from the secretary of the Hilton Park Golf Club:- A History of Hilton Park, Jubilee Year 1977, it was most interesting.

During my time as a player in the club I was fortunate to win a number of club trophies. One record, of which I am very pleased about, was to win 4 monthly medals in succession and tie for a 5th which I ultimately won with scores of 72 scratch. I may also have brought some honour to the club by winning a number of open competitions.

In 1977 it gave me very great pleasure to present to the club a "Silver Challenge Trophy" as under John M Gardner J.P., it is now known as the John M Gardner Stroke Play Championship" played for annually under scratch conditions.

In 1951 I was elected Captain of the Milngavie Golf Club and in 1976 I was made an Honorary member of the club.

Later at the Annual General Meeting of the club on the 19th of November 1982 I was given the top honour of the Club, being elected Honorary President of Milngavie Golf Club.

On the 1st of January 1983 I had now been a member of the club for 50 years, and was chief guest at the Annual Dinner in February 1983.

How fortunate I was to join Milngavie Golf Club in 1933, I have seen many changes over the years.

One experience worth relating happened one Saturday evening when playing over the course a number of years ago in the company of Gilbert Morris, the local Professional and greenkeeper, who had a hole in one at the 12th hole after playing golf for over fifty years. He was an extraordinary golfer who could play either left or right hand, and had the distinction of going round the course in 72 strokes right hand and left hand. The nearest I ever got to a hole in one was at Clober Club 7th hole, being within 1/4" of an inch from having an ace.

As I am now an octogenarian my world of golf has been like a fairy tale having played with so many distinguished golfers and business associates. It has all been very worth while.

There are many other Sports Clubs and activities, especially since the inauguration of Milngavie Week in 1966, also the beginning of the Bearsden and Milngavie District Council of which I participated in.

Having reached the age of 80 years I have retired from all business life and my son and heir who was in partnership with my firm of John M. Gardner and Son, plumbing, electrical and heating engineers at 31 Station Road, Milngavie, has now become responsible for a further activity, having been in partnership since October 1972.

Outwith his business commitments Iain is keen on all forms of motor and water sports, being a highly successful circuit racing driver having gained a considerable number of awards and records in Scotland.

In water sports his interests are mainly in parakiting and jet ski as instructor, with over 300 appearances and winner of the British Jet Ski Championship in 1982.

Honour for Local Champion, October 1986

Presentation Award

Bearsden and Milngavie District Council have seen fit to present Iain Gardner, Milngavie sportsman, with a certificate of merit for his exploits on the racing track and the water.

The presentation took place at Boclair District Council Chambers, Bearsden, when Provost Ray Robinson presented Iain with the Certificate of Merit. The former British Jet Ski Champion and undefeated driver last year thanked Councillors and the Provost for their appreciation.

It is wonderful how the years go by and you look back on times. One feature has given me considerable pleasure, this was when I received an invitation from the editor of the Milngavie and Bearsden Herald on the 11th of May 1984 to visit their office as something was about to happen in connection with "Milngavie Week" that would be of interest to me, as I was the originator of Milngavie Week in 1966. To me it was a trip down memory lane, and was indeed a worthwhile visit. Herewith is an extract of a feature in the Milngavie Herald that week. It could be quite interesting to a great number of readers.

Milngavie Week has weathered every Storm

Milngavie Week is to have a new trophy this year, forging a link with the very first Milngavie Week 18 years ago.

It has been presented by Bearsden and Milngavie District Council, and will be known as the Angus Chapman Memorial Trophy in honour of Milngavie Week's first chairman. It takes the form of a rosebowl, and dates from the time of the old Milngavie Highland Games, when it was known as the Leitch Trophy.

It has since been in the keeping of the local authority who have now renamed it in memory of the late Angus M. Chapman. It will be offered for competition among Milngavie Week golfers.

The 19th Milngavie Week will run from June 2 to June 10 this year. The first week was held back in 1966 and in the intervening years it has successfully negotiated such obstacles as a series of financial crises, sporadic bouts of apathy, reorganisation of local government, relocation of venue, personality clashes, freak weather. (In 1980 the opening Gala Day was hit by a sudden thunderstorm, and Oakburn Park was awash within minutes).

Storm

Reports of its imminent demise always proved to be exaggerated... Milngavie Week has weathered every storm, and in 1984 seems set to have its most successful season so far.

But after almost 20 years how many people remember how it all began? What were the aims of the men and women who ran the first Milngavie Week, and how far have those objectives been achieved?

There is no doubt that the original idea of holding a week of gala activities to be known as "Milngavie Week" came from local plumber and heating engineer John M Gardner, for many years a member of Milngavie Town Council.

He recalled "In the 'Sixties Milngavie was expanding at a tremendous rate, and it made me sad to find when I call on people in the new housing areas that they often didn't know their neighbours - at one time everyone in Milngavie knew one another.

Events

Bailie Gardner was determined to do something about it, and one night in 1965 at a meeting of Milngavie Town Council, he declared that if the defunct Milngavie Highland Games couldn't be revived the town should instead hold a whole week of gala events, and it should be called Milngavie Week.

The idea was enthusiastically taken up by Provost John M Buchanan and his council. An organising committed was formed and Dean of Guild Angus Chapman became its first chairman.

Interest

When Milngavie ceased to be a Burgh in 1975, and joined Bearsden in a new local authority, the future of Milngavie Week seemed in some doubt.

But reorganisation had a rejuvenating effect. Former chairman, Mrs Elma Choat told me, "To our surprise was the amount of interest shown in Milngavie Week. People seemed to want Milngavie to keep its identity and were keen to support anything that helped in that. As a result we found we had no shortage of committed members and volunteers."

This year's chairman Bill Hastings, told me the Milngavie Week Committee were "cutting costs quite a bit", following last year's deficit of £600.

By moving the Miss Milngavie crowning ceremony into the pedestrian precinct he hoped to bring Milngavie Week "closer to the people", he added, "I'm a great believer in trying to bring the community together". Which takes us back to John Gardner. Looking back over 18 years he summed up, "I'm sure the people of Milngavie have been brought together more by Milngavie Week than by any other single organisation. It's been so good and consistent - and we've been so lucky in the people who interested themselves in it."

EVOLUTION

We have travelled a long way since the Industrial Revolution in 1880. How the world has changed. It would appear to be a much smaller universe when you now consider how we live and have our being. And when you think of all the inventions and discoveries of man, it is very difficult to comprehend that your health is a priority with all the advantages of medical science, although we appear to live faster, it is now possible to live longer.

If I may quote some of the discoveries of modern living, the Nature of the Universe, Political Science, Economics, Modern Science, Mathematics, English Literature, Psychology, Architecture, House and Home, Hobbies and Pastimes, Appreciation of Music. From the above you will appreciate education is a must to try and understand what life is all about in this wonderful world. The big question is what man is doing about it. Dare I venture to suggest we are now entering the outer space age.

Over the years, during bad times and good times Scotland has produced many brilliant men from all walks of life during hostilities and peace on land, sea and in the air, also in the world of industry, commerce, and invention, they have been outstanding. Who will ever forget the famous shipbuilding of all kinds of vessels on the "Clyde Built" ships.

If I may quote just two local inventors of great substance, James Watt of Greenock, with his modern condensing steam-engine, and other uses of steam, married Anne Macgregor a Milngavie lady. The other being John Logie Baird of Helensburgh, inventor and television pioneer. He was the first to achieve television over any distance. Two gentlemen that Scotland can be proud of. There were so many other Scots too numerous to mention in the world of discovery and inventions, above and below ground, on the high seas and in the air, with materials from a simple candle, to water power, coal, iron, steel, oils, gas, electricity, alloys, aluminium, plastics, ionization, lead, copper, acids, building materials, medicine, transmission, spinning and weaving, telecommunication, the atom is an invention, ballistics, nuclear power, etc, etc. There must be thousands of discoveries and inventions.

It has always been fascinating to me that during my lifetime, I have seen and done so many things in transmitting services such as water, sewers, gas, electricity, telephones in pipes and cables underground; For the use of man whether it be in town or country, house and home, factory, place of work, business, pleasure or entertainment.

The world of transport with the construction of roads to suit the inventor of the motor car, construction of railways to suit the modernisation of trains from steam to electric drive, transport by air from airports of huge planes carrying passengers and cargo all over the world, transmission by satellite. Everything seems so much closer to home with all the modern conveniences for speed, and the world appears to be a smaller universe. It is all so highly technical, yet sometimes we have to pay a heavy price by disaster for further advancement to take place. Looking back over the centuries it has been the nature of man that the application of particular methods and techniques of one subject or another has contributed much to general progress.

Modern Times

It has been said "All the world is a stage with all the men and women merely players, they have their entrances and their exits, each man and woman in their turn play many parts". How true.

The progress of science during the 20th century has been little short of miraculous, growth of ideas led to the development of new studies, until now the scope of each is so vast and its ramifications so multitudinous that a whole lifetime is needed to master one simple aspect.

If we consider a few headings it will give some idea of what is happening in the modern world.

Astronomy is the oldest of the sciences.

Physics is the mechanical age with relativity and wave mechanics taking place.

Chemistry closely related to other sciences in the fields of physics and biology in many places, is defined as the investigation of the composition and properties of various substances and of their changes.

Geology, Meteorology and Agriculture, a basic problem of geology in recent years is the calculation of the age of the earth. Discovery of radioactive phenomena in the crust of the earth has aided new theories concerning the earth's supply of heat. One of the most important applications of this science is in the field of prospecting for oil. It is also of great assistance in the detection of water supplies and mineral veins. Echo-sounding has made it possible to map the topography of the submerged continental platforms.

Meteorology

The science made great progress with the discovery of the stratosphere, a region of almost uniform temperature. Radar has found important applications in meteorology, where it is used for the detection of storm centres. Radar methods are also used for the measurement of raindrop size and cloud height, also for forecasting sea conditions on landing beaches and for tracing of waves to the storm centres from which they originate.

Agricultural Science

The interdependence of geology, meteorology and agriculture is evident in many ways: the study of the soil is but one instance where their interests converge. The geologist is interested in the weathering of the rocks (a necessary precursor to soil formation), which is obviously affected by climatic conditions; and the farmer is interested in what the soil will grow. Again, one of the most serious agricultural problems in the world today, particularly in warm dry conditions is the damage caused to good agricultural land by soil erosion: an exhausted or poor-quality soil may have its food-producing capacity revived by suitable manuring or by the application of fertilizers, but on eroded soil it is beyond recovery. Only by preventive measures, such as the planting of trees, is it possible to avoid the loss caused by the ravages of wind and water in removing the fertile surface soil. Another advancing front in the field of agricultural science concerns the development of powerful new weed-killers and insecticides. One of the most effective insecticides recently discovered, commonly known as D.D.T. came into wide and prominent use during World War Two.

A further recent discovery of considerable interest showed that certain insecticidal substances could be absorbed into living plants through the foliage or root system and thus render the whole plant toxic to biting insects, such substances are known as systemic insecticides, to distinguish them from contact insectasides such as D.D.T. which act by direct absorption through the external body-surface of the insect.

The development of new hormonal-type selective weedkillers has only been made possible by a further understanding of the natural chemical substances which regulate the life of plants.

materials science had made available. Nevertheless, a way was being prepared for a new and more homogeneous art of building.

Industrial architecture, including all buildings in which manufacture, purchase, sale, exchange and transport of commodities are carried on has attained a position of peculiar significance in this period, nor has the demand for office and store buildings increased, but factories, steel plants, pit-head gear, power plants etc., have for the first time come to be considered as architectural problems.

Until the 20th century such structures were usually handled by engineers, and architects were called in, if at all, only to add a bit of "dressing" to a predetermined structure. On the other hand, a number of engineer-architects of that period designed such buildings as warehouses and railway stations of real aesthetic merit.

Development in specialized fields of architecture such as theatre, schools, laboratories, shops, with a tendency towards larger and larger units through commercial and industrial architecture.

Religious architecture, many new and imposing government buildings and other structures as in "Skyscraper buildings" for offices plus new building techniques in construction heating, air conditioning, lighting, plastics etc., all this changed the environment, and town planning took on a new meaning although planning had been with our ancestors for a few thousand years, historical planning shifted from military security to the addition of aesthetic expression to public welfare.

In its broadest sense city planning means the definition of a desirable objective for community living, which is realized through the operation of public controls of co-ordinated programs for physical, social and economic inprovement of the urban area, its history is the history of man's changing attitude towards his shelter, his means of livelihood and his leisure time. It has also been defined as the application to a town of that process of ordered forethought we have naturally applied to individual buildings.

The philosophy which underlies modern city planning practice stems directly from the great social and economic revolution of the 19th century. Man had never lived comfortably in the worlds cities, but his misery, degradation and poverty increased immeasurably under the juggernaut of industrial development. Old slums became worse and new ones were created by the disorderly sprawl of new factories and tenements into the surrounding countryside. During this period the great influx of population to cities from rural areas began. Almost no public facilities for transportation, communication or recreation, and certainly no public services designed to improve sanitation or protect health were available. Life was unbelievably drab and often dangerous. Only the aristocrats and the wealthy new industrialists and merchants escaped the socially destructive influence of unplanned urbanization. In 1872 and again in 1875, the Public Health Acts were passed, they contained compulsory provisions.

Out of this legislation grew the first Town Planning Act of 1909, designed to improve sanitary conditions and to provide convenience and amenity in the development of land. There were several new town planning acts thereafter, one being the Town and Country Planning Act of 1944, which for the first time granted local authorities adequate powers to control undeveloped land for planned use. It also recognized, with financial assistance and the requirement of standards below which the planning must not fall, the obligation of the central government to aid in the rehabilitation of bombed and blighted areas. Zoning came into it.

In 1929, the Local Government (Scotland Act) was passed which created major changes in local government with the inclusion of the green belt.

Taking advantage of the new Housing Acts, the Milngavie Town Council built in the years between the wars some 350 council houses, and much of the credit for the planning of modern Milngavie in those years is due to the efforts of Mr Frank A B Preston, who was at that time Burgh Surveyor.

The war years 1939-1945 put a stop to building so that in the post war years the need for adequate housing was greater than ever. The Town Council intensified their efforts and in the subsequent years and in spite of shortage of materials, built some 1200 houses (including pre-fabs of late memory) to cater for all sections of the community. House building continues today with 74 houses being built on the site of the former paper mill and a "sheltered" project for senior citizens in Mugdock Road.

From this stage on Milngavie became a very popular place to live.

SOME PERSONAL BUSINESS EXPERIENCES WITH MILNGAVIE DISTRICT MANSION HOUSES AND CASTLES

Over the years as the owner of an old established firm connected with the building trade, tradesman and local councillor, I have been asked to give a short description of the houses and the experiences of having provided various services for them. Unfortunately some have disappeared or have become ruins for various reasons.

The following is my own personal experiences with the owners or factors since my apprenticeship days:-

Mugdock Castle:-

Very historical, in 1923 owner Mr Strang, had flour mills in Bridgeton, Glasgow. The castle was 75% lived in, the remainder ruins of old fortifications, the ancient portcullis still exists and signs of an ancient moat. Mr Strang employed a staff of approximately 10 including cook, servants, an engine man who looked after an oil engine driving generator for electricity, and one gamekeeper. Sanitation was by septic tank system, water domestic supply from Allander water driven by a ram water pump. Up-to-date bathrooms installed; boasted a miniature golf course. The food and social side were quite good, in fact I attended a staff dance in the banqueting hall, unfortunately now more or less a ruin. It is now a part of Mugdock Country Park.

Craigend Castle:-

Formerly called the Gallowknowe, from the Gallows of the Barony standing just above the present house, property of Sir Andrew Buchanan, Ambassador to the Court of Vienna. A lovely house with twin towers, the stone built front of house facing east with beautiful outlook. When I took over the maintenance of the estate the water supply came from an artesian loch on Gallow Hill with an underground pipe to the castle. Sir Andrew Buchanan brought plants and flowers to be planted around the castle. It had a huge conservatory and the lay-out was wonderful including stables and garage. An engine plant supplied electricity to the castle. Half a mile from the castle, it had a substantial market garden with housing accommodation for staff.

The tenant at the time was Sir Harold Yarrow, shipbuilder. I did a number of alterations for him to modernise. He employed quite a staff and in the grounds it was not unusual from time to time to see the odd roe deer. Sir Harold was a gentleman to work and do business with.

I always remember one incident when working as tradesman repairing an underground burst pipe from Gallow Hill to the castle. I was being tormented by his son Eric Yarrow who kept running away with my tools. I had to give him a little spanking to get rid of him, the nanny noticed the incident and congratulated me for my action. That little boy is now Chairman of a National Bank, it could not have done him any harm. However Sir Harold and family gave up living in the castle and went to live in Kilmacolm. Later the estate went to a Mr Wilson who transformed the place into an animal zoo. It failed badly with the result the castle became a ruin and so did the estate.

By 1968 Mr John Lawrence J.P., building contractor, had become the owner of Craigend Estate, Lord Fraser of Allander had become the owner of Mugdock Estate.

In 1970 as Convener of Planning I had a meeting with the gentlemen concerned as they were to build a £9 million leisure complex on their combined lands between Milngavie and Strathblane, including a Championship Golf Course, this would be called Highland Gateway. However, owing to some unfortunate circumstances it never did materialise, and was ultimately altered to become Mugdock Park.

In Mugdock Village there stands a huge mansion house built in 1912 by a Mr Beattie, a well known baker and bread maker. Later it was occupied by a Mr Muir Simpson, a Glasgow draper, for whom I carried out a large contract of leadwork on the roof. It was then purchased by Lord Fraser of Allander. He had a factor from Campsie Glen who looked after the estate. My first meeting with Lord Fraser was rather amusing, it was at 9am one morning while waiting for the arrival of his factor to discuss some work in the mansion house. I was walking up the main avenue when he was just leaving in his Rolls Royce, he came out of the car and asked me if he could help me. I mentioned the reason for my visit was to meet his factor to discuss some business. He asked me who I was and I explained, his reply was "Oh, I sometimes call at your shop to buy some rubber rings for our Hoover," but I said "surely you sell hundreds of machines a week," his reply was, "Well Mr Gardner, my wife always tells me in the morning to bring home some rubber rings for the Hoover and I never remember until I am coming home from business. I always remember you are an agent for Hoover." We always remained good friends.

I can remember a rather unfortunate affair happening later with himself and his son Sir Hugh, as a boy, letting off some fireworks in the grounds. One of them must have gone in the wrong direction, as it landed in the hay shed of the farmer across the road and destroyed part of the farm. It is also sad to relate that in later years the mansion house was sold to an oil sheik, who had five sons and were sent to this country to be educated. The home was not properly maintained and deteriorated, I understand it is again sold and likely to be altered into flats.

Another interesting, rather large house in Mugdock Village, called Westerton House was the home of Professor Barr of Barr & Stroud, scientific instrument makers, Glasgow. It was rather a unique house. It's location allowed one to see for miles in all directions from a specially built large room on the roof top with glass windows all round. I do know the firm were makers of special binoculars and telescopic apparatus, there was also inside the house a fire prevention system with large iron pipes and fire hydrants and outside a most up-to-date sanitary system of drainage with revolving water sprays for purification. The professor had an experimental workshop the like of which I have never seen. A truly remarkable gentleman.

On his death the property was given over and became a childrens home, it has now been turned into dwelling flats.

Craigallion Mansion House:-

Further west we have Craigallion House another very fine large house and estate with a home farm built by a Mr Graham, the father of Mr Allan Barns Graham of Carbeth. Stone built in the form of a rectangle courtyard, and having two stone lodges for outside staff, and one two storey house as a gamekeepers house. The water supply was from a storage tank on a hill at the rear of the house, sanitation was by pipes to a septic tank, there was also a gas main supply from Milngavie.

The house and estate was bought over by the Connel brothers, shipbuilders on the Clyde. They kept quite a staff. I always remember the two bachelor brothers had motor cars, each with yellow coloured wheels and chauffeur driven. I carried on maintenance of the estate for a long period, until the time of their death, when Sir Charles Connel, a nephew from Perth, took over the estate when he was chairman of the firm. It is now in the hands of his son who has converted part of the mansion house into offices for various firms when the shipyard closed down on the River Clyde.

Another brother of the older gentleman bought Dougalston Mansion House. He was married to a lady of Russian descent from the aristocracy and a gifted pianist. During my time in business, my relationship with both families were excellent.

Dougalston Estate has now been sold to Mr Reo Stakis, part has been made into a golf course, with the mansion house removed and replaced by some modern detached houses which were sold privately.

Easterton Mansion House:-

It is sad to reflect Dougalston Mansion the former home of both John Glassford and T. Ripley Ker had now more or less vanished. Ripley Ker having gone on to Boghall at Bardowie and from there to Easterton Mansion House at Craigmaddie, where he had attained the age of ninety. Easterton House was again a well built edifice from an architectural point of view, the only bad feature being the private water supply which was of an iron nature thus discolouring sanitary fittings and eating its way through pipes. It was quite a problem in maintenance, otherwise it had a very good aspect. His son, Major Ker occupied the house for some time after his death. The house went to his son, a lecturer in Oxford, who being unable to live in the house has had it tenanted out since that time.

Craigmaddie Castle:-

We now turn to the very historic estate of Craigmaddie with the ruin of Craigmaddie Castle. It was the ancient seat of the Galbraiths and was part of the old Barony of Cartenvenock close to Bardowie.

The new stone built mansion house stone is now very commodious and the place beautiful. It was built by James Black, Lord Provost of Glasgow, who also laid out the ground. The house has had a few proprietors, these were General Peters a Glasgow family, James Spens Black of the Printfield in Milngavie. It was then bought by Mr Ker of Dougalston, whose daughter married Mr Charles T. Higginbotham and given over to them. During the 1914-1918 World War it acted as a hospital for disabled soldiers. It was then bought by Mr Arnold Wilson, Captain of 1st Milngavie Boys Brigade and founder with Mr Smith of the Boys Brigade in Glasgow, now world wide. Captain Wilson was a Glasgow metal merchant, I carried out a few contracts on the estate. At the New Year in the Boys Brigade of which I was a member and if you were a player in the pipe band or bugle band you were invited to Craigmaddie House to take in the New Year with the Wilson family. Fortunately I was a member of the bugle band so I used to enjoy the walk to the house at Craigmaddie to 'first foot' the family, enjoy a refreshment and return home. Yes, those were happy days.

Bardowie Castle and Loch:-

A picturesque place, very historical. The castle goes back to ancient times. I visited the place quite a number of times as a boy for pleasure and later on business. Some dastardly deeds have been committed here.

Above the front entrance to the castle a stone sticks out from the wall where hanging took place. The walls are six feet thick, the windows fairly small, the attic full of bats "a flying mammal with wings attached and very poor eyesight", which could be called vermin. In early times around the fourteenth century it was the property of the Hamiltons. The east part of the house is very ancient and is a fine specimen of the massive and faithfully built mansions of that early date. There have been several extensions since I knew it best when one of the Dewars, the whisky people, occupied it. I remember the thick walls during central heating alterations, I also had bother with water supply.

Duntreath Castle, Blanfield, in the Blane Valley:-

Another ancient and well built mansion house. I have been shown the charter by the late Sir Charles Edmonstone, who called me in to do the maintenance work of the castle and farms. It was managed for a short time by the Dowager Lady Edmonstone, until she removed to Lettre Cottage. They were very nice people to do business with.

Sir Archibald Edmonstone, the son, took over the running of the estate and property, during this period I carried out a new central heating system and other works. There was a sad happening during the alterations when an accident to one of the tradesmen, Robert Lamont, son of Robert Lamont & Son builders, fell from the scaffolding to the ground a few minutes before I arrived on a visit. I rushed to Killearn Hospital to pick up a surgeon and get an ambulance, I was most fortunate as at the entrance of the hospital I met a surgeon who collected some splints and bandage while I turned the car. We covered the ground back to the castle at great speed to discover Robert Lamont lying on stone rubble with severe injuries. With the aid of a stretcher he was on his way to the hospital in an ambulance. After a long illness, he recovered.

Although he was unable to do any manual work, having a good knowledge of the building trade he got employment as a Clerk of Works at the construction of the Clyde Tunnel and so continued to lead a normal life. How fortunate, and thanks to the staff of Killearn Hospital.

Balvie:-

This was a very old building. Early in the 13th century the Earl Maldoven of Lennox allowed a daughter to marry a Logan and he was made The Laird of Balvie. They were much engaged in public affairs. He was also a leader in one of the many attacks upon Dumbarton Castle. The Logans of Balvie ended about the beginning of the 17th century. The Campbells are connected by marriage with the Douglases. Mains House is not the original mansion, this stood about a mile to the south.

The present house was purchased with some land from a Mr McNair by Mr John Campbell Douglas, the present Mr Douglas's father who built a very fine addition and changed the name of the whole from Balvie to Mains.

I was an apprentice when I worked at Douglas of Mains, I can always remember the method of lighting was by gas supplied from Learmonts Gas Works. Other than that the only work done was what we termed jobbing. The Mansion House was ultimately closed down to make way for private houses and the building of Douglas Academy.

Clober Mansion House:-

Not a large estate, but quite important. The house and grounds belonged to the Duke of Montrose who granted a long lease to James McGregor, who as already explained was the merchant in Glasgow who started Clober Bleachworks. There is a peculiar interest attached to Clober from its being the scene of some of the works of the celebrated natural philosopher and engineer James Watt, the inventor of the steam locomotive. The bleachfield here, which has been long famous was planned by him for his father-in-law Mr McGregor and during its construction he superintended the making of the water courses and the erection of the machinery.

Here again I was quite young when I came in contact with the new owners of Clober Mansion, Mr John Blackwood and his two sisters who owned Craigton Bleach Works. The method of lighting was by gas from the local gasworks with gas mantles and glass globes. They employed a staff of servants and had a chauffeur. The method of calling on the servants was by mechanical bells in the dining room, bedrooms and front door. It was quite a well built stone house, the aspect being quite good. For some reason the dining room had an electric bell with a foot push switch on the floor near the dining table for convenience. It was run off a motor car battery, my job was to repair this apparatus as it was not working. In the process of the repair I found it necessary to lift part of the carpet on the polished floor. After making the necessary repair I was accused by Miss Blackwood of marking the floor, I pointed out it could not have been me as I had on rubber shoes. It was rather funny that a few years later when I owned my business, Mr John had died and I had to assist them with a new water supply, I found myself in the same taxi with the Miss Blackwood who accused me of marking the floor going into George Square to discuss with water officials the question of a new water supply to the mansion house. Fortunately we managed to get a new supply allowed. I was now friendly with the two sisters for a number of years until they passed on, and the usual trend of events occurred, the estate sold to build private houses and the mansion house removed, a small part of the ruin still remains.

I do hope I have given a rough sketch of castles and mansion houses with estates round Milngavie as I knew them.

Some local items of interest you may appreciate
Tannoch Loch Constructions

Tannoch Loch as an overflow from Mugdock Reservoir was originally a small stream on the Heathfield Drive side of the loch. On the Montrose Garden side where the depth of water is very shallow and before the building of the houses of Montrose Gardens were built, a football field existed, started no doubt by the work force used for the construction of the reservoir and other works.

The football team was called the Allander and was a first division team, playing against all the superior teams in Scotland, later to be transferred to Mains Estate, at a site near Clober Road before the First World War.

When Tannoch Loch was completed, Mr Woodburn, the builder of the houses in Heathfield Drive, had the idea of using the outfall water to operate a small water wheel to operate an early type of dynamo to generate direct electric current for lighting houses. At Clober Crescent remains of early type wiring can still be seen in the attics of the houses, however, owing to the untimely drowning of Mr Woodburn in the Mugdock reservoir the scheme was abandoned.

From time to time in winter conditions the loch has been used for skating but it can be rather treacherous. I can remember a very great tragedy of a young girl and boy being drowned because of the thin ice unable to take the weight. The girl was C. Graham and the boy A. Laing from two well known families in Milngavie.

Fire

One of the tragedies which the Town Council had to cope with occurred on a Monday morning in April 1940 when the Town Hall and Council Chamber were completely destroyed by fire. However, the Town Council were fortunate in obtaining the use of the Parish Church Halls in Station Road which served for community purposes until the new Town Hall and Council Chambers were built in 1962.

Included in the complex is the Lillie Art Gallery, the result of a benefaction by the late Robert A. Lillie, a citizen of Milngavie.

Ancient and Modern

There is no doubt over the years sport and recreation has always been popular with all classes of the community depending on the seasons of the year. In earlier times a great deal depended on your status in the community and financial position. That has all changed in modern times, depending now on your own selection and ability from a very great selection, in sport both outdoor and indoor plus hobbies and pastimes it is considerable and can be financially very rewarding.

At the beginning of the industrial revolution in our district or barony, archery, golfing, curling and yachting seemed to suit the "prodigious swells" who came to reside in our district in the many respectable family mansions. Milngavie has been very fortunate with the high quality of person arriving here especially in the commercial and shipbuilding industry, to add to the good old business men of yore, who did so much to make Milngavie what it is today.

T. Ripley Ker, Esq.

In sport there is one gentleman, and his good lady, worthy of note. One time owner of Dougalston Mansion House and Estate, including Douglaston Loch and Dovecot field, his name was T. Ripley Ker, Esq., and his wife Mrs T.R. Ker, M.B.E., both did some very good work for Milngavie.

Mr Ker being a keen sportsman, when the loch became frozen in winter, used to organise a curling bonspiel or curling match of some importance. He also had shooting parties over the estate usually from the dovecote field. He was one of the founder Captains of Milngavie Golf Club. In addition he gifted a piece of ground on Crossvegate Farm to the inhabitants of Milngavie as a public park or recreation ground, later called "Lennox Park". Some years later he removed to Eastertoun Mansion House, Craigmaddie, where his good lady did a considerable amount of work associated with the Red Cross Association, being awarded with the Member of the British Empire. I did some business with them at Eastertoun House and for his successor, his son Major Ker. A well respected family.

Archery is now considered old fashioned. It is a sport of shooting with bows and arrows, mostly done by the wealthy. Yachting is another sport suitable for wealthy friends sailing on the River Clyde and Loch Lomond. Very popular.

Bearsden and Milngavie District Council

On the 16th May 1974 Scottish Local Government was reorganised and the local authority for the area of Bearsden, Milngavie, High Craigton and WindyHill was to form the District Council.

Strathclyde Regional Council was also to take control of major services such as education, social work, police, roads and sewage and their functions will be advertised elsewhere.

The area of responsibility of the District Council was to be:-

Local Planning and Industrial Development
Building Control
Housing
Environmental Health
Refuse Collection and Disposal, Street Cleansing
Food Hygiene
Clean Air
Cemeteries, etc. Shop Acts, Offices, Shops and Railway Premises Act and Health and Safety at Work Act Provisions
Parks, Recreation etc.
Libraries and Art Gallery
Licensing Functions (Liquor, Betting, Gaming and Miscellaneous).

Having been elected again for first ward Barloch as Councillor for another period of three years, it was quite convenient as my business was situated in the ward. In addition I was made convener of Local Planning and Industrial Development, also of Building Control, which was more or less the job I was doing in Milngavie Town Council and Dunbarton Town Council. Added to all this I had just completed the Central Area Redevelopment of Milngavie so I had all the experience necessary for the job.

As an Ex Senior Bailie I had to take my turn on court duty as Magistrate on the Bench.

At this stage of the proceedings I should like to quote a few of the officials I had the pleasure and privilege to work with over the years.

Mrs. S.V. Peters	Chief Librarian
Mr Frank A. Preston	Burgh Surveyor
Mr Arthur Millar	Burgh Surveyor
Mr William W. Dudgeon	Burgh Surveyor
Mr A.R. Rae	Chief Executive
Mr David L. Cuthbert	Director of Administration
Mr John M. Hornby	Director of Finance
Mr Walter D. Hemfrey	Chief Planning Officer
Mr Clive Richardson	Building Control

Milngavie Boys Brigade 1921 - 22, Cpl. Neil McDougall with award winning best drilled section

COMMENT

It is with some regret we have to pass on to a new administration as the future is so uncertain, in doing so I would like to make a few comments on the place they call Millguy.

It is a beautiful place, which cannot be beat, for the scenery around, is one perfect treat, I am sure you will praise it, right up to the sky, if you just take a run out to "Bonnie Millguy".

A local historian has described Milngavie as "a child of the Allander". The first consideration in dealing with a community is the amenities both physical and cultural. That being the case the first cultural activities recorded in the community was the "Milngavie Mechanics Institution" founded in 1836. The object was the "the dissemination of useful knowledge, by the delivery of public lectures at such times, on such terms, as would enable all who felt inclined to participate in the advantages which must be derived from the spread of general knowledge."

One year later in 1837 a library was formed which contained 1,000 volumes. Subsequently the building was used as a school, known as the "Bridge School".

Later a new Town Hall was built, both were the focal points for cultural and community activities. Clubs were formed, some of which continue until today. So far as sport is concerned I have already given some details on this. There are so many hobbies and pastimes today it would be most difficult to itemise them.

Nevertheless, it can be said with some truth that today, whatever your interest or activity may be, it is likely to be catered for, helped by "Milngavie Week" which started back in 1966.

Is it any wonder why I am so proud of Milngavie, having been born at 26 Main Street, 100yds away from the mill of Davie Guy.

All my life I have been more or less associated with business and other affairs in Milngavie. The people have always been very kind to me and in return I have always tried to do my best for the community. It has not been easy. I have had tragedy and happiness, coupled with some success. I did what I had to do at the time and have no regrets.

We now turn to the Bearsden and Milngavie District Council. It commenced on the 16th May 1974, you could say into the unknown for better or worse. Some of the detail I have already given, however this was local government reorganisation on a large scale.

It is easy to understand the first year did not accomplish very much when you consider a new administration had to be built up, smoothly, efficiently and economically as the great majority of officials and staff of the new District are drawn from Bearsden and Milngavie Town Councils. You would have thought with the high technology, with new machines, that the staff would be cut, this, however was not the case. Sometimes it is better to leave things as they are, after all I had a job to do and I got on with it.

The second year in the District Council was a year of reports, legislation and mistakes. Sometimes double work. And politics were coming into the scheme of things. This, of course, I had no time for in local government as I was elected as an Independent Candidate over the years and I was not going to change now. The atmosphere was beginning to change.

As convener of planning and building control most of my time was spent with Mr Hemfrey on Planning and a Mr Richardson on Building Control, the office being in Milngavie. Other than the regular meetings of the Council, I did not visit the offices at Boclair, Bearsden, more than I could help.

It was a peculiar situation as there seemed to be far more work going on in Milngavie than Bearsden despite the fact Bearsden area was much bigger. I seemed to be handling much bigger contracts in Milngavie.

During the third year it was a little better. The starting of a new supermarket at Kessington and some new housing programmes were on line. Having attended conferences and being a member of the Scottish National Housing and Town Planning where discussions would arise as to the future of Town and Country Planning, most interesting and informative to me.

At the end of my third term I had become rather disenchanted with my lot at district level as I now found myself unable to help Milngavie in the way I used to. With another election coming up I had to go into hospital for a bypass operation, and with pressure from my family I decided the time had come to retire.

I will give a brief description of the future of planning as I see it.

Local Plans will be prepared, mainly by the district for those areas or subjects which require fairly immediate development, often within the next ten years.

It will be the responsibility of the Region Planning Authority, in consultation with its districts, to work out a scheme of local plans, specifying the nature, area and scope of each one and setting out a programme for their preparation. There will be a wide variety of different types of local plan.

Typical subjects for local plans might be:-

- A town centre scheme, incorporating changes in the road pattern and a new by-pass
- A plan for the expansion of a small town
- A plan for the rehabilitation of an area of older housing where the quality of the environment needs improvement
- A plan for a city aimed at producing better open space provision for recreation and leisure
- A plan for a new township on the edge of a city incorporating a new district shopping centre
- A plan for a country park in a rural area.

It will be apparent, even from this brief description of the new planning system that there is an important differentiation of planning function implied as between structure and local plans. The structure plans of the regions are intended to be concerned with broader questions and relationships, even, in some cases, national considerations.

They will be concerned almost entirely with location, with the pattern of services (especially transportation), with the quantity of development allocated between different cities, towns and villages that may feel, at the more parochial levels, that they have rival claims either to have development or to avoid development. The structure plan will therefore play an important plan in the determination of the allocation of resources and the quantity of development.

Local plans will tend to be concerned with different things - with the siting of development and its arrangement, with localised movement and access, with the mixture of uses and activities on a more localised scale, with the control of development where there is a mixture of old and new building, with conservation and preservation as well as development and change.

Above all, local plans will be concerned with quality; it will be local plans that determine, by detailed treatment and design, how our future environment looks, feels and impinges on all our senses. The first point is the working relationship between the new regions and the new districts. No one who has the real interests of better planning at heart will regret the passing of the bickering, squabbling and of the open strife that has often gone on about planning matters between the Counties and Burghs.

But the new system demands a new relationship of collaboration, not conflict. There will, of course, be differences of approach and differences of opinion as between the new regions and their District Councils. The new process of planning will make it essential for there to be this continuous dialogue between technical officers and between elected representatives from the two tiers of authorities. They will just have to get on with each other better.

The future of town planning is not determined in advance: nor is the success of the new system guaranteed. The future of town planning depends on the determined efforts of all of us to tackle the new problems of the new system and the determination of all those concerned, especially government, to tackle these urgent resource problems, particularly providing the right sort of skilled manpower at the right places and solving this serious problem of producing urban designers on which improving the quality of the environment so largely depends.

Highland Gateway Proposed

Further to my exploratory meeting with Mr. John Lawrence, his architect and surveyor, in agreement with Lord Fraser of Allander given earlier, some items which you may find interesting.

Highland Gateway has been designed as a unique tourist project. The proposed site is 400 acres of unspoiled countryside at Strathblane, only 15 miles from Loch Lomond and the Trossachs - one of Scotland's world famous beauty spots.

Professor A. S. Travers produced a development and conservation plan for the site, the plan includes hotels and three massive sky domes enclosing sports, trade and conference facilities. Included in this unique group of central buildings are restaurants, cinema/theatre, night-clubs, shops, discotheques, etc.

The remainder of the 400 acre site contains a new championship golf course, designed for T.V. coverage; a nature reserve with an educational centre for visitors; a restored castle for banquets and dramatic presentations; an angling loch; and illuminated landscaped gardens.

Lying between the Kilpatrick Hills and the Campsie Fells, the site, containing the old castles of Craigend and Mugdock, is a natural gateway to the Highlands - only half an hour from Loch Lomond and the Trossachs. The area was chosen because of its convenience for travellers. Glasgow is less than half an hour away by road or by electric service. Prestwick International Airport is one hour away and, of course, Glasgow Airport - within easy reach is less than an hour's flying time from London. The site is well connected too, with the main motorway routes to Glasgow, Edinburgh, Carlisle and London.

For conference use, it is planned that the project would be equipped with the most modern telecommunications systems - making it possible for sound and vision links with other centres elsewhere in the world. Television facilities would be available throughout the central building complex.

Highland Gateway is designed however as more than a magnet for tourists and conferences from overseas and England. Despite a superb location with outstanding views, there is a potential local market of 2 million people within a twenty five mile radius. This population would be offered a completely new and remarkably varied blend of entertainment, sports, and hotel facilities, suitable for everything from evening visits to full-scale holidays.

The study produced by Professor Travis makes Highland Gateway the only project of its kind in the world - first, because it combines such a wide variety of interests and, second, because of its unique architectural design.

The central group of buildings would include a luxury 300 bedroom multi-storey hotel and a two-storey terrace of family apartments. Linked to them would be three massive sky domes, each enclosing 10,000 square metres (approximately 100,000 square feet) which would provide an artificial temperature controlled indoor landscape. Within the domes there would be a conference, assembly, and concert area, with committee rooms, studies, translation rooms and a wide range of audio-visual facilities; an indoor recreation area with swimming and diving pools, saunas, gymnasium, indoor tennis, squash, golf range, etc; and an exhibition area for permanent and temporary displays. The facilities would be suitable for everything from industrial exhibitions to show-jumping.

The three domes would be of a unique construction. Their translucent roofs would be made of glass fibre and vinyl supported by a slight differential air pressure. The intention would be to create a sky-like effect. Internally, the domes would have a constant pleasant temperature and would be laid out with a variety of different floor levels - in some cases adjustable to allow for the creation of amphitheatres or exhibition areas. At all times, the intention would be to establish the illusion that the whole area beneath the domes is out-of-doors, with profuse use of trees, plants, grass-like carpeting and involving special lighting effects.

Knitting the three domes together would be a series of "decks" - some open but most totally enclosed. Along these decks would be shops, restaurants, cafes and entertainment venues such as night clubs and a cinema/theatre. The decks would lead to the multi- storey hotel and on to the two-storey flatted accommodation. Built into the complex, also, would be a luxurious golf club-cum-country club.

This club house would overlook a new 18 hole championship course. This course would be the first in the world specially laid out with television in mind. Already, there have been preliminary discussions with relevant interests regarding the special design that would be required to assist the production of television and filmed golf.

Other facilities close to the central group of buildings would include a large outdoor space with planting, fountains, children's play areas and a creche. Across an ornamental bridge-way there would be a hillside of laid out gardens for floodlighting and other special lighting effects.

Relatively close to the hotel, there would be stables (for horse-riding and pony trekking), an artificial dry ski-run, and a site for a helicopter landing pad suitable for an air link with Scottish airports. Further away, across the golf course, it is planned to renovate historic 14th Century Mugdock Castle and make use of it as a heritage site with historical displays allied to evening use as a banqueting hall. Near to the castle there would be a visitor centre with exhibitions and information about local history and ecology. This centre would be the base point for nature trails and other specialist activities in the nature reserve.

The development of the nature reserve is based on the fact that the area - known as Mugdock Wood and including Mugdock Loch - is already recognised as a site for special scientific interest, particularly because of its plants and trees, butterflies and moths, insects and beetles, birds, roe-deer and other animals. Over 400 species of wild life have been observed in the area. This whole area would be subject to a conservation programme including tree planting and replanting as part of an overall scheme of landscape management.

Site Analysis

In summary, having considered alternative possibilities and made further analysis, a number of key factors emerged encouraging development in some parts of the site and limiting or discouraging the development of others. Notable points are as follows:-

1. The elevation, site form, aspect and prospect of the land area in the immediate vicinity of Craigend Castle encourage its development.

2. Site access private roads for development at Craigend Castle involve much lower capital costs than those for opening up the Mugdock Castle end of the site.

3. Site profile in relation to drainage and sewerage appear to make Craigend preferable to Mugdock for extensive development.

4. The natural character of Mugdock Loch and of Mugdock Wood support their positive retention as nature reserves. Their development would be expensive as well as undesirable.

5. The appropriate reconstruction of Mugdock Castle could both conserve the historic feeling and natural setting for the heritage site as well as provide an asset for profitable uses.

6. The woods and gardens on the hill at Craigend should be retained and reconstructed for intensive recreational use in association with adjacent indoor facilities.

7. The varied shelter and exposed conditions on the site shown in the survey required detailed consideration in respect of new landscaping and building forms. The landscaping of much of the site will have to be related to the design of the proposed new golf course.

8. Full advantage should be taken of the views from the site in deciding on locations for buildings and outdoor focal points.

After protracted negotiations with all the responsible Authorities and Trusts, an agreement was reached and the formation of Mugdock Country Park took place.

My Father

Author and Grandson

THE ENVIRONMENT

In the modern world we are being advised how important this subject is. It can be many things for instance, the aggregate of all external and internal conditions affecting the existence, growth and welfare of organisations, one's surroundings or external circumstances collectively in most cases a nuisance, that which annoys, vexes or harms. In law that which by its use or existence works annoyance or damage to another.

During my term as a Magistrate the main code of statutory nuisances is contained under the Public Health Act 1897 and other acts such as the Clean Air Act, Noise Abatement Act, an additional factor in the concept of common law nuisance, namely injury or danger to health as any premises etc. in such a state.. .as to be a nuisance or injurious or dangerous to health.

Any work manufactory... so conducted as to be injurious or dangerous to hea1th. In the first example it would be sufficient to prove nuisance only without reference to health although it has been known for the Courts to want more than this.

In the second example proof of injury or danger to health would be required before nuisance could be established. There is no need to go into obvious difficulties of proving injury or even danger to health.

What does all this lead to and what has it got to do with modern nuisances? The point is: modern nuiances call for a modern approach in law. The Public Health Act was drafted to deal with conditions in the late Victorian times - to deal with gross conditions of bad environment and sanitation which by and large no longer exist.

There is throughout the notion of foul or obnoxious conditions and conditions associated with epidemic diseases but the Act was also born in an age which hesitated at interference with industry and trade, and it is perhaps something of a paradox that in certain sub-sections the word "nuisance is dropped leaving the inhibiting words "injurious or dangerous to health". Today living conditions and standards have changed out of all recognition from seventy years ago and we are no longer just emerging from the grim conditions of the Industrial Revolution. More freedom from physical disease is not the ultimate in environment. We should enjoy our environment.

Surely in this day and age reference to injury or danger to health in the context of a nuisance is an anachronism. Just as the 1897 Act widened - in theory if not in practice - the scope of the 1867 Act by inserting the words "or dangerous" into the phrase "injurious to health", today the scope is needing to be widened further.

If any specified circumstances in an Act are a nuisance that should be enough: there should be no need to prove injury or danger to health. To illustrate a factory immediately adjacent to dwellinghouses installed a new proceess which emitted a rather offensive and even nauseating odour which permeated the neighbourhood and into the houses. This varied in degree with weather conditions, it was considered that nuisance could be proved but under the sub-section that was not enough. No actual injury to health could be proved and it seemed that danger to health would be no less easy to prove. Fortunately, after negotiation, the management agreed to co-operate. But the fact remains that had recourse to law been necessary the action might well have failed. In a case like this it should be sufficient to prove nuisance only.

The concept of nuisance also needs to be widened beyond the idea that there must be material physical discomfort or interference and beyond the often accepted limiting factor "within a man's property". To illustrate: a vacant feu in a residential street becomes a dumping ground for say, builders refuse. There is no offensive matter, no smell, it does not directly interfere with any individual in the occupation of his own property. It is very doubtful if nuisance in terms of the Public Health Act could be proved and yet in the aesthetic sense it can be an undoubted nuisance - an eyesore. Nuisance law needs to be altered to deal with any similar situations. To sum up so far: a change is required to remove the inhibiting idea of injury or danger to health; also, to deal with circumstances which by modern standards spoil amenity, offend public taste and standards and in general cause nuisance in a wider sense than previously accepted.

Some Modern Nuisances

Noise

Noise is fast becoming one of the worst features of modern life. Few people however would like to live in a silent world and in moderation, human activity can be very comforting. Much more, therefore, needs to be known about the effects, assessment and control of noise. At present the assessment of what constitutes a noise nuisance is extremely difficult. Human reactions to noise vary greatly: one individual may react differently to the same noise according to circumstances and time. Instruments for the measurement of noise are only aids to the investigating officer. He must use his own judgement. He must try, so far as possible, to be objective and to base his assessment on the reaction of "an average reasonable person" for it is reasonable to assume that legislation was not meant to provide for the ultra-sensitive or the crank. In the final analysis, however, the inspector can never avoid a subjective assessment and this can often put him in a difficult position visa-vis the complainants. All the circumstances - place, time, nature of the noise - must be taken into account. Generalisations cannot be made but it seems certain that if one has to strain to hear a noise no nuisance exists. To be a nuisance a noise must - this may have little to do with actual loudness - impinge itself on the senses. One investigator has suggested that the reaction against the author of a noise can be greater than against the actual noise - that sometimes a sense of grievance against the author can lead to a form of neurosis even in cases where the noise itself is trivial.

There are of course genuine noise nuisances and the truth is that it is rather astonishing just how much annoyance and discomfort people will put up with without complaining.

Perhaps, of course, noise is regarded as inevitable just as years ago smoke from industry was regarded as inevitable. Many noises can, in fact, be eliminated or reduced below nuisance level.

It is suggested, however, that the great problem of noise is not the isolated nuisance; it is the total mass of noise to which modern life subjects the whole community. One of the worst sources is traffic. The remedy for all this is beyond nuisance legislation. Far more attention should be given to noise in the design of all modern machinery, vehicles, buildings, etc.

Dumping

It is a paradox that with improved environmental services and higher standards of living, indiscriminate dumping is one of the most prevalent and insidious modern nuisances. It takes many forms.

One form of dumping is a product of the affluent society. In the vicinity of almost every community - even well into the countryside - hideous accumulations, large and small, of household furniture and other domestic commodities are to be found. What is the answer? The emphasis should be on prevention and local authorities should provide a service for the removal of what is after all household refuse. Even so dumping will occur from time to time. Local authorities cannot be expected to provide a regular public service for cleaning up privately-owned ground; this would in any case only encourage dumping. Further, such accumulations are not necessarily statutory nuisances as the law stands. But it must be made possible for all such eyesores to be treated as statutory nuisances and, however unfair it may seem, ultimate responsibility for removal must rest with the owner of the ground. Builders refuse is another similar problem and the ultimate answer here is the same. It might be a good thing, however, if all local authorities could provide on a payment basis well operated dumps for this and other innocuous wastes.

Dumping of garden refuse can be another problem particularly in large built-up areas. This is not household refuse although some local authorities have provided a service and at least one local authority has abandoned it because the depositing points created nuisances. The ultimate answer where dumping has occurred is the same as already given and indeed is the same for dumping of whatever nature (It is appreciated that certain accumulations of garden refuse could be dealt with under present nuisance law).

Dumps

Over the country there seems to be a rash of dumps appearing. These may be local authority or privately-owned dumps. They may or may not have town planning approval. In some cases it may be the owner of the ground is just tolerating the dumping. Many of them do not seem to be subject to any control and if not nuisances within the present legal definition, are certainly nuisances in the broader concept - blots on the landscape.

Quite obviously such dumps while in use as such cannot be things of beauty but they can be operated with the minimum offence to amenity. If such dumps are not approved, they should be automatically treated as nuisances:- if approved, there should be far more rigid day to day control and the law of nuisance should operate.

Abandoned Vehicles

This is already a nuisance problem in some of the larger cities and there is no doubt that it has already touched many smaller communities. It is likely, too, that this will become an increasing problem. Abandoned cars, besides being a nuisance to amenity, can be dangerous to children and accidents are not unknown. Under the Removal of Vehicles (Scotland) Regulations 1961, local authorities have powers to remove and dispose of vehicles abandoned on roads. The Act however does not appear to cover vehicles abandoned elsewhere than on roads or car parks. It is understood, too, that the procedure under the Act is rather cumbersome and takes time. One London burgh has cut through the procedure of the equivalent English regulations by classifying such vehicles as dangerous litter and taking action under the Highways (Miscellaneous Provisions) Act 1961. This Act, however, does not apply to Scotland. There is a case, therefore, for adjusting the law to bring abandoned vehicles clearly within the specification of nuisance. If it is argued that the present regulations are adequate to deal with abandoned vehicles on roads there is a need for nuisance procedure in relation to places other than roads or car parks.

Derelict Industrial Premises

Few people have not seen abandoned industrial premises with their derelict buildings, old accumulations of industrial waste, ground overgrowing with weeds and pools of stagnant water - and most likely being used as a general dumping ground. Surely such places are a nuisance and should be treated as such. It is however doubtful if they can be dealt with under the present Public Health Act and again this type of circumstance requires specification under a concept of nuisance.

Uncultivated Gardens and Other Ground

There is little need to stress the nuisance which can be caused by uncultivated gardens and other ground, namely spreading of weeds and loss of amenity. This may not be a modern nuisance but the growing number of houses with gardens has made it more prevalent. Again in many tenement properties with gardens, the increase of owner/occupiers has increased the incidence of the uncultivated for the old control that the factor exercised is gone.

In housing schemes it may be argued that this can be controlled through factorage but everyone knows the difficulties here and that of applying the ultimate sanction of eviction which creates its own problems.

The time is ripe, therefore, for uncultivated gardens including vacant parcels of land in urban areas being specified as nuisances. Perhaps it should be said that the Weeds Act of 1959 which is directed against the spread of certain injurious weeds is really an Agricultural Act and does not cover the problem being discussed.

Quarries

Quarries are not a new source of nuisance but a few which have been observed appear to be emitting more dust than, say, ten years ago. They have probably escaped attention because of the injurious or dangerous to health qualification in the Act and because they are seldom situated in densely built-up areas. But anywhere - even in the country - nuisance from dust can be widespread and the harm to vegetation and to general amenity can be severe. Here again, new thinking on nuisance is required.

Schools

Certain circumstances in schools may be treated as nuisances, namely, lack of cleanliness, overcrowding, etc. This sub-section needs to be extended to include such things as sanitary accommodation not being adequate, not readily accessible, not protected from the weather and not properly ventilated, lack of washing facilities attached to such accommodation or washing facilities to which pupils are not given free and ready access at all times.

These conditions apply wholly or in part to the vast majority of pre-war schools which are in use. Despite the provision of new schools it would appear that in many areas most of the pre-war schools are still in use. The difficulties of education authorities are appreciated but there seems to be a tendency for these grossly unsatisfactory conditions to be lost in programmes of budgeting and priorities for school buildings. Health authorities need some powers of intervention to enable them to cut across such priorities when circumstances warrant it.

Streets

Most Environmental Health Officers would generally accept (and act accordingly) that an accumulation of water in a street caused by a choked gully is a nuisance. What about accumulation of water including oil, etc. caused by uneven street surfaces and potholes? The frequency and speed of modern traffic can make such the source of considerable nuisance to pedestrians. It may be argued that this is already the responsibility of the local authority and that no other powers are needed. But, like schools, so often street maintenance, etc. is a question of programmes and priorities where circumstances warrant. Similarly, there may be a case for including pavements which are uneven and dangerous as nuisance; indeed, such pavements caused more damage than some items of disrepair in houses which are regularly dealt with under nuisance law.

Other Environmental Matters for Consideration

As stated in the introduction, many conditions which adversely affect our environment could be described loosely as nuisances but they do not lend themselves to remedy by nuisance law.

Some probably call for specific and positive legislation; some may call for action by local authorities and some call for education. One thing is certain : some will never be remedied until there is a determined will to achieve that end.

There seems to be a curious streak in the British character which shrinks from taking a firm line in certain matters. We applaud the end but avoid the means. Litter is one example of this kind of thing. There is no doubt that the Litter Act has been a complete failure. Many reasons and excuses can be put forward but the simple fact is that the will to ensure success of the Act is not there. Many things which used to be common place are not so today, not so much because of penal legislation, education or even self-interest, but because certain things are simply "not done". In other words, the will of the community is being exercised.

This takes two forms. Litter in the streets of urban areas and tourist litter both in the highways and in beauty spots. Some may take the view that the only answer here is education. On the other hand, it is suggested that a more direct answer lies in the determined enforcement of an improved Act - this after all can be a form of education - in which the will of the people in the community is expressed. In beauty spots and beaches perhaps litter wardens are needed. After all, we have traffic wardens (perhaps in towns they could act as litter wardens).

Are parking offences any more important than despoilation of the countryside or the appearance of towns?

Motor Car

The streets of our cities, towns and villages have become repositories for the parked motor car. In town centres and holiday resorts they are everywhere - almost as permanent as the buildings themselves. They obstruct our movement, our vision and we walk in tunnels with the cars forming one side and the buildings the other. In a visual sense and in other ways the car is a blight on our towns. They also interfere with street cleansing. Some residential sterets, too, have been turned into outdoor garages and workshops with the added hazards of water, oil and detergent foam. Apart from the hazards to pedestrians, especially children, nothing detracts more from amenity.

These remarks are not directed against the motor car as such but against allowing it to become the master of our environment. There seems to be a curious reluctance to admit that the motor car is here to stay and to make proper provision for it we must come to terms with the motor age.

Petrol and Diesel Fumes

So much has been written and said about this in recent years that further commentary seems needless. There appears to be some uncertainty about the health hazards and no doubt this will be dealt with. Whatever the ultimate findings on the' medical aspects there is no doubt that the emissions cause nuisance and discomfort and for these reasons alone should not be tolerated beyond the technically possible minimum. Poor maintenance seems to be the cause of excessive emission of diesel fumes and perhaps there is a case for stricter surveillance and the introduction of road tests.

Kerbside Refuse Collecting

This is still the practice in a number of cities and towns. The answers, of course, to this lies with the local authorities concerned. It may be that such local authorities have good reasons - economics, labour, etc. - for continuing the practice. There is no doubt whatsoever that on public health and amenity grounds kerbside refuse collection is anything but a desirable practice.

It is true to say that today we are in a transitional state in the matters of environment. The gross insanitary conditions have largely disappeared, the objective now possibly a more difficult one is to create and maintain an environment which is not only safe but attractive - one which satisfies our aesthetic needs.

There are for example such matters as better and adequate public conveniences with allied services in towns, the provision of such on main highways and tourist areas, contamination of beaches by sewage, beach cleansing, the subject of radiation and radioactive wastes and pollution of the atmosphere.

The Dog

Having discussed some modern nuisances and the various problems they cause I have refrained to mention one "The Dog". This is rather difficult as I learned from my six years as a senior magistrate there are always two sides to a story.

Having already explained my own personal experience, I will refrain from going into details except to state that in 1959 I got in touch with a lady breeder. She offered me a Golden Cocker Spaniel puppy. It was a pedigree dog, male, his parents being Sunkist Sir Harold, the sire, and Golden Chorus Girl, the dame. Little did we realise until some time after they were both champions. I called the pup Caesar.

Caesar was all that could be expected from a dog. He was a beautiful dog and an excellent companion, always in good health for thirteen years when he took a heart attack and died.

I could never have another dog. I thought so much of my Caesar. I was so fortunate.

Your Dog

I came across a book published by Spillers with a preface "Your Dog" by Harper Cory as follows, it is excellent and to the point, and here I quote.

"Dogs are creatures of habit. The best habit your dog can get is one of absolute confidence in you. He will then be your friend, guardian and willing slave, but - this is the important thing - you alone can give him that confidence. Nobody can do it for you.

Your dog asks for little in return for his loyalty and utter devotion - a bed, correct food, water, your understanding and complete confidence in him. Like the child, he becomes what you make of him.

Dog-owning can be a joy or a nuisance. My dogs are, in every sense of the expression, "members of the family". We enjoy having them in the house and they enjoy being with us. There is complete understanding and confidence on both sides. This is not for the expert but it is simply a friendly attempt to help the average householder who wants a dog about the house. I try to show you how to win your dog's confidence speedily, to care for him or her in health and sickness, to train him for the home and the road; to make him a "member of the family" whom you will love as he loves you.

There is not much to learn and that little is simple to understand and to practise.

The Dog

The adult dog is only a grown-up puppy. However old he may be in years he will always have a mentality which is juvenile when compared with that of a human being. People forget that simple fact when buying a dog. The animal comes to its owner with a variety of habits, some pleasing and some displeasing. He cannot drop the old habits and gain new ones in a matter of days just to please you, no matter how simple those habits may be.

You will never teach him to forget the bad habits completely; they are part of his personality. The most you can do is to teach him new habits to win his confidence and affection so completely that he will obey the new habits

Suggested feeding charts are available.

A final word, it is a simple matter to rear and train a dog. The animal has inherited a centuries-old desire to please and to serve man, he is anxious to respond to good training and correct feeding.

Enjoying a dog is quite a different matter. To enjoy a dog you must try to see life through his eyes and appreciate his many limitations. Endeavour to understand the message he is trying to pass to you when he sits beside your chair and touches you with his paw or head. You will often find it difficult, but sometimes his message will be very clear. At such times, if you will remember that although he cannot speak, nor read, nor write your language, yet he has learned to do exactly what you wished him to do, that he has won your admiration, sympathy and affection by his obedience, devotion and loyalty, then you will begin to realise what a fine intelligent animal the dog can become when you co-operate full-heartedly with him. You will enjoy your dog.

Author with "Caeser"

FLUORIDATION

Fluoride is a natural element that is found in many water supplies and most foods, and thus everyone ingests small quantities of fluoride every day, but most people do not receive adequate amounts to give them maximum resistance to dental decay.

Fluoridation is the controlled increase of the fluoride content of drinking water in order to strengthen the resistance to dental decay of those who consume the water throughout their lives. In Britain the correct level is one part of fluoride to every million parts of water (1 part per million: ppm).

The problem. Dental decay is one of the most prevalent diseases of western civilisation. It attacks mainly the young but, as it is an irreversible disease, its effects remain throughout the life of the individual affected. The amount of dental disease in Britain is far in excess of the dental profession's resources to treat it. Within the National Health Service the cost of its treatment is second only to the cost of mental illness.

Apart from bringing pain and infection to most members of the community at some time or other in their lives, it is a particular hazard of some chronically ill and handicapped groups. As a result of dental decay, many pre-school children are subjected to general anaesthetics for the extraction of painful teeth, some teenagers suffer disfiguring mutilation of their mouths through rampant decay of their front teeth and working hours are lost by adults of all ages.

Much of this suffering and loss of productive time could be eliminated by a very simple, inexpensive and harmless procedure: the addition of a minute and carefully controlled amount of fluoride to the drinking water supply.

Fluoridation is not a new idea. It has been the subject of intensive studies throughout the world over the last forty years; some communities in the United States and Canada have fluoridated their water supplies for nearly thirty years, whilst two in the British Isles have been fluoridated for more than fifteen years. Many communities throughout the world (including some in the United Kingdom) consume water that naturally contains fluoride at 1 ppm or more. Studies of these have shown that the prevalence of dental decay is about half of that in comparable communities with little or no fluoride in the water.

This reduction in the amount of dental decay has been seen consistently in many countries and has been confirmed in areas throughout the world where fluoride has been added to water supplies in trials of fluoridation, including the Departments of Health's studies in Britain.

Benefits in areas where fluoridation has been undertaken, slow the rapid decay resulting in total destruction of the teeth of very young children, and considerably reduce the disfigurement of teenagers. In addition, in one major city with fluoridation of the water supply children of pre-school age who form a very difficult group to treat and often require surgery under general anaesthesia, have been withdrawn as a priority group.

Although these benefits have been mainly demonstrated on children and young adults, it is clear from studies of communities receiving naturally containing effective fluoride levels the beneficial effects extend into later life.

In addition to the advantages to the individual outlined above, which are of prime importance, other benefits accrue. For example, in communities receiving fluoridated water, dentists can care for approximately 40 per cent more children than in communities suffering the effects of too little fluoride: the routine dental inspection of schoolchildren can also be reduced by 50% and all this for a few pence per head per annum.

Perhaps the greatest advantage of such improvements is that dentists can take a positive role in promoting dental health. Once they become less occupied with what is in effect the emergency surgery of gross dental disease, they can spend more time improving the dental side and hence the general health of their patients. It will not be possible in the foreseeable future to provide enough dentists and their assistants to cope with dental disease as it occurs now in Britain; but if the incidence of dental decay can be reduced by fluoridation then the other dental diseases can be managed by the dental resources which are likely to become available.

More than 130 million people throughout the world (including 4.3 million in Great Britain) are receiving artificially fluoridated water. Over 17 million in the United States have now consumed fluoridated water for about 20 years. Millions more older generations have consumed water that naturally contains the correct level of fluoride. Despite this enormous population exposure over many years, no adverse effects on health have been demonstrated. On the other hand, if the water contains too much fluoride adverse effects may be detected particularly in bones and teeth and a number of communities have reduced the content of fluoride in their water to levels recommended by the World Health Organisation. It is clear that fluoride is a trace element that should be present in the water within a range of concentrations - and thus the control of the fluoride level is important to the well-being of the community. The Food and Nutrition Board of the United States National Research Council has stated that fluoride is an essential nutrient.

The Committee on Research

The Committee on Research into fluoridation set up by the Department of Health and the Medical Research Council to monitor the British studies into fluoridation in its report of the results achieved after eleven years concluded that the fluoridation of water supplies at the level of one part of fluoride per million parts of water is a highly effective way of reducing dental decay and is completely safe. Further recent evidence has confirmed a continuation of this benefit following 15 years of fluoridation.

Fluoride can be utilised in other ways to protect the teeth but these are less effective and more expensive than fluoridation. None of these techniques have been adequately tested in this country, nor in any part of the world have any been established as of benefit to the whole community over a life-time. Fluoride remains the only adequately tested and successful dental public health measure.

Current World Situation

Over 30 countries in every continent of the world except Africa have some artificially fluoridated areas and at least three - Ireland, Greece and Brazil - have made it mandatory by law. Among many cities that have fluoridated their water supplies are New York, Toronto, Philadelphia, Dublin, Washington, Leningrad, Los Angeles, Basle, Canberra, Sydney, Birmingham and Newcastle.

The fluoridation of public water supplies has been consistently supported by the World Health Organisation (co-sponsored by 37 nations) who reiterated this as recently as May, 1975.

Among other groups supporting fluoridation are the British Medical and Dental Associations, the American Medical and Dental Association, the Royal Society of Health, the Central Health Services Council and the Federation Dentaire International. It has been the subject of a large number of extensive national and international enquiries. Commissions of Enquiry in the United States, Canada, New Zealand, Tasmania, South Africa and Norway have all decided in favour of its adoption.

Technical Considerations

Fluoride is added to the water by water engineers and a variety of different fluoride compounds can be used. It is generally simpler if liquids are used and it is new practice to use hydroflero-silicic acid. The equipment used incorporates a system of continuous monitoring, and experience over many years has shown that there is no difficulty in maintaining the required level of fluoride.

Legal Consideration

Under the National Health Service Re-organisation Act the responsibility for deciding whether water supplies should be fluoridated rests with the Departments of Health but has been delegated to the Area Health Authorities or Boards who request the Regional Councils in Scotland to implement the schemes.

The judicial Committee of the Privy Council stated "The addition of fluoride adds no impurity and the water remains not only water but pure water, it becomes greatly improved and still natural water containing no foreign element."

The Supreme Court of the Republic of Ireland ruled that there was no legal objection to fluoridation of public water supplies and the Department of Health in the United Kingdom have encouraged the appropriate authorities to proceed with fluoridation offering to indemnify them against legal proceedings brought for introducing this valuable public health measure.

Conclusions

It has been established for many years that the fluoridation of public water supplies is a safe and effective method of dramatically reducing the amount of dental decay in a community. Much suffering and disease will be prevented, especially in young children, and under these circumstances it would appear unethical to deny a new generation these undoubted benefits.

Summary

Fluoridation of the public water supplies is the most effective and inexpensive method of reducing the amount of dental decay in a community.

The protection given by fluoride lasts into later life so benefiting adults as well as children.

Fluoride is a natural trace element and has been classified as an essential nutrient.

Over 130 million people are receiving water to which fluoride has been added to bring it to the optimal level.

The Departments of Health in Britain are encouraging the Area Health Boards to agree to the Fluoridation of public water supplies.

Author and house built in 6 days by Lawrence Construction Ltd.

STONE CLEANING AND REPAIR OF BUILDINGS

A few years ago when on council business in Edinburgh I was given a pamphlet on the above subject which I found most interesting and here I quote.

There is considerable concern about the effect of the cleaning of the stonework of buildings of special architectural or historic interest in Edinburgh. Damage is being caused by inappropriate abrasive cleaning methods and the cleaning of individual buildings in the New Town is having a disruptive effect on the character of the streets.

The Planning Committee has adopted a policy intended to improve the standard of stone cleaning and consequently its effect on the "townscape". The importance of carrying out necessary repairs to stonework and other maintenance work at the same time is also stressed.

A listed building is a building considered by the Secretary of State to be of "special architectural or historic interest" and information about Statutory Listed Buildings (category A and B) and those on the supplementary list (category C) is available at the Planning Department.

Listed Building Consent is required for work which affects the character of any listed building, including stone cleaning and it is the owner or his agents responsibility to make an application for Listed Building Consent. Four copies of the application form are required together with three copies of plans (one coloured).

The plans should indicate the location of the buildings and show elevations giving the extent and details of any repairs that are to be carried out.

The method of stone cleaning and the product to be used should be stated on the application form.

Method Description

1. New Town

a) Only cleaning fluid - hydrofluoric acid based (with agreement certificate) - should be used on statutory listed buildings in the New Town area.

b) As part of the application for listed building consent each building should have a very inconspicuous part cleaned with an approved cleaning fluid to demonstrate the cleaning effect. The trial area should not be more than 2 or 3 stones in size.

c) The trial sample must be inspected by a member of the Planning Department and the Director of the New Town Conservation Committee and in some cases before the application is determined by the Planning Committee.

d) If after repeated trial applications of an approved cleaning fluid the process does not appear to be satisfactory it may be necessary to try an alternative cleaning method or abandon the proposal.

e) In granting listed building consent the notice of consent will state the approved cleaning method.

f) Owners of supplementary listed and non-listed buildings within the new town are advised that stone cleaning proposals should comply with the above policy.

2. Designated and Proposed Conservation Areas outwith the New Town

a) Buildings of polished, v-jointed, rusticated, droved and decorative stone should be cleaned with an approved cleaning fluid.

1. b-e above also apply.

b) Undressed stone buildings may be cleaned by an approved cleaning fluid and/or abrasive blasting.

c) Buildings on the supplementary list within a designated or proposed conservation area should be cleaned in accordance with 2 a) and b) above.

3. Authorities

a) Listed buildings of polished, rusticated, droved and decorative stone should be cleaned with an approved cleaning fluid.

1 b) - e) above also apply.

b) Listed buildings of undressed stone may be cleaned by an approved cleaning fluid and/or blasting.

c) Buildings on the supplementary list should be cleaned in accordance with 3 a) and b) above.

Townscape

1. New Town

a) Streets, terraces, crescents and similar continuous elevations should be cleaned in block lengths working uniformly along the front elevation as part of a comprehensive scheme. Very long blocks might have to be split into a number of segments to ease administration.

b) Rear elevations may be cleaned individually where they are enclosed by adjoining blocks. A list of streets where the rear elevation should not be cleaned on an individual basis can be seen at the Planning Department.

c) Both sides of a street, groups of buildings forming a square and in general continuous street elevations adjacent to each other should be cleaned with a minimum time interval between each elevation being cleaned.

d) The cleaning of individual buildings will be granted consent only where buildings are detached from the street elevations, e.g. churches and other public buildings.

e) A list of streets where individual cleaning of buildings may be acceptable can be seen at the Planning Department. Individual cleaning in other streets might be permitted if a considerable amount of stonework repairs are being undertakcn at the same time.

f) As part of consent for exterior decoration of doors, windows and railings within the two New Town Article 4 Direction Areas, paint should be removed from the stone architraves of entrance doors where possible, subject to approval of the method. Depending on the particular design of the doorway, cleaning may proceed separately to the rest of the building.

2. Designated and Proposed Conservation Areas Outwith the New Town

a) Continuous front elevations should be cleaned in block lengths working uniformly along the street where buildings are of dressed stone.

b) Rubble stone buildings forming continuous elevations may be cleaned individually.

c) Where consent has been granted for the cleaning of an entire street elevation there should be a minimum time interval between each elevation cleaned.

3. Other Areas

2 a) - d) above apply to all other listed buildings.

Repairs

1. New Town

a) All necessary building repairs and maintenance work should be carried out before stone cleaning takes place. All open joints in stonework should be sealed before cleaning and thereafter pointed with the appropriate mortar. The Edinburgh New Town Conservation Committee regards stone cleaning as the last stage of a comprehensive scheme for repair and restoration and stone cleaning by itself is seldom likely to be eligible for a grant from the committee.

b) Paint should be removed from all main stonework on front elevations (e.g. outfacing basement walls) during stone front elevations. Many small items of stonework are pointed in the new town especially architraves. Cleaning of these on an individual basis is unlikely to disrupt the street scene and is preferable to re-pointing in a stone colour.

c) Adhesive bonded veneers and similar artificial stone finishes should not be used as a stone substitute in the repair and maintenance of listed buildings.

2. Designated and Proposed Conservation Areas outwith the New Town

See 1 a) - b) above. A very limited use of artificial stone finishes might be appropriate on occasion.

3. Other Areas

See 1 a) - b) above. Limited use of artificial stone on occasion.

LOCAL GOVERNMENT

It is now 1973 and a new experience is about to start for me. I have always had a soft spot for Bearsden in my life, which I hope to explain later.

However, great changes were taking place in Local Government Organisation by the formation of District Councils with the proposal that Bearsden and Milngavie Town Councils should amalgamate but Glasgow had other ideas.

MANIFESTO

A Manifesto by Glasgow Peripheral Authorities on Re-organisation of Local Government for the case for five Additional Districts, within the proposed West Region, with a foreword on behalf of the Steering Committee and a Statement by Bearsden Town Council and a Statement by Milngavie Town Council.

Foreword

This manifesto has been prepared for the information of the members of the Scottish Grand Committee by a Steering Committee set up by the peripheral authorities who are vigorously opposed to the proposed Glasgow District as defined in the White Paper (Cond. 4583 Reform of Local Government in Scotland). These authorities are the Burghs of Bearsden, Bishopbriggs, Clydebank, Milngavie and Rutherglen with the District Councils of Old Kilpatrick, Eighth Lanark and Eastwood (First) Renfrew. These councils lodged objections at the appropriate time to the recommendations in the White Paper that the present City of Glasgow should be extended to absorb certain peripheral areas but all were most aggrieved that the Secretary of State (or one of his Department Secretaries) did not respond to the objections, the general and unconvincing reply through the local authority associations being completely unacceptable. A request for a meeting with the Secretary of State subsequent thereto was rejected out-of-hand.

These authorities, with reservations, accept H.M. Governments' remit for Regional Authorities, but agree with the Wheatley Commission Minority Report that the number of District Councils should be substantially increased. The eight authorities responsible for this submission representing over 240,000 people are quite unanimous in their recommendations that the present Glasgow city boundary should not be extended and that there should be at least five additional District Councils on the periphery of Glasgow with more District Authorities in the west region.

Case Statement by Bearsden Town Council

Due to an increasing realisation that the remoteness of county administration was not producing the best results for Bearsden and that the Bearsden rate payers were not receiving value for their rates, a campaign was instituted in the late 1950s to gain some measure of control of their own affairs, culminating in Burgh Status being obtained in 1958. Since then, Bearsden has been a happier and better place in which to live and there has been continuous improvement not only in small burgh functions carried out by the Town Council but in the wider sphere of county administration and the burgh has doubled in population since its inception to a present population figure of around 26,000; larger than some large burghs.

Not long after the Town Council came into being a policy was evolved with local authority housing that anyone who had an income sufficient to purchase an appropriate house through a building society would not be eligible for a local authority house subsidised by rates and taxes. This policy has proved acceptable and well worthwhile. There was also an initial drive to improve inadequate street lighting throughout the whole burgh and this was achieved in record time. A conscious effort was made to improve the general amenity of the area and recreation grounds, parklands and woodland of very considerable acreage were acquired either by gift or for very nominal considerations. The number of public halls were increased and local authority housing generally greatly improved and this with many other improvements has induced a feeling and interest in Bearsden that was never in existence before. The formation of the Burghs of East Kilbride, Bishopbriggs and Cumbernauld followed in regular succession, impelled by the same reasons in every case show accelerated progress and more efficient administration. They have been able to sort out their own priorities in accordance with local requirements and have them dealt with them more quickly and more effectively. With the Glasgow City District this has all to go by the board into a cauldron at a district level of well over a million people with a cumbersome council in which Glasgow will play a leading role and which will have powers similar to existing small burghs.

The Secretary of State on 22nd December, 1971 issued explanations on his intentions and states in relation to our proposals "The White Paper emphasised the need for the structure of district authorities to reflect community of interest consistently and for authorities to have sufficient resources to discharge their functions effectively. Some of the additional districts now proposed would correspond with genuine local communities but not on the scale on which the district structure has been created. On this scale the Secretary of State does not think that more district authorities can be established without cutting across important links between major centres of population and their surrounding areas or without fragmenting possible patterns of growth and prejudicing the provision and development of local services.

The Secretary of State has examined very carefully the proposals for additional districts around Glasgow in particular, but he considers that the Glasgow District should remain as proposed in the White Paper.

The existing city boundary is out of date and anomalous in many ways and detailed research has confirmed that a very close interdependence exists between the peripheral burghs and Glasgow for employment, shopping, education, leisure, recreation and many other services.

That is the whole case against our proposals and a little examination will show that taken sentence by sentence, it is quite untenable to support the conclusion it reaches, and it makes a complete mockery of the constructive independence and attainments of the new authorities referred to, and is a disparagement of the other peripheral authorities' past efforts. Glasgow the Secretary of State would have us believe is the missing influence which we need to fulfil a happy destiny and although we are too stupid to realise it' without Glasgow to hold us together we would disintegrate. What utter nonsense! Any problems and there are many, engendered by the Glasgow and surrounding authorities conurbations will find their solutions in the upper tier functions. The district will be exercising the same functions as we have always been exercising and no one can reasonably contend without tongue in cheek that these functions will be carried out better for us in a Glasgow City juggernaut. We therefore strongly reiterate our proposal to join with Milngavie, Clydebank, Old Kilpatrick and Duntocher to make a vigorous, viable and independent District.

What we are trying to do has the support and endorsement of the Convention of Royal Burghs in the presentation of its case to the Secretary of State on 19th November, 1971. The Convention, supported by ourselves, are trying to increase the number of Districts proposed in the White Paper of 49 to about 60 and this is in line with what we as a Town Council have propounded for some considerable time. We have pointed out that the White Paper increased Wheatley's number of Districts by 12 but allocated only one of these to the western region where with half of the population of Scotland within its ambit, at least half that number should have been given to the western region. We, along with the Convention, are trying to increase the number of Districts in the Western Region from the 13 of the White Paper to 20 or 21 including the 5 additional Glasgow peripheral area Districts. This is not only in line with our thinking, but is in line with the Secretary of State's thinking when he made the following statement at a conference in Dunblane in May of 1971, as follows:- The Commission recommended 37 District Councils. I should like to see something nearer 60 or 70. This would produce Districts of a better size. There would be less danger of Councils becoming remote from residents of their area; and the many towns and the country areas around them would more easily fit into this pattern. I think that the feeling of community that there is in different areas and the loyalties that go with it will find a pattern much more easily in the kind of figure which I have mentioned. The figure of 37 is much too small - and support was also given by George Younger, the Under-Secretary of State for Development, Scottish Office, when he addressed a conference in Rothesay, again, before he came into office. These additional Districts pre-suppose as a corollary the containment of Glasgow within the existing boundary and the Secretary of State for Environment, at the second meeting of the English Local Government Bill, again gave us valiant support when he made the following statements. I believe that it is right for this country to say that it is no longer correct to solve the immediate problems of the major conurbations by steadily spreading their boundaries further. I accept that if the land is not available within the boundaries of the metropolitan areas it is the duty of Governments to see that their housing problems are met. I take here the example of Birmingham. I accept that such a regional approach does not entail that the region as a whole has to cope with this problem but I do not consider that it is correct in planning terms to say that it should be met by a steady extension of boundaries. For to do so would aggravate the problems of congestion, of communication, of job opportunity and of the availability of the countryside to people living in the inner parts of the major conurbations.

These are exactly the sentiments which we have profounded and these are proposals which give a more democratic and logical representation and should be adopted.

The reasons which Wheatley gave for evolving the proposed Glasgow District were somewhat more robust than those given by the Secretary of State above referred to. Wheatley stated:- The course we propose is to enlarge the city boundaries from their present line but only so far as to take in those parts of the hinterland that would be better served and more effectively administered from the city than from the centre of any other District Authority. In other words we adopt the principle that the areas to be included within the city boundary are those which genuinely form part of the city community, not of any other community. In other words, he emphasises that the perimeter areas would be better served and more effectively administered from Glasgow than from the centres of our proposed districts and he contends that we genuinely form part of the city community, and not of our own communities. These are clear statements of his grounds for taking into one district almost a quarter of the population of Scotland. This, of course, is self-contradictory shown by the fact that we are striving as separate communities, to remain such, and in the sure and certain knowledge that Glasgow with its paramount problems cannot serve any of us better in the realms of housing, local planning, cleansing, refuse collection and disposal or any of the other functions allocated by the White Paper to District Authorities. Let us maintain our vigour and our districts.

Case Statement by Milngavie Town Council

Milngavie has enjoyed small burgh status since 1875 and until very recently was an entirely distinct and separate entity. Even today, it retains a most distinctive community spirit. It now lies on the fringe of the built up area, separated from the Blane Valley on the north by three miles of "green belt" area. It has a population of 10,700 (1971 Census) and a well balanced mixture of local authority and private housing, commercial and light industrial development. There are over 1,400 Local Authority and S.H.A. houses (about one third of the whole).

The Town Council are united (and are confident that they express the view of the great majority of their citizens) in resisting the attempt to incorporate this area in the Glasgow District. While accepting the need for some reorganisation they felt that there was a strong case for matters to evolve naturally under the present system, e.g. by amalgamation of authorities, extension of burghs to take in adjoining areas, etc. This would be more in accordance with the stated aim of retaining local democracy and would have removed the artificial division between burghal and rural areas created by local government legislation of the past century. However, if reorganisation is inevitable, then they wish to remain part of a district separate from Glasgow but associated with their neighbouring authorities, viz, Bearsden Burgh and Strathblane District and would not oppose amalgamation with Clydebank and Old Kilpatrick. These proposals were accepted by the Convention of Royal Burghs in their submissions to the Government. The whole area has strong local ties and a growing population (including Clydebank) now over 95,000.

As already stated, Milngavie is an old established Burgh (even older than Clydebank) and while it is accepted that a large proportion of the working population work outwith the Burgh, the figures used by the Wheatley Commission are not necessarily accepted as accurate and are in any event six years out of date. Many residents work in Clydebank and also locally. Indeed, there is a flow in the reverse direction, local factories employing workers from Clydebank and Maryhill. In any event, on this basis and on the argument regarding changes of residence (which seem to be points for the Government) there are areas within the conurbation, where volumes and percentages are greater than those of Milngavie, which are excluded from the Glasgow District. Even on the Wheatley figures, the overall percentage travelling to work in Glasgow from Clydebank, Bearsden, Old Kilpatrick and Milngavie is only 40%. It is stressed again, that while there may be an argument for this area to be in the same regional or top tier authority as Glasgow City on the basis of the Government proposals, there is no justification whatever for its inclusion in a district authority of 1,170,000 people with powers roughly equivalent to those of a small burgh now and from the viewpoint of local democracy representation by approximately 2/3rds of an elected member instead of 12.

The Council resent very much the continued refusal of the Secretary of State even to discuss the reasoned and valid objections put forward to the disappearance of so many well established local authorities into the anonymous mass of Greater Glasgow and to the consequent extinction of local democracy. It is noted that the latest refusal gives ground, lifted almost verbatim, from the Wheatley Report viz: The very close interdependence between the City of Glasgow and the areas of a number of the authorities contiguous with it for the purposes of employment, shopping, education, leisure, recreation and many other services and facilities.

In rejoinder, it is pointed out that employment, education and shopping are matters which planning-wise would be dealt with by the new West Regional Authority and not by Glasgow District. With regard to leisure and recreation, it may fairly be said that this community now contributes at least as much to Glasgow, as it receives. In the absence of specification of "other services and facilities" no comment is made beyond remarking that public transport will also be Regional responsibility.

We support our fellow "peripheral" authorities or "sacrificial lambs" all the way, in demanding five new district authorities in the area surrounding Glasgow. We would also, not necessarily, regard the existing Glasgow City boundaries, as sacrosanct.

They should be liable to adjustment in the interest of efficient and democratic administration, always bearing in mind that the new Glasgow District will not be the all purpose authority which Glasgow Corporation is at present. If Milngavie must celebrate its centenary by disappearing as a Burgh, then at least let its successor authority retain some minimum of local representation and interest.

Having given the case statement by Bearsden and Milngavie the Glasgow Herald made out a case against the Glasgow District, why Bearsden and Milngavie should not be included in the Glasgow District. In addition, we had the support and endorsement of the Convention of Royal Burghs in the presentation to the Secretary of State on 19th November, 1971. We now know how grateful we are to the Members and Officials of both Bearsden and Milngavie Town Councils who did so much in the formation of Bearsden and Milngavie District Council in May, 1974.

The new District extends well beyond the old burgh boundaries to the bridge over the Allander Water at Carbeth and to Windyhill in the west. Bearsden and Milngavie District is fortunate that within its area it encompasses towns, small rural communities, farms, attractive hills and open countryside and it is extremely important this desirable balance be maintained in the future.

THE TERM, HOUSE AND HOME

The term "House and Home" is in wide use and of universal appeal. It is used in its widest connotation, embracing the home not merely as an architectural unit, but also as a design for living. Modern labour-saving devices have so mechanised housekeeping that it has in many cases ceased to be an instinctive function. Science has been applied to all aspects of home-life, house construction, household appliances, furnishing, lighting and heating and with the increasing knowledge of dietetics supplements and new methods of food preparation, such as pressure cookery.

Home-making is an art that attracts all women, as it is an art all may practise even in the lowliest homes: mere drudgery never makes a home; it is the care and the cherishing of household possessions that give to a house its particular aura and make it a well-beloved home. The making of such a home not only gives happiness through the sense of achievement and artistic expression but means that through the application of knowledge for its smooth running, the ordinary everyday routine becomes merely a part of the constructive effort of home making and not an end in itself.

The Selection of a Home

The selection of a home naturally depends on a great variety of factors, the most important of which must be its accessibility from your place of work and its situation in relation to train and bus services, its nearness to good shopping centres and schools, clubs and other social amenities. The class of a neighbourhood too, plays an important part in the choice, because it is reflected in the aspect and general surroundings of a house. Town and country conditions are very different, and both rents and the prices of property will be found to vary considerably within the district. To avoid noise and vibration, it is best to select quiet neighbourhoods away from railways and busy streets.

The needs of the family will also have to be taken into consideration: a small and compact bungalow, for example, will be ideal for a young married couple but inadequate for the growing needs of children. It might therefore be better to choose a less modern house, perhaps in a fashionable district, in order to obtain more roomy accommodation. The use of a garage, or at least of garage space, may also be required. A garden too is important, not only from the point of view of providing a delightful hobby, but as a safe and healthy place for children to play in, and for the means of ensuring a fresh vegetable and fruit supply. A pretty and well-stocked garden should not, however, be the determining factor in the selection of a home: House design and structure, sufficient room, plumbing in good condition, freedom from damp and domestic amenities should be given a very high priority as they affect the ease and economy of home management.

Building a Home

The removal of licensing restrictions, a legacy from World War II, and the immediately following years, has greatly smoothed the path of the prospective private builder. Even so, before a start can be made, a number of essential formalities must be observed. Application will have to be made to the following authorities: the Local Council, under the provisions of the Building bye-laws and Public Health Acts, the Planning Authority, under the Town and Country Planning Act and the Central Land Board for the determination of the development charges where applicable.

These authorities will each stipulate the necessary plans and documents that must accompany their applications. The most important authority is of course, the Council Surveyor. All plans and sanitation arrangements must be passed by him before construction can begin. Responsible to him, too, are the building inspectors who inspect the actual building process and ensure a specified standard of work and compliance with building regulations.

Before a site is bought, it is wise to ascertain future assessments for making roads and pavements, sewers and water installations or any other district improvements and, if possible, to obtain a guarantee from the seller as well as from the Local Authority. In new building estates the roads are generally roughly made for building purposes and the local authorities can at any time, and after due notice, make up the road and put down water or sewage systems. The property owner will be legally obliged to bear his share of the cost as assessed by the local authority. It is also as well to find out if there is a likelihood of road- widening or the construction of airfields. If the local authorities find that land or property is in the way of a road or building improvement, they have the necessary powers for compulsory acquisition of such land or property. You will of course receive financial compensation but whether it will be really commensurate with the resulting devaluation in the property, plus the annoyance caused, will remain a moot point.

It is also sensible to investigate any of the so-called "burdens" that might have to be borne by property owners in respect of frontage walls or fences. Ancient lights are a form of building restriction which prohibits the erection of any building which will obscure the view of an adjoining property which has had 20 years' uninterrupted enjoyment of that view. The burdens and easements of a building site are matters of title deed and it is strongly advised to seek legal advice to interpret them. Your solicitor will arrange the title deeds, including the deed plan, and will also verify the land titles.

The Town and Country Planning Act, 1947 which came into force on July 1, 1948 aimed to prevent speculation in land by restricting its value to that of its "existing use". Speculators, therefore, cannot buy agricultural land at agricultural land value and resell it as building land. The district valuer decides the "existing use value" and he should be referred to before the site is bought. The Central Land Board assesses a development charge when any building (there are some exceptions) is erected. This charge, which takes into account any compensation to be paid, makes the ultimate cost of the land approximate to its market value before the act came into force.

The best foundation for a house is a chalk soil or a thick bed of gravel so that the surface water can drain off quickly. Clay soils are uncertain and are usually damp.

When building a house it is wise to find out whether the soil has been "made". This "made" soil might be formed from an ashpit or refuse dump and there will be the danger of escaping foul gases as well as of damage to the structure of the house through the foundations subsiding. Peaty and marshy ground is also a bad foundation and unhealthy.

If it is possible to choose the position of the house it should face south east. The kitchen and bathroom can face north. The pantry must be in a position where it does not get direct sunshine: it should be both cool and dry with a good ventilation; an ideal situation is to have rising ground behind to afford good protection. A house should never be built in a hollow even though the background might look attractive, because efficient drainage of the soil would be difficult, and dampness would result.

To guard against dampness, a damp-proof course is placed horizontally in the thickness of the wall below all the woodwork of the floors, but above the level of the ground outside. A space should be left under all floors for the free circulation of air, so that all the walls should be provided with air bricks inserted slightly above the level of the soil. Many points in house-building, such as the minimum heights for bedrooms, are governed by local bye-laws; and it is advisable to obtain a copy of these from the town hall and to give them careful study. Chimneys have to be at least three feet in height.

When they are available, local stone and other building materials may blend well with the landscape. Good brick-work is, however, superior to stone in strength and durability as well as in colour and texture. Cavity walls are made by thickness of brick with a space left between them. These hollow walls, when properly built and fitted with good damp-proof courses, give warmth and dryness. If uncovered brick is not liked, or in order to afford extra protection, rough-cast and pebble dash can be added. Concrete blocks are also used in some modern houses. Concrete is also used for flooring where government restrictions on the amount to be spent on a house make its use necessary, but it is colder and less attractive than timber.

Doors and window frames should be constructed of well seasoned wood to guard against warping and to prevent poor fittings and draughts. Timber can also be used for roofs. Great attention must be paid to the construction of the roof. Its chief purpose is to keep rain, wind and snow out. It must withstand changes of temperature and may at the same time contribute to the beauty of the architectural design. Slates used for roof covering should be non-absorbent. Tiles are ornamental but as they tend to absorb rain a tiled roof needs a steep pitch to throw it off. In rural districts, timber and thatch can be used artistically and effectively. There is, of course, a greater risk of fire with these two materials and thatch can harbour vermin.

Buying a House

There is much satisfaction to be obtained from house ownership. Labour put into it, and improvements added to it, are for your own benefit and increase the value of property. It gives security of tenure, and constitutes property that can be left to dependants. The payments made on it are a form of saving and, if they are paid monthly, amount to little more than would normally be paid in rent.

It is essential for all conveyancing to be done through the medium of a lawyer. He will investigate titles and draw up the title deed and the mortgage deed, if one is used, and will find out whether any easements or ancient lights affect the property.

When selecting a house one must decide how much one can afford to pay. Cost will not only mean the initial purchase price but yearly outgoings which must be taken into consideration when estimating final cost. Outgoings will include Schedule A income tax, general rates, water rates, electricity, ground rent if the property is lease-hold, fire and personal insurances, repairs and the interest and repayment of a mortgage if one is used. When viewing a potential home, it is wise to make a note of any repairs to be done and to get an estimate of cost. It is particularly advisable to pay attention to plumbing, to notice if tanks and pipes show any signs of having been patched up, and to keep a sharp look-out for damp patches on walls and ceilings. Plumbing is among the most expensive items for repair. In new estates and in country lanes, see whether any roads at the front or side are likely to be made up in future.

When a house is freehold, the owner and his heirs can hold it forever; and unless it endangers somebody else's property they will not be compelled to make any repairs to it. A leasehold, however, is usually granted for 99 to 999 years, at the expiration of which time, the property has to be returned by the purchaser to the owner in exactly the same condition as it was purchased, usually in good decorative and structural condition. If this is not done, the owner can sue for damage.

For the number of years that the lease has to run, the purchaser can let or sell the house, provided that he does not sell or let it for a longer period than that for which he has it. A sinking fund can be taken out to safeguard against being left with neither the purchase money nor the property. This is a form of insurance for capital to purchase a fresh property unless the lease runs out, if it cannot be renewed.

When purchasing a leasehold property, the longer the lease the better. Ground rent will, of course, have to be paid for leaseholds. As the lease runs out the selling price of the property will fall. That is why a leasehold house is cheaper than a property which is freehold, but otherwise similar to it in other respects : for when the property is valued, ground rent and sinking fund premiums are taken into the calculations.

Mortgages

A mortgage is really a system whereby business men, corporations or societies who wish to invest money can do so at a low but secure rate of interest. The borrower is the mortgagor, the lender is the mortgagee. The onus is on the purchaser to inspect the property to see that it is structurally sound : the vendor will be under no liability if the house turns out to have some serious defect. So, when you feel you have decided upon a house, be careful to state to the vendor that your purchase is "subject to contract". The 10% of purchase price that is usually paid as a deposit is then still recoverable by you if you do not proceed. You will thus have time to get the property inspected by a surveyor. For obtaining a mortgage this is, of course, indispensable, but even if no mortgage is required it is most strongly advised. The fee charged in relation to the purchase money is a small one, and certainly worthwhile.

There are several methods of borrowing the purchase money. You can apply to private persons and arrange a suitable rate of interest - though there is of course the difficulty that an individual may suddenly need the money back and demand the repayment of his capital. Money can be borrowed from the vendor who can arrange to lend the borrower part of the purchase money in return for a fixed rate of interest on it. Banks will only lend the money on a first mortgage i.e. provided that no money has already been borrowed. Building societies, too, will only make an advance on a first mortgage. The yearly or monthly amount of money to be paid does not decrease, but remains the same, so long as the mortgage is still being paid off.

Insurance companies will advance the capital in consideration of the mortgagor's taking out an endowment policy for 20 years or less and a life insurance, both of a value at least equal to the sum advanced. Therefore when the endowment policy matures the deeds are handed over to the mortgagor : or, if he should die before the policy matures his next of kin will receive the house free of mortgage under his life insurance policy. The additional security that this affords naturally entails higher repayments. The insurance companies also have what is termed a deferred house-purchase scheme.

The building societies have similar schemes so that the prospective house-buyers can start saving the amount of the deposit as soon as they wish. In these cases, the societies will often be prepared to grant a larger loan.

Many local councils will be prepared to advance money for the purchase of suitable property in their district. Borrowing from public bodies rather than private individuals has distinct advantages. The loan can be paid in small fixed amounts and the capital will not be recalled.

In applying for a mortgage, it must be remembered that mortgage value is always less than the market value especially where house market values are inflated. The mortgagee is concerned with the security of his money and will reckon with the danger of the house deteriorating in value. The mortgagor can sell the house but the mortgage must either be redeemed out of the purchase money or the sale must be made subject to mortgage.

The mortgage systems of most societies are usually prepared to lend a generous proportion of the value of the property. They will generally make the most favourable advances to owner-occupiers and to tenants (described as sitting tenants) purchasing their houses at advantageous prices. No preliminary charges will be made by a building society but the prospective purchaser will have to pay the surveyor's fee. On his confidential report the directors of the society will decide the amount of loan which can be offered. If this loan is not large enough, together with the cash deposit, to meet the price of the house it may be possible to obtain a larger loan by depositing with the society some collateral security in the form of war-loan stocks, savings certificates, life-assurance policies or the title deeds of other approved property.

The mortgage deed is drawn up by the mortgagee's solicitor. If you do not wish to choose a solicitor, the society's solicitor will act for you. He will set out all details covering the loan. His knowledge will safeguard and protect you from legal pitfalls. His fees will be proportionate to the land value. The solicitors of vendor and purchaser will then exchange contracts. After this, both parties will be obliged to go ahead with the conveyance. Should the purchaser decide to withdraw after this he will forfeit his deposit to the vendor. As soon as contracts are exchanged the purchaser must see that the house is insured against fire. The total cost will comprise the following items: the purchase price, the surveyor's or valuation fee, the solicitor's fees; and in the case of a mortgage, a further stamp duty, the mortgagee's charges and the fire insurance premium. In all, slightly complicated.

Some Hints on Home Decorations and Repairs

The things that any handyman or handywoman can do in a house are innumerable. Frequently the services of a craftsman are not easy to obtain and in any case the cost of employing one may seem excessive in relation to the work to be done. If, however, you are prepared to do many jobs yourself, you can considerably reduce the total cost to yourself and at the same time have some fun and a lot of satisfaction when the task is complete.

Obtain the best equipment that you can: cheap tools and brushes are shortlived and insufficient and will only make the task of the amateur more difficult. The same applies to paint. Cheap paint is unsatisfactory and can be very disappointing in the results. Choose a good dealer and do not be afraid to confide in him.

Measure roughly the area that is to be painted and he will tell you the amount of paint you will need. Buy enough for your purpose so that colour and quality will be the same throughout your work. The woodwork, if previously painted, should be stripped before any painting is started.

There are several preparations on the market for removing old paint. Alternatively, a blow lamp can be used, but this needs some practice in its handling and care must be taken with old and rotted wood to prevent smouldering. Woodwork which has once been painted will not need so oily a priming coat as new woodwork. Before applying the priming coat remember to treat all knots in the wood : cracks can be neatly filled with plastic wood.

New woodwork needs the preliminary priming coat which is made of white lead, linseed oil, drying agents and turpentine. The aim of this priming coat is to penetrate the surface of the wood and act as a preservative.

As this is a comparatively slow process the paint should not be allowed to dry too quickly : raw linseed oil can be added to prevent this. White priming can be used for bare plasterwork. Paint must be well stirred before being used. New woodwork and bare plasterwork usually require priming and three coats of paint. For a very special finish a fourth coat may be used. This sounds very extravagant but the paint should be applied thinly.

Priming paint should be applied evenly in all directions. The next coat should be brushed up and down and then across (for finer work the paint should be brushed in two diagonal directions). Wait for each coat of paint to dry, then rub the whole surface with glass paper to obtain a perfectly smooth surface before the next coat is applied. To lay-off the work it will be necessary to smooth the surface drawing the brush very lightly over it with a succession of strokes all in the same direction as the grain.

At the end of a day's painting suspend your paint brushes in a pot of cold water. They are suspended to prevent the bristles bending. This will also prevent the paint hardening on them by the next day. When the task is complete the brushes need several washes in paraffin and a final rinse in hot soapy water.

Distemper, like paint, must be well stirred before being applied. Care must be taken on mixing to see that the distemper is of the right consistency, for if it is either too thick or too thin it will look decidedly patchy. This will apply both to ordinary soft distemper and to washable distemper. A distemper brush must have good quality bristles to provide the necessary spring. Brushes should be soaked in water before use and after.

Remove all furniture from the room so that the work can be carried out without unnecessary delay. Remember to work away from the light : work in strips from the window side of the room. Cover the brush evenly with distemper and when applying it, turn the brush back on itself as the strokes are made from side to side. It is best to begin from the top and work downwards. Unlike paint, which must be finished off in straight parallel strokes all in the same direction, distemper can be applied up or down or across. Make quite sure that the first coat is thoroughly dry before the second coat is applied. Try not to leave any gaps as touching up afterwards will spoil the appearance.

When distempering any surface that has been previously distempered, examine the surface carefully for flaking. Scrub the surface with hot water, using a stripping knife for obstinate surfaces. Fill any holes neatly with a plaster stopper, mixing a little coloured distemper with it as if you are using colour. Painting should always be completed before papering is begun : any paste spilt on paintwork is far more easily removed than splashes of paint on new wall paper. Ceilings and friezes should also for the same reason be whitewashed before papering.

When choosing your wall paper, go to the shops where it is displayed in long pieces. This enables you to judge much better how it will look when hung than if it were just selected from a book. Always consider the suitability of a particular paper for your room, bearing in mind the direction which the room faces, whether it is sunny or cool; the furniture and soft furnishings in the room with which it will have to tone; and the use to which the room is put - nursery, bedroom or drawing room. There is a great range in the price of wall papers and this of course affects one's choice. Some of the more expensive papers are said not to attract dust. A heartening fact is that durability and cost are not necessarily related: some of the cheaper papers can be as strong as more expensive ones. Do not choose too large a pattern for a small room and remember that some colours, like mauve, will fade in a room with strong sunlight. The modern tendency seems to be towards plain or small-patterned papers. These also have the advantage of being easier to match and therefore less wasteful than large patterns. If a fairly large pattern is chosen it is as well to buy an extra roll and in any case it is better to err on the side of generosity as it will be exceedingly annoying to find one has insufficient paper to complete the task. If a house is sold however with the walls not too smooth, it may be found that a patterned paper will tend to mask defects which might be more readily noticed if a plain paper were used.

The first task is to measure the area of the walls to find out how much paper will be needed. A roll of paper or "piece" is usually between 10 and 12 yards long and approximately 20 inches wide. It will therefore be possible to calculate how many rolls will be needed by measuring the area of the walls and allowing for such interruptions as windows, doors and fireplaces.

If the room is already papered, it will be simpler to go round and count the number of present strips and make calculations from their number and length.

It is possible to hang paper over previous layers but if there are two or more of these it is more hygienic to remove them and to strip the walls bare to the plaster. This can be done by damping them with brushes and cloths which loosens the paper and makes it easy to remove with a stripping knife. The walls must be sized to help the paper to adhere and to prevent porosity. If the paper has not already been trimmed by the dealer this can be done on one edge as the next piece of paper will overlap the remaining edge (this is known as lap-jointing). When both edges are trimmed the pieces will be hung flush to each other (this is butt-jointing). It is usual to hang the first piece of paper at one side of the door and then work round the room to the other side, finishing with the short pieces, if any, above the door.

After measuring the length required lay the paper on its face, preferably on a trestle, covering its whole back thinly with paste. In folding the paper to move it, take care that the sticky sides do not touch the face; and clean the trestle after pasting each piece. Fix the paper to the top of the wall and smooth it down with a clean brush to the skirting. Paper is liable to stretch and you will find that there is a piece left over at the skirting. This can be cut off with sharp scissors or a razor blade. The next piece can be matched for pattern, measured off and hung in the same way, care being taken that the joint is true all the way down the strip. As the work progresses and rolls are used up, the end pieces which are too short for a complete "drop" may be accumulated and used for under windows and over doors and fireplaces.

Obstructions such as light-fittings may either be removed and papered over (after which the flex may be allowed to poke through and the fitting be re-fixed) or a star-effect may be cut in the paper to allow them to appear through it (the paper can then be neatly trimmed around the fittings).

Before staining the floors remember to scrub them well and remove any loose tacks. Glass-paper the rough bits until they are quite smooth. Inexpensive varnish-brushes can be purchased and there are a great variety of stains and varnishes on the market. If the floor has not been stained before, a solution of potassium permanganate may be first applied and allowed to dry. Two coats of varnish will be necessary, one being allowed to dry completely before the other is applied. Always take care that the varnish does not become gritty by the brush picking up dust from the floor. To guard against this, it is advisable to work with only a small quantity of liquid in the pot at a time.

Management

Planning and forethought are essential not only in the structural layout of a house and in its equipment and furnishing but also in the routine of day to day housekeeping and still more in the balancing of the housekeeping budget.

Time and money are both precious commodities and the art of housekeeping is to make the best of both.

Expenditure must be apportioned correctly and every homemaker must make an effort to live within her income and to save at least something against emergencies and the proverbial rainy day. A household that has a lower income than another may have a far higher standard of living owing to wiser expenditure and housekeeping.

The bottling of fruit when it is cheaper for use than it will be out of season and expensive; the making of good soups, jams, cakes and pies instead of buying them in shops; the growing of one's own vegetables and fruit, even though only on a tiny plot; home sewing and dress-making and the conversion of partly-worn garments into children's clothes - these are only a few of the means by which money can be saved by the home-maker, while the improvident will neglect them because at the time the amount to be saved will seem small and not worth the trouble. A knowledge of the market is another prerequisite, as well as a knowledge of the varieties and qualities of goods offered. It is always wiser to buy well known brands that have a reputation to keep up than purchase cheaper goods that are often unbranded.

This is particularly true of food, where the cheaper brands will often have less nutrition value. Experience is by far the best teacher. The young housekeeper should never be afraid to ask the shopkeeper's advice as much useful information can be picked up in this way. With care and planning the budget can usually be made to balance satisfactorily. There are items like lodging, food, clothing and fuel which are universal necessities:- then there are the conventional necessities such as newspapers, radio, holidays. What constitutes conventional necessities will naturally vary with the individuals and the class of society to which they belong. The size of the family and the varying needs of children at different ages will also affect the household budget.

The locality, in its bearing on rent, will also have its effect on the budget. Hobbies, sports and amusements should not be forgotten either for they play their part in our general well- being and happiness. Good management should never be replaced by mere parsimony for stinting of necessities such as the quantity of food or warm clothing, this will never compensate for the loss of comfort or health. The whole aim of budgeting is to prevent any undue excess of expenditure in one direction.

Electricity

The electric mains of a house are stated to be either D.C. (direct current) although A.C. (alternating current) is becoming the standard in this country. When purchasing electrical equipment for the home it is best to ascertain whether they are fitted with universal motors and can be used for AC or DC mains.

A conductor is any material through which electricity flows freely: water and minerals are conductors. Insulators are material through which electricity does not flow and which are therefore used to guard and enclose wires containing current: air, rubber, wood, plastics, porcelain, ebonite and glass are insulators. The human body is itself a conductor of electricity and the current may flow through to a second person who touches it.

If one person receives a shock immediately switch off the current or, if the switch is not near, try to pull the person free with the aid of any dry articles such as wood, rubber, paper or rugs.

The electrical connections in a house are composed of the main fuses of the company which are sealed, the meter and the householder's main switch and fuse boxes. The fuse is a safety device and constitutes the weakest link in the house current. The wire used in the fuse box is purposely made weaker than the cable used in the circuit. This means that when a fault occurs anywhere in the circuit the trouble can be remedied in the easily accessible fuse box and not under floor boards and other difficult places. Make sure that all switches are turned off at the main before attempting to join a fuse. Only the company can attend to anything that goes wrong with their fuse box.

There are usually alternative methods of paying for electric current. Payment can either be paid in advance through a slot meter or else a meter can be installed which registers the amount consumed to be paid for quarterly. There should be plug points or outlets for power purposes throughout the house as well as sufficient lighting points and there are many wiring accessories for both types of points.

The danger of using electrical equipment in a bathroom is only that a fault may occur in the circuit and a person standing in water can come into contact, and cause the current to pass through his body. The switch should be outside the bathroom door and should be earthed. The only electric fire suitable for a bathroom is one attached to the wall and controlled by hanging cords.

Much of the larger electrical equipment can be hired from the company (e.g. cooker and pans and electric washing machines) or it can be purchased by deferred payments. The most popular electric equipment in the home consists of cookers, kettles, irons, clocks, washing machines, towel driers, hair driers, mowing machines, fires, immersion heaters, toasters, polishers, refrigerators, mixing machines, sewing machines, vacuum cleaners, as well as plate-warmers and electric blankets.

The Unoccupied House

Having given you some detailed information on your house and home, possibly one of the most important matters in your life, certain precautions must be observed during the changing seasons of the year.

If for instance you go on an extended holiday in summer or autumn conditions, you will have under the building regulations some protection by overflow pipes terminating outside your house say from storage water tanks and sanitary fittings. It is however good advice to have the main stop cock bringing the cold supply into your house turned off.

During winter if a house is unoccupied it is necessary to have further action taken when all tanks for storage purposes and pipes should be run off and emptied. You should, therefore, acquaint yourself with all control stopcocks and have a label attached stating what it controls.

Each house has its own system. Herewith some hints that may be helpful.

If your home is unoccupied during cold weather, either:-

1. Turn off water and drain down the system (including central heating)

or

2. Turn off water and leave adequate space heating

and

3. Leave key with a neighbour if possible.

<u>Frozen Pipes</u>

1. Apply warm air or warm water to affected pipes, but if in doubt call a plumber.

2. If pipes frozen are in part of hot water system, turn off source of heat and call plumber.

3. To prevent frozen pipes ensure an adequate safe supply of heat to apartments likely to be affected plus leave hatch to loft open (if tank in loft).

<u>If a burst occurs</u>:-

1. Turn off water at main stop valve of supply coming into house; also the two stop valves at the cold water storage tanks (usually) in attic.

2. Turn on all taps.

3. Flush W.C.

4. Turn off immerser/water heating and withdraw fire.

5. Call plumber.

6. If water has penetrated electrical fittings switch off at mains and call electrician.

Get estimated costs of the damage to property and advise your claims to your insurance company, who may wish to send out their assessor before payment is made.

Insurance

Insurance can do much to relieve our natural anxiety. Sir Francis Bacon tells us that "he that hath a wife and children hath given hostages to fortune".

For such a person, insurance will bring peace of mind, for in addition to being a form of security it is also a good way of saving money. There is of course a variety of policies that can be taken out, but the majority of them are based on two principles:- (1) whole life insurance when the sum is paid on the death of the policy holder and who shall receive a fixed sum at the end of a certain period if he is still alive and that if he dies before that date the same fixed sum shall be paid on his decease to his dependants.

The different insurance companies have different terms. The competition between them is keen, and this, together with the law's control over their operations, is your safeguard. Some people declare that they cannot afford insurance. They will argue that it is better to invest the money where it can earn a much higher rate of interest than it can in insurance. Life, however, is very uncertain and few can be certain of providing for their dependants the amount that an insurance policy would offer. Herewith are a few of the types of policy available:-

Accident Insurance Personal
Annuity
Fire Insurance
Life Insurance
Motor Vehicle Insurance
Fire Protection
Lighting and Lightning
Insurance, Miscellaneous

Protection against Housebreaking

Never make the intruder's job an easy one through negligence or oversight to which, as police officers will tell you, a great many house-breakings are due. Thieves do not like difficult jobs; they are fighting against time and afraid of being disturbed.

First of all, do not let the thief know that you are away. Cancel your milk deliveries by telling the milkman directly and not by leaving a note in an empty bottle. Do the same for the baker and inform your newsagent too since a lot of newspaper sticking out of the letter box give a tell-tale sign to the thief.

When you go out do not leave notes stuck on the door with instructions for friends or tradesmen. Lock up and take your keys with you; do not try to hide them under mats and flower pots. If you are going away on holiday, inform your local police station; then a policeman on his beat in that area will keep a special watch on your home. Bolts should be fixed to all external doors and internal doors should, if possible, be locked. All accessible windows, particularly ground-floor ones, should be secured.

Money spent on good locks is money well spent and mortice locks which fit right into the door and are not screwed on should be fitted to back and front doors. Glass panels near the latch on doors can easily be broken; either back them with wood or add bolts to top and bottom of the door where they cannot be reached by an intruder. Remember also to put your valuables into safe keeping.

Should you hear anything which arouses your suspicion go quickly and quietly, and telephone for the police. Even if it turns out to be a false alarm, they will not mind if the call is made in good faith.

INTRODUCTION TO ARCHITECTURE

The problem that architecture sets itself is how best to enclose space for human occupancy. Strictly speaking, it is concerned only with those buildings that embody elements of beauty and the term implies that the building concerned has been designed to last for some time. Thus although architecture arises directly from the need for shelter, primitive huts and dwellings are not usually regarded as examples of the art. The study of architecture begins with the more enduring and carefully thought-out buildings of the higher civilizations.

The history of architecture runs parallel with that of the other arts in many ways; but the architect is bound far more closely than any other artist by the necessities of utility, by the technical knowledge of his time and by the available materials. Furthermore, the aesthetic effects which he can achieve are conditioned by the requirements of his time. In several periods of the world's history, ecclesiastical buildings have been the only important expressions of architecture. At other times they have been rivalled by public buildings and by domestic architecture. With the Industrial Revolution the new field of industrial architecture was added.

The weight and bulk of building materials have made it impossible until comparatively recently to move them for any great distance. Therefore, local styles of architecture have commonly appeared based upon prevailing trends but modified by the capacities of the immediately available materials. Sandstone, marble, brick, wood, concrete, etc. have different structural and ornamental possibilities and throughout the greater part of architectural history, builders have had to adapt their designs to those materials which were available within a fairly short radius.

The use of reinforced concrete, in particular, revolutionizes structural possibilities. A form of unreinforced concrete was discovered by the Romans but its use lapsed during the middle ages. It was not until the 19th century that its possibilities were scientifically studied but it has now become one of the leading materials for buildings of all kinds.

Three basic structural principles have governed all building of a permanent character - the post and lintel, the masonry arch and the modern steel skeleton. Each of these has given a new impetus as it evolved, but the first two have been known since an early period. The use of steel, on the other hand, is very recent and its appearance coinciding with the new demands of industrialism has revolutionized construction. Architecture has been freed from the shackles of stone-weight and gained the ability of almost unlimited verticality and flexibility.

The historic architectural styles have come from distinct and more or less isolated localities. Each has represented the needs and individual characteristics of the society that evolved it. During the past 150 years these styles have been widely copied and adapted by architects all over the world who have been impelled by the unprecedented demand for buildings and confused by the rapid progress of architecture.

But buildings produced by such adherence to stylistic forms cannot express contemporary culture. It is now becoming apparent that new requirements and the use of steel construction have revolutionized architecture so completely that new methods of design are required. Thus, the old forms, which were once used as models, are now important chiefly for their historical interest.

ECONOMICS

Economics are a social science concerned with the relationships of men in their various wealth-getting and wealth-using activities and the ways in which these activities affect the welfare of the community. The significance of economics to every individual may not always be apparent in our industrial society but analysis of the economic activities involved in such an everyday thing as buying a loaf of bread at a bakers shows that everyone is a part of a complicated system of wealth - getting and wealth-using activities.

In a primitive society, getting food was an individual matter. A man who was hungry found his own food and prepared it without the aid of anyone else. Today it is very different. First of all, the ingredients for the loaf of bread you wish to purchase must be produced - perhaps each ingredient in a different section of the country. These ingredients are bought by the baker, probably from a wholesale house, and made into bread, perhaps in a large bakery where many people work.

When bread is baked, it is transported to markets many miles around by a fleet of vans or by train. Among those who buy bread is your baker who, in turn, sells to you one of the loaves which he has bought.

In producing wheat for that loaf of bread the farmer had need of capital for buying the seed, for tending the crop, for paying wages to his labourers and for machinery used in growing the wheat; the baker required capital to build his bakery, buy the necessary equipment, pay his employees, buy and run his fleet of vans, pay rent on the land where his bakery stands, if he does not own it, pay for heat, light, etc. He is required to conform to certain standards of quality, cleanliness, hours of work and many other things and he has at all times to consider his relations with his employees in order to be certain that his bread was baked and ready to be bought.

Then there are all the money transactions involved. You, who bought the loaf of bread, paid for it with money earned at a particular job, perhaps in the procedure of some other commodity, or perhaps in rendering some service, medical, legal and so on. Or you may have asked the baker to give you credit at his shop, promising to pay at a later date and then settled the whole account with a cheque from the bank where your money has been deposited.

This illustration shows only a few of the many intricate transactions involved in even the simplest economic activity, transactions of which most of us are only vaguely aware. Economists have found in the course of the development of economic service that these complicated relationships of economic life can be analysed and classified to a certain extent. Of course, economics deals with human beings, just as the other social services do, and to the extent that human behaviour enters into economic activities, the economist can only guess at its effect. For that reason, economic theories may appear too general and too abstract, but these theoretical foundations are necessary before an intelligent approach to the complex practical problem of our economic society can be made.

Some Economic Definitions

Our definition of economics is that it concerns the relationship of men in their wealth-getting and wealth-using activities. To understand this definition, it is necessary first of all to know what is meant in economics by the term "wealth".

In the broadest sense, wealth may mean all material things that are or may be useful to human beings. Economists, however, make a distinction between "free" goods and "economic" goods. Free goods possess utility, but they are available in relatively unlimited quantities to anyone, and require practically no effort or payment to obtain them, e.g. sunlight, rainfall, etc. Economic goods also possess utility but are relatively scarce and so can only be obtained with some effort of payment, e.g. food, clothing, motor cars, legal advice, and most other goods and services.

Wealth, then, is another term of economic goods and services on hand at any given time. Claims to goods and services, such as money, mortgages, bonds, licences and contracts cannot be considered wealth in the economic sense because human desires are not satisfied by the claims in themselves, except possibly for a very miserly person, but rather human wants are satisfied by the goods and services which can be commanded by means of the claims.

The basic economic activity is the creating of wealth or production. Production involves not only the actual growing or construction of an economic good, but its transportation, its storage, its purchase and resale, and the services of all those connected with the whole process. Production may be direct as exemplified by a hand-made product sold in the maker's shop or it may be roundabout, using tools, machines and power production. Most production in industrial nations today are roundabout and the goods and services made available by most people are not for their own immediate use, but are exchanged for the goods and services which they want, and which are produced by others.

There are four essential factors or agents of production which are only briefly defined here. Land is the first and most essential factor of production, for all economic goods come in the first instance from the land or the natural resources it contains. The second factor of production is labour. This includes all human effort used in the production of economic goods and services, and is indispensible to production, since effort is required to make use of the resources of the land. The third agent of production is capital, or capital goods. The combination of land and labour is sufficient to create a simple sort of wealth, but the goods required in an industrial nation can only be produced if devices such as tools, machinery, factory building, etc. are used in production. The fourth and last important factor in production is organisation or management.

The human intelligence which directs the creation of wealth is present in the simplest sort of production, usually provided by the same person who supplies the labour.

In an industrial civilization, however, a special type of worker, the entrepreneur or business man, has the task of organising the other three factors into an operating unit, directing its operation and assuming responsibility for production.

The wealth-using activity is known to economists as "consumption". Thus all the economic goods are services used in the direct satisfaction of human wants are known as "consumer's goods" to distinguish them from "producers" or "capital goods" which are used only indirectly in the satisfaction of wants.

If wealth is regarded not as the fund of goods and services on hand at a given time, but as a flow of economic goods and services over a period of time, it is known in economics as "real income". To produce wealth which yields income involves "costs". "Real costs" consist of the human effort expended in the process of making goods and services available for consumption. The national income stated in terms of goods and services corresponds to the real income of the nation and the division of income among the four factors or agents of production is known as "distribution". The share of land in income is rent, the share of labour is wages, the share of capital is interest and the share of management is profit.

An individual's real income consists of the goods and services which his money income will buy. The value of any economic goods or services is the quantity of other goods and services which can be obtained in exchange for it. Value is usually expressed in terms of money which is a convenient medium of exchange, but an illustration of barter may make the meaning of value more clear. If ten bushels of wheat are exchanged for one pair of shoes, then the shoes have a value of ten bushels of wheat, and vice versa. If the wheat is exchanged for fifty shillings, the fifty shillings represents the value either of ten bushels of wheat or one pair of shoes.

The "price" of goods or service is the amount of money which is obtained in exchange for one unit of it. Price is always expressed in terms of money, whereas value may be expressed in terms of any goods or service, and whereas value can be used for any quantity of goods and services, price relates only to one unit of the goods or service.

THE DEVELOPMENT OF MODERN INDUSTRIAL SOCIETY

From the earliest times, systems of economic activity can be traced by means of which man produced the goods he wanted or could exchange for what he wanted. In primitive society, needs were satisfied directly from nature - by hunting, fishing, gathering food, etc. and the only tools man used were crude stone ones, chiefly weapons for obtaining food, together with some implements of wood.

Stone Age man eventually left behind his primitive food-gathering and hunting existence when his life was affected by the so-called "Neolithic Revolution". During this stage he learned first to domesticate certain animals and then to prepare the soil for planting the seeds he had garnered for the purpose. At about the same time pottery was invented and, with the development of new skills, the first steps in specialisation were taken. But the family, clan or tribe still formed the earliest sort of economic unit. There was some external trade, e.g. in special stones for tools or in amber, but not a great amount until metal was used for tools. This led quite early to the establishment of overland trade routes. As life became easier, inventions and discoveries in technology increased, laying the foundations of science.

During the Middle Ages, the agricultural life in European countries was organised on the basis of land tenure and personal services in what is known as the Scottish and English manor system or the feudal system. The head of the manor was subject to the King who, in turn, was subject to the church. The lord ruled over his lands tenanted by serfs and freemen who were expected to give a certain number of days of work as well as part of their product to the lord in return for protection. The manor was practically self-sufficient, only such commodities as salt, metals and tar being brought in from the outside. With the crusades and frequent wars, trade grew and the manor declined. Towns began to grow where trade routes crossed or around castles and monasteries.

With the development of towns came the beginnings of specialisation in economic life. The handicrafts flourished and the cobbler, the smith, the tailor, the weaver, etc. began producing quantities of goods for others to consume. Money became more important and the towns competed with each other for commercial and political influence. This handicraft period saw the growth of the merchant guilds, composed of traders within a certain town, and craft guilds, made up of members of the various trades.

The guilds declined in strength about the 16th century and were followed in economic life by the domestic system which has been called the first step to capitalisation. The appearance of the middleman who bought raw materials, furnished it to the workers and then sold the finished product on the market, marked the beginning of the separation of the craftsman from the ownership of his tools. The middleman needed capital to function since he often supplied the tools for the workman, bought the raw materials and paid wages for the production of goods for an unknown market.

Nationalism arose, particularly in England, as a result of the breakdown of the old feudal economic and political system. The system of regulation over economic and social activity with a view to maximising national wealth which grew up along with a new feeling of nationalism is known as mercantilism. The doctrines of mercantilism were followed by a policy known as laissey-faire or "let things alone". The commercial class and the traders found that their interests and those of the state were not always the same and the laissey-faire doctrine expressed their views that the state should not interfere with individual economic activity.

Towards the end of the 18th century, especially in England, the industrial revolution which had been slowly gathering force for many generations came to a climax with the establishment of the factory system in place of the domestic system. The invention of machines run by water or steam power, such as the spinning jenny, the power loom, the steam engine and blast furnace, necessitated the location of centres of production near coal, iron and water. Industrial towns sprang up where the factories were located and labourers moved to the towns to work for wages.

Employers vied with each other to turn out the largest quantity of goods, hours of work were long, wages low and working conditions miserable. With the factories came the new means of transportation, the railway and steamboat and local markets expanded into national and world markets.

As a result of this Industrial Revolution production had increased rapidly, and the people could now have necessities in greater abundance and an ever increasing number of goods and services of which earlier generations had never dreamed. The old policy of laissey-faire failed to protect the consumer and the labourer in some instances, and has been replaced by a system of control which more or less regulates activity by means of laws concerning hours of work, factory conditions, state education, social insurances, etc.

Conflicts have developed between labour and capital under the industrial regime. Labourers are no longer in personal contact with their employer and their skills and knowledge have become less important in competitive bargaining as machines have replaced handwork. Great cities have grown up as a result of the machine industries and all sorts of problems of housing, health, protection, etc. have resulted.

Large-scale production and specialisation have made all units of the industrial system dependant upon each other with the result that fluctuations in business have become more severe for both the wage earner and the business man than before the industrial revolution.

The present system of economic organisation in Great Britain is still that of capitalism and is characterised by private property and private enterprise. The fundamental legal framework for such a system of free enterprise is furnished by government enforcement of private property rights and freedom of contract. Private property has encouraged the accumulation of capital so important to industrial progress, and individual initiative has been stimulated under the system of economic freedom. Of course, the word "free" is used in a relative sense in the modern organisation of economic activity, since control has been found increasingly necessary in many of its aspects to protect the welfare of the whole community.

Staff at Tambowie distillery

FUNCTIONS OF THE STATE

The functions which modern governments perform can be divided into those which are essential and those which are optional. Essential functions of any government are in turn based on the power of the government or on the rights of the citizens as guaranteed by the government.

In the group of essential functions of government based on the power of the state are included, international relations - relations between states, both diplomatic and military; powers of taxation and eminent domain exercised by the state for its own support; and the police power of the government for the maintenance of law and order.

Essential functions of the government based upon a recognition of individual rights have meaning only in governments where the rights of citizens to share in government and the protection of certain civil liberties are recognized as fundamental. In a totalitarian state, such functions are not considered essential, in fact civil and political liberties do not even exist in the forms in which we find them in popular governments. They are accepted for the sake of enforcing discipline.

The functions of government which may be classed as optional are also of two types. In the first group are those functions which almost every government in the world takes upon itself today, such as the care of the insane, of paupers, and other classes of unfortunates, and the maintenance of public parks, sanitation systems, elementary educational institutions, postal service and the construction of bridges and highways. The second group of optional functions has increased tremendously during the 20th century, and the tendency of all kinds of government today is to expand even further into the economic realm in the interests of the general welfare of the people, or in the interest of the state, as the case may be. Included in this group are all forms of social security, public health and child welfare measures, maintenance of public utilities, government employment agencies, regulation of labour, capital and other sections of the economic life of a modern nation.

EXPERIENCE OF LIFE

Man is by nature an enquirer, a being beset by curiosity. He is continually asking questions about his own life and destiny, and about the mechanism and purpose of the world around him plus his own life experience.

It has been stated that "all the world is a stage, and all the men and women are merely players, they have their entrances and their exits, each one of which plays many parts". How true.

My own experience of life has been one of variety, a man of quite a few parts. That as may be, having been an employer in business for over forty five years, the older you get life appears to be more complicated. Evolution takes place and our problems with the environment must be solved.